On Holy Ground

Other Books by Charles Stanley from Thomas Nelson Publishers

Enter His Gates
Eternal Security
The Gift of Forgiveness
The Glorious Journey
How to Handle Adversity
How to Keep Your Kids on Your Team
How to Listen to God

The In Touch Study Series
Advancing Through Adversity
Becoming Emotionally Whole
Developing a Servant's Heart
Developing Inner Strength
Experiencing Forgiveness
Listening to God
Living in His Sufficiency
Ministering Through Spiritual Gifts
Overcoming the Enemy
Protecting Your Family
Relying on the Holy Spirit
Sharing the Gift of Encouragement
Talking with God
Understanding Eternal Security
Understanding Financial Stewardship
Winning on the Inside

In Touch with God
Our Unmet Needs
The Power of the Cross
The Reason for My Hope
The Source of My Strength
Winning the War Within
The Wonderful Spirit-Filled Life

On Holy Ground

A DAILY DEVOTIONAL

CHARLES STANLEY

OLIVER
NELSON

THOMAS NELSON PUBLISHERS
Nashville

Published in Nashville, Tennessee, by Thomas Nelson, Inc.

Unless otherwise noted, Scripture quotations in this publication are from THE NEW KING JAMES VERSION. Copyright © 1979, 1980, 1982, Thomas Nelson, Inc., Publishers.

Scripture quotations noted NASB are taken from the NEW AMERICAN STANDARD BIBLE®. Copyright © The Lockman Foundation 1960, 1962, 1963, 1968, 1971, 1972, 1973, 1975, 1977. Used by permission.

Scripture quotations noted NIV are from the HOLY BIBLE: NEW INTERNATIONAL VERSION®. Copyright © 1973, 1978, 1984 by International Bible Society. Used by permission of Zondervan Publishing House. All rights reserved.

Scripture quotations noted KJV are from the KING JAMES VERSION of the Bible.

Library of Congress Cataloging-in-Publication Data

Stanley, Charles F.
    On holy ground : a devotional / Charles Stanley.
      p. cm.
    ISBN 0-7852-7662-9
    1. Devotional calendars—Baptist Church. 2. Bible Devotional literature. I. Title.
BV4811.S817 1999
242'.2—dc21

                  99-15321
                  CIP

Printed in the United States of America
1 2 3 4 5 6 BVG 04 03 02 01 00 99

Contents

Introduction . . . . *vii*

JANUARY
Journey of Faith *1*

FEBRUARY
Journey Out of Egypt *33*

MARCH
Journey to the Promised Land *63*

APRIL
Journey to the Cross *95*

MAY
Journey to the Battlefield *127*

JUNE
Journey into the Wilderness *159*

JULY

Journey to Freedom *191*

AUGUST

Journey to Jabbok *223*

SEPTEMBER

Journey to Receive a Spiritual Mantle . *255*

OCTOBER

Journey to Revival *287*

NOVEMBER

Journey to Mount Horeb *319*

DECEMBER

Journey Down the Damascus Road *351*

About the Author *383*

Introduction

You are invited on an exciting spiritual journey. Everything you need is provided. Your passport—the blood of Jesus—was secured for you at Calvary. Our Guide is the Holy Spirit. We will learn much from Him along the way. The Guidebook—the Bible—is crammed full of information about our destinations.

You hold in your hands our itinerary. Each month during the coming year we will visit a different spiritual destination that is drawn from actual journeys of biblical characters. My prayer is that you will find these journeys lead to holy ground, a meeting place with God.

- In January, we make a journey of faith, illustrated by Abraham who packed up and started down the road by faith, not knowing where he went.

- In February, the focus is on Israel's journey out of Egypt, symbolic of our deliverance from sin.

- Devotions in March emphasize claiming the promises of God—our spiritual inheritance—just as the nation of Israel claimed the promised land.

- In April, we journey with Jesus to the cross, with devotions focusing on its powerful meaning in our lives today.

- In May, we travel to the battlefield, following the example of Jehoshaphat, who faced a formidable enemy but moved forward in confidence to win the conflict.

- In June, devotions focus on the wilderness experiences of life—the difficult times of brokenness and adversity—as we travel with Jesus into the wilderness of temptation.

- July's devotions are illustrative of Israel's return from Babylonian captivity, emphasizing deliverance from negative emotions, habits, and behaviors.

- Like Jacob—whose life was changed at Brook Jabbok—we will travel in August to our own spiritual "Jabbok" for renewal, consecration, and change.

- In September, the emphasis is on ministry to others as we trace the footsteps of Elisha who traveled with Elijah to receive the double-portion anointing for ministry.

- October will find us journeying with Ezra to return to Jerusalem for renewed emphasis on the Word of God, meditation, and prayer.

- In November, we will stand with Elijah at Mount Horeb and come to know God's voice.

- In December, we conclude our journey as we walk with Paul down the Damascus Road to our divine destination.

Before you start on a long trip, you usually check to make sure you have everything you need. Nobody wants to be caught unprepared. The good news is that the Lord has already supplied you with everything needed for your spiritual journey:

As His divine power has given to us all things that pertain to life and godliness, through the knowledge of Him who called us by glory and virtue. (2 Peter 1:3)

You are provisioned to the maximum, with nothing left out or forgotten. And just like a traveler, you appreciate your full suitcase the most when you have the greatest need. The times in which you come to the end of your ability are the very times you realize the abundance of His provision. These special moments can be defined in many ways. In the Scriptures, when men and women experienced a meeting with God, they often responded with awe, brokenness, and repentance. Moses slipped off his sandals. Isaiah cried, "Woe is me, for I am undone!" (Isa. 6:5). All of these fellow travelers, however, inevitably came to the understanding that, at that special moment in time, exposed and in the presence of God, they were standing *On Holy Ground.* May this be your experience too.

Don't try to lug along your own resources for this spiritual journey. Stop striving. Let the Word of God work effectively in you. Trust God and enjoy your trip.

On Holy Ground

JANUARY

Journey of Faith

REPRESENTING: Trusting God

KEY VERSE: Hebrews 11:8

By faith Abraham obeyed when he was called to go out to the place which he would receive as an inheritance. And he went out, not knowing where he was going.

Abraham's roots were firmly entrenched in the city of Ur. It was a civilized culture. His business was thriving. His family lived there. Yet God spoke to him at age seventy-five to leave all that was familiar and travel to an unknown territory. God promised to bless Abraham if he started down the road by faith.

Like Abraham, we enter this year unsure of the paths we will walk, but we can make our journey in faith and confidence that God will be with us each step of the way. He has given us His Word and the Holy Spirit to guide us: "That you may know the way by which you must go, for you have not passed this way before" (Josh. 3:4).

Perhaps God has been speaking to you about leaving familiar territory, making new steps of faith, or moving on to a new job, a different ministry, new relationships, a new geographical location, or a new spiritual commitment. If so, pack your bags. Our journey of faith is beginning.

The Pathway of Faith

SCRIPTURE READING: Romans 4   KEY VERSE: Romans 4:18

Who, contrary to hope, in hope believed, so that he became the father of many nations, according to what was spoken, "So shall your descendants be."

Hannah Whitall Smith once wrote, "Sight is not faith, and hearing is not faith, neither is feeling faith; but believing when we neither see, hear, nor feel is faith . . . Therefore, we must believe before we feel, and often against our feelings if we would honor God by our faith."

As you read the account of Abram's life, you realize he was a man of faith. God asked him to do something most of us would find very difficult, and that was to leave his family and friends and go to an unfamiliar land.

Yet God's reassuring words lessened Abram's fear: "I will make you a great nation, and I will bless you, and make your name great; and so you shall be a blessing; and I will bless those who bless you" (Gen. 12:2–3 NASB).

Abram, or Abraham as he was later called by God, gave little thought to the fact that his name would be made great. The most important thing to him was the exercise of his faith through obedience.

Anytime God calls you to step out in faith, He will provide the reassurance you need to go forward by faith. Your only responsibility is to obey and follow Him. Abraham left everything simply because God said, "Go."

Are you willing to obey Him even if it means letting go of something you care for dearly? Pray that your response to the Lord is always one of faith, love, and devotion.

> *Heavenly Father, help me to believe, even when I do not see. Help me to trust when I do not hear Your voice. Give me the reassurance to step out in faith, even if it means letting go of something I care for dearly.*

Faith Defined

SCRIPTURE READING: Psalm 24   KEY VERSE: Hebrews 11:1

Faith is the substance of things hoped for, the evidence of things not seen.

What is faith? Faith is not a power or force that we can use to manipulate God to fit into our agenda. We're not that smart. Faith is not just confidence. It is not believing in yourself or feeling sure about the outcome of a certain event.

For example, you could visit the bleachers in a ball game, and each side would be confident its team would win. This is not biblical faith.

Faith is not confusing or complicated. It is not the domain of educated men but is meant to be sought and applied by everyday folk in everyday life. Faith is not connected to circumstance. When all is well, we often think our faith is intact. But when foul conditions set in, what happens to our trust? As long as our faith is no deeper than our circumstance, we're set up for failure.

Authentic faith is simply this: God is who He says He is and will do what He says He will do. Our faith is in the person of Jesus Christ, in His character and attributes. It is completely trusting in the faithfulness of God to do what is right.

Is this the kind of faith that is deposited in your heart? If not, rid yourself of all false notions, and tell God that you are trusting Him as your all-sufficient Savior, Lord, and Life. It doesn't necessarily mean all will go well, but it will be very well with your soul.

> *Dear Lord, give me authentic faith. I believe You are who You say You are, and You will do what You say You will do. My faith rests in Your faithfulness to do what is right in my life.*

Getting God's Viewpoint

SCRIPTURE READING: 2 Corinthians 4:7–12   KEY VERSE: 2 Corinthians 4:7

We have this treasure in earthen vessels, that the excellence of the power may be of God and not of us.

If you have ever flown in an airplane and peered out the window, you were probably enraptured with the view. In clear weather, you can see a vast landscape in one quick glance, allowing you to momentarily transcend the restrictive barriers of earthbound living.

It is but a minute portrait of how our omniscient, omnipotent God views the life of the believer. He sees all. He knows all. He is aware of every detail of your life from birth (even before you were conceived) until death.

Since God knows your future perfectly and how today's ordinary events fit into His plan, you can rely on Him every moment. The timeless principles of Scripture help you make wise decisions from God's viewpoint.

We are related to an all-seeing, all-knowing God who has given us resources to face life's challenges and obstacles from His perspective. We are not limited by our own strength or wisdom.

We are hemmed in too often by our circumstances, unable to see through the fog of our finiteness. But if we seek God prayerfully and consistently, regularly digesting His Word, we can break through barriers with His insight.

Father, You see all, know all, and are aware of every detail of my life. You have planned today's ordinary events to fit into Your long-range purpose for my life. As I travel through this day, help me break through barriers with Your insight.

The Call of Faith

SCRIPTURE READING: Genesis 12:1–9   KEY VERSE: Hebrews 10:23

Let us hold fast the confession of our hope without wavering, for He who promised is faithful.

Suppose you plan a wonderful surprise vacation for your family or friends. The big day finally comes. The car is loaded, everyone has taken care of all those last-minute details, and your tank is full of gas. Everyone piles in the car and fastens seat belts in anticipation.

Finally someone asks the fateful question, "Hey, where are we going?" And you say with great authority, "Well, I don't know exactly." After the bewildered looks and cries of dismay, probably the only one left in the car with you is the dog, and he isn't looking too certain either. People simply don't make big trips without knowing where they're going—unless God asks them to. And that is precisely what God asked of Abram and his family: "Go forth from your country, and from your relatives and from your father's house, to the land which I will show you; and I will make you a great nation, and I will bless you, and make your name great" (Gen. 12:1–2 NASB).

God gave them some very important information, but He did not hand them a road map. Why? He wanted them to trust Him for the journey. Abram did not know where they were headed, but he knew their future was blessed, more than he could conceive.

Are you letting God take you in His direction, or are you still insisting on a travel plan?

Lord, take me in Your direction. Help me learn to walk by faith. I know my future will be blessed, more than I can imagine. No travel plan is necessary for my journey—I need only You as my Guide.

Faith Versus Reason

SCRIPTURE READING: 1 Corinthians 1:18–29   KEY VERSE: Hebrews 10:38

Now the just shall live by faith; but if anyone draws back, my soul has no pleasure in him.

From man's point of view, not everything God does seems logical. There are times when we know what God is doing. Other times, all we can do is scratch our heads and think, *Lord, I don't understand, but I trust You because You know what is best.*

The basis of faith is not in knowing, but in trusting. Many people are tripped up in their faith at this point. When we insist on seeing and understanding where God is leading before making a commitment to trust Him, we are living by human reason and not by faith.

Yet God calls each of us to live a life of faith. He says, "My righteous one shall live by faith" (Heb. 10:38 NASB). The author of Hebrews continued by writing: "Faith is the assurance of things hoped for, the conviction of things not seen" (Heb. 11:1 NASB).

Abraham lived by faith. He trusted God for a son, and God was faithful. But it wasn't until he was quite old that he held God's promise in his arms.

Are you trusting God or reasoning your way through life? When you live by faith, things may not always turn out the way you think they will. God answers our prayers according to His will and timing. He knows some of what we ask for would lead only to heartache and grief. Therefore, He protects us by giving us the things He knows will bring blessing to us and honor to Himself.

O God, there are times when I do not understand what You are doing. Let me learn to trust that You know what is best. Thank You for protecting me by answering my prayers according to Your will and perfect timing.

Three Principles of Victory

SCRIPTURE READING: Joshua 1:1–9   KEY VERSE: Joshua 1:9

Have I not commanded you? Be strong and of good courage; do not be afraid, nor be dismayed, for the LORD your God is with you wherever you go.

Jesus calmed the raging sea not so that the disciples could witness another miracle, but so that they might be caught up in the reality of His strength and personal care for them. Jesus allowed fear to captivate their hearts briefly so they could learn of Him. After the first few opening chapters of the book of Acts, we see His principles come to life in the lives of His followers. They found their strength in Jesus.

Joshua faced a similar situation as he prepared to lead Israel into the promised land. Chosen by God to complete the task, Joshua struggled with thoughts of fear and failure.

The angel of the Lord gave him three principles to keep him focused on the victory of God's strength: (1) meditate on the Word of God daily; (2) focus, be watchful and not distracted by the turmoil around him; and (3) do exactly what God told him to do.

When you begin to realize who Jesus Christ is and how much He cares for you, your faith level will increase. The greater your faith level, the clearer His strength will become.

Remember what the angel of the Lord said to Joshua: "Have I not commanded you? Be strong and of good courage; do not be afraid, nor be dismayed, for the LORD your God is with you wherever you go" (Josh. 1:9).

Master, I choose to meditate on Your Word today instead of my own circumstances. I want to be watchful and not distracted by the turmoil around me. Help me to do exactly what You tell me to do. Increase my faith level today.

Stepping Out

SCRIPTURE READING: Matthew 14:22–33   KEY VERSE: Matthew 14:29

He said, "Come." And when Peter had come down out of the boat, he walked on the water to go to Jesus.

Many remember watching the news coverage of a young Olympic runner who fell as he came out of the backstretch before the final curve. Wrenching in pain, he tried to stand but collapsed back onto the track's surface.

A hush enveloped the crowd as eyes turned from the race's victor to the lone runner struggling to his feet at the far end of the stadium. Suddenly he was joined by an older man who eluded Olympic guards and jumped onto the track. It was the runner's father. Together, arm in arm, they pressed toward the finish line. The runner might have fallen, but he was not defeated.

When Peter stepped out of the boat and began to walk on the water to Jesus, his one goal was to reach the Savior. And though the darkened waters caused his heart to momentarily doubt, Peter would not settle for defeat, and he called out, "Lord, save me!"

This is not an account of faithless peril. Had Peter truly doubted Jesus' power, he never would have gotten out of the boat. Never allow the enemy to tell you that you are worthless and defeated because you stumbled in your race to the finish line. Just like the loving father who ran to his son's side, Jesus runs to be near you and to carry you to victory. Call out to Him as Peter did, and He will save you.

Precious Lord, thank You that when I stumble and fall, You are like the loving father who ran to his son's side. You are prepared to carry me on to victory. Together, we can make it to the finish line!

Fear or Faith?

SCRIPTURE READING: Matthew 8:23–27   KEY VERSE: 2 Timothy 1:7

God has not given us a spirit of fear, but of power and of love and of a sound mind.

Wolf eels, which grow to be approximately six feet long, live in the cold waters of the northern Pacific Ocean in rocky dens on the sea floor. They have large, almost human-size eyes and formidable teeth, which give them a fierce appearance.

It is no wonder that for years, many marine scientists and divers believed them to be predatory and vicious. A recent discovery, however, has debunked that myth forever. Wolf eels actually use their long, sharp teeth to crack the shells of mollusks in order to get the meat inside. They do not bother humans at all. In fact, they are so docile that some have even played with the divers who studied them.

Something that looked fearful turned out not to be worthy of fear at all. Appearances can be deceiving, especially in spiritual matters. Peter was fine until he put his eyes on the waves at his feet and allowed the seeming impossibility of walking on water to rule his belief.

In an earlier scene, when the disciples were caught in a storm and awakened Jesus in a panic, He asked them, "You of little faith, why are you so afraid?" (Matt. 8:26 NIV).

Jesus does not want you to evaluate situations with your senses and human reason, which can be led astray easily. He wants you to walk by spiritual sight that is guided by faith in a Lord who cannot fail.

Dear heavenly Father, do not let me evaluate situations by my carnal senses and human reasoning. Let me walk by spiritual sight guided by faith in You—a God who can never fail!

The Faithfulness of God

SCRIPTURE READING: Psalm 102   KEY VERSES: Hebrews 13:5–6

Let your conduct be without covetousness; be content with such things as you have. For He Himself has said, "I will never leave you nor forsake you." So we may boldly say: "The LORD is my helper; I will not fear. What can man do to me?"

At times in our spiritual walk we feel as though all of heaven is shut up before us. We find ourselves wondering whether God has forgotten us or we have done something to disappoint Him. But nothing we do surprises God. He is omniscient and perfectly in tune with our every thought.

God has chosen to love you, even in sin, with an unconditional love. His love is based not on your performance but on His grace. You could never in your own strength perform up to God's standards. He loves you just as much when you stumble and fall as He does when you closely follow Him. This is not an excuse for sin but an opportunity to learn to love Him better.

Along the pathway of faith each of us can expect to face times of trials and difficulty when it appears that God is distant and removed from us. Yet we walk not by sight but in the reality of the promise that He will never leave or forsake us (Heb. 13:5–6). Faith always looks beyond the immediate to the eternal.

The times you feel God is doing nothing in your life are usually the very times He is doing His greatest work. Be of good courage; He may simply have you protected under the cover of His hand while He works out the necessary details for your advancement. Trust Him, and you will find Him faithful.

Almighty God, even when I feel You have forgotten me, You are still there. Thank You for Your unconditional love. I know You love me just as much when I stumble and fall as when I follow closely. Thank You for the great work You are doing in my life.

The Mind-Set of Faith

SCRIPTURE READING: Exodus 3:1–14   KEY VERSE: Exodus 3:14

God said to Moses, "I AM WHO I AM." And He said, "Thus you shall say to the children of Israel, 'I AM has sent me to you.'"

We often think faith begins when we step out and trust God for something He has promised, but actually faith begins even before this point. Faith is an attitude, a mind-set that has the power to chart our course through life.

Those who bypass faith in God experience discouragement because they are left to trust in their own abilities. What is human capability in light of God's omniscience?

Moses faced several critical points in his walk of faith. One came very early in his relationship with the Lord. The first time God spoke to Moses, He challenged Moses' ability to trust Him: "Come now, and I will send you to Pharaoh, so that you may bring My people, the sons of Israel, out of Egypt" (Ex. 3:10 NASB).

The situation appeared overwhelming to Moses. How could he possibly go to Pharaoh and tell him to let God's people go? He couldn't! At least, he couldn't in his own strength.

Are you facing a situation in which you know God wants you to trust Him, but the way seems dark and unsure?

Moses felt totally inadequate to do what God wanted him to do. God understood. This is what is so endearing about our Savior; He understands our frailties. All He asks is for you to be willing. Trust His love and care, and be strengthened by His power.

Precious heavenly Father, thank You for understanding my frailties. Even when my pathway seems dark and unsure, I know You will strengthen me. I rest in Your love and care.

Growing Your Faith

SCRIPTURE READING: Matthew 17:14–20   KEY VERSE: Matthew 17:20

[Jesus said to them,] "Assuredly, I say to you, if you have faith as a mustard seed, you will say to this mountain, 'Move from here to there,' and it will move; and nothing will be impossible for you."

How do you respond when presented with a challenge that calls for a surge of faith in God? Hesitantly? Tentatively? Fearfully? Optimistically?

The key to breaking the faith barrier and anchoring our trust in God is an exalted view of God Himself.

"But I thought to have more faith, I had to work at it more," you say. You do, but your work is to see God for who He really is, not to struggle to obtain more faith or have a more positive mind-set.

When the disciples thirsted to have more faith, Jesus told them all that was necessary was faith the size of a mustard seed. "Use what you have," Jesus was saying, "and your faith will grow in the process."

We use what faith we have, as little as it may seem, by magnifying the heart's view of God. When Moses was scared to go to Pharaoh, God exploded Moses' worries with the revelation of Himself: "Thus you shall say to the sons of Israel, 'I AM has sent me to you'" (Ex. 3:14 NASB).

We grow in faith by seeing God in a new light. Our faith is as big as our God. If your notion of God is grand, your faith will soar. If it is little, your faith will sag. How big is your God? See Him as He is, and the faith barrier will shatter before you.

Dear God, let my faith soar. Grow faith in me that is as big as You are. O God, I want to see You as You are. Shatter the obstacles of fear, disobedience, and faithlessness in my life. I want to break through the faith barrier.

Breaking the Faith Barrier

SCRIPTURE READING: Exodus 4   KEY VERSE: Hebrews 12:27

Now this, "Yet once more," indicates the removal of those things that are being shaken, as of things that are made, that the things which cannot be shaken may remain.

The journey of faith is not always safe; growing up in the Lord involves seasons of pain, testing, and uncertainty. Sometimes questions go unanswered for a long time. But as Moses discovered in the wilderness and as you will discover, the outcome is worth it.

Penelope Stokes describes the process in her book *Faith: The Substance of Things Not Seen:*

When we respond to the call to leave the walled garden and venture out into the woods beyond, we take the gamble of having our preconceived notions shattered. We open ourselves to new truth and new ways of perceiving; we embrace "the removing of what can be shaken . . . so that what cannot be shaken may remain" (Hebrews 12:27). We commit ourselves to exploration.

If we intend to be spiritual explorers, to follow the unknown paths and journey into unmarked territory, we must learn to trust God. Like Christian in *The Pilgrim's Progress,* we must put our hands to our ears, shut out the voices that would call us back to safety and sameness, and run with all our might toward the woods, where God waits to lead us on our way.

We need to embrace our own explorations, even when we can't please everybody, even when others are afraid we are taking the wrong path . . . even if we risk falling down the mountain and breaking an arm in the process.

O Lord, help me shut out the voices that call me back to safety and sameness. I want to run with all my might to where You wait to lead me on my way. Let me move forward by faith to explore and penetrate unmarked territory.

Matters of Faith

SCRIPTURE READING: Exodus 5   KEY VERSE: Isaiah 55:9

For as the heavens are higher than the earth, so are My ways higher than your ways, and My thoughts than your thoughts.

You did something kind for a neighbor, and your gesture was considered to be self-serving. You put in extra hours on a project at work helping a coworker in a bind, and others said you were just trying to look good to your boss. It hurts when people misunderstand your intentions. Not only is the good effect lost in the process, but you end up with blame you don't deserve.

Think about how Moses felt. He was God's special messenger on a divinely appointed mission of mercy, and the people accused him of trying to make their lives more miserable. They were absolutely wrong, as they would later discover, but in the meantime submissive Moses caught the brunt of their grumbling.

Such misinterpretations often happen in matters of faith. Why? God's ways do not always make sense in a sinful world. His methods sometimes turn human reasoning on its head or go against popular opinion. And sometimes the benefits or rewards of obedience are delayed or delivered in a way that nonbelievers cannot recognize.

If others mock you for doing what the Lord says instead of walking in the world's path, you can stand firm. The true and ultimate victory belongs to Him.

Dear heavenly Father, even though Your ways don't always make sense to my human reasoning, I know the ultimate victory belongs to You. Let me stand firm in this knowledge and walk Your way instead of the pathways of this sinful world.

Suffering a Faith Failure

SCRIPTURE READING: Numbers 13–14   KEY VERSES: Proverbs 3:5–6

Trust in the LORD with all your heart, and lean not on your own under-standing; in all your ways acknowledge Him, and He shall direct your paths.

The spies' report was very negative and discouraging. The Israelites spent the entire night weeping and mourning. The situation seemed hopeless.

Under God's direction, Moses had led them triumphantly out of Egypt toward their final destination—the promised land. But now they were stuck in the desert outside a land filled with menacing giants.

At a critical point in time—the moment of challenge—the Israelites took their eyes off the Lord and looked only at the obstacles. Because they forgot God's promise and listened to false information, an entire generation wandered and died in the desert, never even getting a glimpse of the land of milk and honey.

Are you facing a challenge to your faith? Is God calling you to a task that seems unreasonable? Don't assess the situation by your limited resources; failure to see things God's way may cause you to miss His blessing, and others may be hurt. Disobedience is always followed by disappointment and disillusionment.

Remember what God has done for you in the past, and trust Him to deal with the impossible. You cannot be defeated when you follow God's plan in confident faith.

> *Precious Father, as I face my spiritual journey today, help me view each challenge in terms of Your resources instead of my limited strength. Give me faith to deal with the impossible.*

Facing Giants in Faith

SCRIPTURE READING: 1 Samuel 17:1–11   KEY VERSE: 1 John 5:4

Whatever is born of God overcomes the world. And this is the victory that has overcome the world—our faith.

Tomorrow she has to face the committee and tell them what she thinks. Last month they asked her to review books for a children's reading club, and she feels that three of the books are detrimental and advocate unbiblical values. She also knows that most of the committee members are not believers and will not understand her arguments.

As she thinks about the conflict to come, panic sets in. It isn't until she recalls past victories in the Lord that she calms down and recognizes that the battle is really His.

Look at David's words of positive confession before he faced the sneering giant, Goliath: "The LORD who delivered me from the paw of the lion and from the paw of the bear, He will deliver me from the hand of this Philistine" (1 Sam. 17:37 NASB).

David could say with unwavering confidence that God would give him the resounding victory. He called to mind former defenseless times when God delivered him from destruction, and he relied on God's might to do it again.

What giant looms in your future? What battle are you headed for today? Are you claiming the victory right now in His name? Always remember—you have a faith that conquers.

Father God, there are giants ahead—tremendous battles to face. Give me the faith that conquers. I claim the victory right now in Your name.

Victory Through Faith

SCRIPTURE READING: 1 Samuel 17:12–37   KEY VERSE: Philippians 1:6

Being confident of this very thing, that He who has begun a good work in you will complete it until the day of Jesus Christ.

As a young shepherd boy, David did not possess all the qualities of a strong, conquering faith. God took years to train him for his future role as a king of Israel. However, he never lost sight of God's goal for his life by fretting over the future.

When facing his first major challenge with Goliath, David mentally went through several steps to ensure himself of the victory through faith:

Recall past victories. David remembered God's past faithfulness and was encouraged.

Reaffirm the reasons for the conflict. Make sure your motives and heart are pure before God.

Reject discouragement. Always be wary of pessimism. Instead, practice recalling God's promises to you.

Recognize the true nature of the battle. Claim your position in Christ as a joint heir and a beloved child of God.

Respond with positive confessions of faith. God is in control, and He will give you the victory.

Rely on God. All your hope and security is in Christ. You struggle with human abilities and limitations, but God knows no limits.

Reckon the victory. David did, and you can too! Whether the victory comes today or in ten years, God will complete what He has begun in your life (Phil. 1:6).

> *Dear Lord, thank You for past victories. As I face the battles of life, make my motives pure. Help me resist discouragement and claim my position as a joint heir with Christ. Your power knows no limit, and You will complete what You have started in my life.*

Conquering Faith

SCRIPTURE READING: 1 Samuel 17:38–51   KEY VERSE: 1 Samuel 17:45

David said to the Philistine, "You come to me with a sword, with a spear, and with a javelin. But I come to you in the name of the LORD of hosts, the God of the armies of Israel, whom you have defied."

David's faith may seem to be of an almost superhuman kind—one beyond reach—if you focus on the feats he accomplished. Killing a giant with only some stones and a slingshot seems unbelievable.

But that is exactly the point. It was impossible and unbelievable. David's simple, childlike faith in a great God produced the decisive victory for the Israelites that brought much glory to their Lord's name.

The faith David had—conquering faith—is yours when you understand the true nature of his trust in God. Conquering faith is a faith that rejects the discouraging words of others.

What if David had listened to the taunts and questions of his brothers, or what if he had let Saul's doubts coerce him to wear cumbersome, oversize armor? David knew that if he let God do the job that God had called him to do, success was the only possible outcome.

Conquering faith also recognizes the true nature of the battle. When Goliath in arrogance came against the army of God, the issue became spiritual, and David understood this principle immediately.

Are you facing a spiritual "Goliath" right now? God does not expect you to manage the situation on your own. Ask Him to handle the conflict. Conquering faith knows the One for the job.

Heavenly Father, give me conquering faith—a faith that rejects discouraging words from others and recognizes the true nature of the battle. Handle my conflicts. Defeat my spiritual Goliaths.

Faith When God Says No

SCRIPTURE READING: 2 Samuel 12:1–23   KEY VERSES: Psalm 138:7–8

Though I walk in the midst of trouble, You will revive me; You will stretch out Your hand against the wrath of my enemies, and Your right hand will save me. The LORD will perfect that which concerns me; Your mercy, O LORD, endures forever; do not forsake the works of Your hands.

The prophet Nathan came to David and, under the direction of God's Spirit, spoke words that convicted David's heart of the guilt he bore and the sin he had committed against the Lord. The days that followed the event were filled with tension and despair as David learned that Bathsheba was carrying his child—a child that God had already revealed would die.

The heartache, the misery—none of us can truly know how deeply this man suffered. Not only had he hurt family and friends, but he had grieved Someone much nearer and dearer than his earthly companions—the Lord Himself.

But in the midst of this tragedy, don't miss the sensitivity of David's relationship with God. When the king received news that the child would surely die, he went straight to the Lord in prayer. That was the one place David knew he could find forgiveness and restoration. Even though the Lord allowed the child to die, David was ever hopeful God might change His mind.

When a person is broken in sin, he is not alone. God is with him, and He is quick to restore the person's fellowship with Him when he acknowledges his sin. You can praise God for His sovereignty in your life, even in times when His answer to your prayer is no. He will always give you His best at just the right time.

Father, I rejoice that You are sovereign over every detail of my life. Even when Your answer to my prayer is no, I know You will give me Your best at the right time.

Faith to Dream

SCRIPTURE READING: Psalm 71:13–21   KEY VERSE: 2 Corinthians 5:7

We walk by faith, not by sight.

When God gives you a promise for the future, He is responsible for opening the right door at the right time for you to accomplish the task. Author and teacher Henrietta Mears had a motto: "Dream big whenever God is involved." In life, she did just that and turned an unheard-of Sunday school department at First Presbyterian in Hollywood, California, into a program that drew thousands into a deeper walk of faith in Christ.

However, in 1937 she faced an interesting problem. Her ever-increasing youth program had outgrown its retreat facilities. God made it clear—He would provide a new retreat area that would meet the need.

Property, once an elaborate resort, in the San Bernardino Mountains became available. But the price, even though greatly reduced, was still too high. Henrietta resolved, "If this was God's meeting place, He would provide the means to purchase it."

The owner's poor health along with a damaging storm opened the way for the purchase of the property at an "unheard-of" low price. Henrietta concluded that the way of faith is never by sight or human reason; it is always by the sovereignty of God.

Is there a need in your life that seems overwhelming? Trust God; He has His best in store for you.

O God, give me the ability to dream big. Remove all that limits my vision.
Let me see beyond natural circumstances that restrict my faith.

Obeying in Faith

SCRIPTURE READING: Luke 5:1–11   KEY VERSE: Luke 5:5

Simon answered and said to Him, "Master, we have toiled all night and caught nothing; nevertheless at Your word I will let down the net."

Jesus was speaking to a group gathered along the shores of Galilee. When He finished, He turned to Peter and told him to raise the boat's sails, head back out into the open water, and lower his nets for a large catch of fish.

Tired and wishing only for a few hours of rest, Peter seemed to hesitate. Did Jesus know what He was requesting? Everyone there knew the best time for fishing—especially with nets—was at night; the worst time was during the day.

Peter tried to reason: "Master, we worked hard all night and caught nothing." But Jesus remained firm: "Let down your nets for a catch" (Luke 5:4–5 NASB).

Every time we are called to obey God, our faith is challenged and our true nature revealed. The miracle of the tremendous quantity of fish was the result of Peter's willingness to trust and obey Christ by faith. In obedience he replied, "At Your bidding I will let down the nets" (Luke 5:5 NASB).

When our hearts are set on obedience, God responds mightily. There will be moments in life when you may ask, "Lord, is this a matter of obedience?" If so, choose to obey in faith, then "let down your nets" and prepare for a tremendous blessing.

Lord, I set my heart this day to obey Your Word. As I move forward in obedience, I am "letting down my nets" spiritually and preparing for a tremendous blessing. I know it is coming, so thank You in advance!

The Test of Faith

SCRIPTURE READING: James 1:2–8   KEY VERSE: James 1:12

Blessed is the man who endures temptation; for when he has been approved, he will receive the crown of life which the Lord has promised to those who love Him.

M ost of us know the story of Joseph and the depth of his faith. Genesis 39–50 records the events of his life and how God provided emotional strength for him to rise above discouragement. The principle involved in Joseph's life is one of extreme faith.

He didn't enjoy being sold into bondage. Like any of us, he probably fought feelings of rejection, loneliness, and fear. He had worshiped and trusted God. Yet he ended up in a foreign land with no immediate hope of returning home to his family. Even there, Joseph held fast to his conviction—God had a plan for his life. He had been given a vision, and he refused to fall prey to sin and discontentment.

Each of us will face times of trial and discouragement. But it is here among life's darker moments that God exposes the depth of our faith.

For the psalmist to write about his victorious journey through the valley of the shadow of death, there had to be a valley experience. For Joseph to testify to God's faithfulness, there had to be an Egyptian encounter. For you to affirm the eternal love and strength of God, there must be a test of faith in your life as well. Remember, God will never abandon you. Just as He was with Joseph, He is with you—forever!

Precious Lord, despite the feelings of rejection, loneliness, and fear that sometimes flood my soul, I know You have a plan for me. Through all my trials, expose and then strengthen the depth of my faith.

Trusting God

SCRIPTURE READING: Genesis 39   KEY VERSE: Genesis 39:23

The keeper of the prison did not look into anything that was under Joseph's authority, because the LORD was with him; and whatever he did, the LORD made it prosper.

People who have spent time in prison talk about the mind-numbing effects of incarceration. Days slide into days, months into months, and an inmate's perception of time and reality may become stunted. It is easy to lose motivation or the will to live without hope, a goal, something to work toward.

Such was not the case with Joseph. If ever anyone had a reason to be bitter, it was Joseph. He did not even deserve to be in jail. Joseph could have allowed his frustration to deepen into resentment and then taken it out on his fellow prisoners and the guards. He could have made life miserable. Instead, Joseph chose to trust God:

But the LORD was with Joseph and extended kindness to him, and gave him favor in the sight of the chief jailer. And the chief jailer committed to Joseph's charge all the prisoners who were in the jail; so that whatever was done there, he was responsible for it. The chief jailer did not supervise anything under Joseph's charge because the LORD was with him; and whatever he did, the LORD made to prosper. (Gen. 39:21–23 NASB)

Joseph understood that God's plans for him extended beyond the negatives of the here and now; in faith he could look past the present pain, and as a result, God turned his circumstances into a beautiful testimony of His love and provision.

I trust You, Master! By faith, I look beyond the past and present into the tremendous future You have planned for me. Turn my negative circumstances into a testimony of Your love and provision.

Faithful Obedience

SCRIPTURE READING: 1 Peter 1:1–15   KEY VERSE: 1 Peter 1:7

The genuineness of your faith, being much more precious than gold that perishes, though it is tested by fire, may be found to praise, honor, and glory at the revelation of Jesus Christ.

Though Joseph was sold into slavery, he refused to become embittered. As a result, God blessed him through Potiphar, an Egyptian officer who purchased him. He was taken into Potiphar's home and given great responsibility. The Bible tells us that Joseph was a successful man (Gen. 39:2). All that Potiphar had was left in Joseph's care.

However, what happened next in Joseph's life was certainly a test of his character and obedience to God. It is fairly common for God to test our level of obedience. One day as Joseph was going about his duties, Potiphar's wife approached him with an alluring temptation. She wanted Joseph to commit adultery with her, but Joseph immediately recognized the error and refused her advances.

Joseph said, "How then could I do this great evil, and sin against God?" (Gen. 39:9 NASB). His first thought was what such a sin would do to his relationship with God. Obedience was far more important to Joseph than a moment of physical pleasure.

Potiphar's wife was furious and turned on him by lying to her husband. Potiphar had Joseph imprisoned. However, God was with him, orchestrating the circumstances of his life for even greater blessing.

If you are facing a situation that calls for obedience, ask yourself, Am I about to do something that will lead to my ruin or damage my faith? Faithful obedience always leads to blessing.

Precious Lord, thank You for the faith already instilled in my heart. Help me continue growing stronger each day in my spiritual journey of faith.

Faith to Cling To

SCRIPTURE READING: Genesis 7   KEY VERSE: Hebrews 11:7

By faith Noah, being divinely warned of things not yet seen, moved with godly fear, prepared an ark for the saving of his household, by which he condemned the world and became heir of the righteousness which is according to faith.

It is an old saying that people are "creatures of habit." Of course, we love occasional variation in the routine, but we strive for stability as much as possible.

If you ever feel stressed when dealing with the unknown, then you have a small idea of how Noah felt when God told him to build an ark. An ark? He probably didn't have a clear idea of what it even looked like until God's blueprint began to take shape.

In a single encounter, Noah's concept of daily life took a violent twist. Though he was surrounded by a self-serving, sensual society with no interest in God, he knew where he and his family stood. But suddenly his vision of the future changed forever. No more neighbors, no towns, no noise of crowds, no marketplace—what would the world be like?

Hebrews 11:7 (NASB) notes that in spite of the questions: "By faith Noah, being warned by God about things not yet seen, in reverence prepared an ark for the salvation of his household . . . and became an heir of the righteousness which is according to faith."

Faith was all he could cling to; God was literally his only port in the storm. When your circumstances turn upside down, when you don't have the answers, trust the Lord. His plan is perfect.

Almighty God, You are my port in every storm of life. When my circumstances are confusing, when I don't have all the answers, help me trust You. Your plan is always perfect.

The Foundation of Faith

SCRIPTURE READING: Matthew 7:24–29   KEY VERSE: Romans 8:35

Who shall separate us from the love of Christ? Shall tribulation, or distress, or persecution, or famine, or nakedness, or peril, or sword?

I magine that someone walked up to you today and said, "Here's one million dollars. Build yourself a dream house." Chances are, you're not going to pick a poor lot filled with sand. You're not going to use the cheapest, knottiest, half-rotted lumber you can find. Of course not. You search for the choicest acreage and the highest-quality building materials you can afford.

But when it comes to constructing a sturdy foundation for their lives, many people settle for inferior supplies—possessions, fame, or financial security. On the surface, these things seem reliable enough, but in the hard blast of a personal crisis they crumble away. A fire can eat up possessions; fame can disappear with one piece of negative press; a failing economy or a layoff can destroy financial security.

That's why Jesus wanted you to see beyond the temporal to the eternal. He said, "Everyone who hears these words of Mine, and acts upon them, may be compared to a wise man, who built his house upon the rock . . . The winds blew, and burst against that house; and yet it did not fall" (Matt. 7:24–25 NASB).

You need the shake-proof foundation of Christ to make it through the storms of life (Rom. 8:35). Only on His sure footing can you find security that survives every trouble. Build your life on the foundation of faith—Jesus Christ.

Dear God, I do not want to build with inferior supplies—possessions, fame, or financial security—because these things crumble. Empower me to build my life upon the foundations of Your Word and Your Son, Jesus Christ.

The Humble Step of Faith

SCRIPTURE READING: 2 Kings 5   KEY VERSES: 1 Peter 5:5–6

You younger people, submit yourselves to your elders. Yes, all of you be submissive to one another, and be clothed with humility, for "God resists the proud, but gives grace to the humble." Therefore humble yourselves under the mighty hand of God, that He may exalt you in due time.

Sometimes great examples of faith come in small, unappealing packages. For Naaman, the leprous captain of the army of Syria, his moment of faith came when he dipped in dirty water far from home.

Naaman was insulted. After all the trouble it took to travel to a foreign country, the prophet he came to see did not greet him as a proper host should. Even worse, Elisha sent him orders by a lowly servant to wash in the Jordan.

Naaman was so outraged by Elisha's supposed affront that he refused to perform the one act that would save him from his ravaging disease. Finally his servants came to talk him out of his pride. They asked him pointedly: "Had the prophet told you to do some great thing, would you not have done it? How much more then, when he says to you, 'Wash and be clean'?" (2 Kings 5:13 NASB).

When Naaman paused to consider their words, he realized that his refusal to humble himself before God would cost his life. He hurried to obey Elisha's instructions from the Lord, and his flesh was made whole.

Do you say yes to God in the little things? Are you content to follow His will when you do not receive any of the glory? No matter what the task, God always rewards the humble step of faith.

Father God, make me content to follow Your will, even when I do not receive any glory. No matter how small or great the task, let me step forth in humble faith.

Unshakable Faith

SCRIPTURE READING: John 20:24–39   KEY VERSE: John 20:29

Jesus said to him, "Thomas, because you have seen Me, you have believed. Blessed are those who have not seen and yet have believed."

The apostle Thomas felt deserted. The One he had followed closely and served for almost three years was gone. A cold cave of stone held Jesus' battered, torn body, and no one knew what to do next.

Later that Sabbath when Thomas arrived at the disciples' meeting, their mood had changed completely. "We have seen the Lord!" they cried. But Thomas couldn't share their enthusiasm. He had not seen the Lord, and he did not want to be set up for yet another disappointment. His focus was gone, his grand vision of the future shattered, and his faith shaken.

Have you been there? A negative experience left a bad impression, and you are afraid to trust again. One more letdown, and you aren't sure how you might respond. If you could have a glimpse of God in the dark times, you would have hope.

Jesus met Thomas right where he was in wavering faith. The living Christ stood before him face-to-face and told him to feel His hands and side. Thomas responded with one of the most moving confessions of faith in the Scriptures: "My Lord and my God!" (John 20:28 NASB).

Look at Jesus. He is real, and He is there to meet you in the bleakest hour. You will have the same reply when you see Him as He is.

O Lord, sometimes the shadows of the past make me afraid to trust. During these dark times, meet me where I am. Let me see You as You are. Let me touch You with the hand of faith.

The Way of Faith

SCRIPTURE READING: Hebrews 11   KEY VERSE: Hebrews 11:6

Without faith it is impossible to please Him, for he who comes to God must believe that He is, and that He is a rewarder of those who diligently seek Him.

Hebrews 11 is an emotional chapter. Spread before you are the spiritual sagas of generations who placed their unwavering trust in God, who took them on adventures beyond their imaginations. Some never saw the end result of their faith, but a great many did. Do you notice some common denominators among their experiences? No matter how different their particular stories might have been, certain principles held true for them all.

Faith was the way of trials. Noah certainly didn't ask for the ridicule and doubt of his neighbors. Moses would have preferred an easier way out of Egypt. But God used the rough times to sharpen them for the future and to be an even more powerful testimony to others.

Faith was the way of the most misunderstanding. Abraham's choice to follow God wherever He led was surely confusing to some. It didn't make sense from an earthly point of view for Rahab to hide the Israelite spies. From God's perspective, however, their unquestioning obedience opened the door to His blessing.

Faith was the way of patience. David had to wait many years before God fulfilled His promise of giving him the kingship. And many of the believers of the New Testament were put to death after prolonged periods of persecution. God's ultimate rewards for them were (and are) worth the wait.

Dear heavenly Father, I realize that the way of faith is often a journey of trials. Use the rough times to prepare me for the future. Give me patience to endure the darkest hours.

Standing in Faith

SCRIPTURE READING: Daniel 6   KEY VERSE: Hebrews 11:33

Who through faith subdued kingdoms, worked righteousness, obtained promises, stopped the mouths of lions.

A plot was afoot. Some political advisers decided it was time to put a negative spin on the efforts of one of the chief officials, to make sure he was put in the bad graces of the executive in chief. Their plan worked. The official's loyalties were cast into question, and it wasn't long before he paid the price.

That sounds as if it could be part of a plot for a modern novel, but it's really a very old story about how Daniel came to be in the lions' den. Daniel took a stand of obedience by refusing to pray to anyone besides the Lord God, and his decision ran in the face of the new law that demanded worship of King Darius alone for thirty days.

Taking a stand in faith very often entails negative consequences, at least from an earthly perspective. Those who do not honor God as Lord are usually angered by those who do, and radical displays of humble reliance on Him can incense them even more.

If you have ever been the victim of harassment by peers, "friends," coworkers, or supervisors as a result of sticking by a scriptural conviction, then you understand a little of what Daniel felt. You have probably not experienced retribution this dire in your own life, but the principle is the same. God will turn negative response into something for His glory. God shut the mouths of the lions, and He can silence your detractors as well.

I take my stand, Lord! I honor You as Lord of my life. I rely on You to turn the negative to positive in every area of my life. You plead my cause. I rest my case with You.

Barriers to Faith

SCRIPTURE READING: Psalm 25   KEY VERSE: Psalm 25:14

The secret of the LORD is with those who fear Him, and He will show them His covenant.

B arriers to faith keep us from accomplishing God's will. A poor self-image; ignorance of who God is; doubt; feelings of inadequacy; fear of failure; selfish desires and actions—all display a lack of faith in God. Anytime our eyes of faith drift from Jesus Christ we run the risk of losing our spiritual focus. At some point, everyone fights feelings of doubt and low self-esteem. However, these are feelings, and feelings have nothing to do with truth.

Jesus was quick to point out that Satan is the father of lies (John 8:44). He is relentless in his attempt to draw you away from God. Whispering thoughts of doubt and feelings of self-pity easily assist his disabling work.

How can you break through barriers to faith such as the ones just mentioned?

First, learn to listen only to God. If you are unsure of what you are hearing, go to God's Word and ask Him to reveal His will to you.

Second, be courageous and not afraid to trust God. He has never failed anyone, and He won't fail you.

Third, when He tells you to go forward in faith, do it, and allow Him to take care of the consequences of your obedience.

Fourth, once you have obeyed God, look for evidence of His blessing in your life. Obedience is the gateway to blessing, and God blesses those who honor Him with their lives.

Father, I choose to listen for Your voice and trust You in every circumstance. Let this day be one of new direction in my spiritual journey as I move forward in faith and obedience.

Walking by Faith

SCRIPTURE READING: Romans 8:35–39   KEY VERSE: Romans 8:37

In all these things we are more than conquerors through Him who loved us.

Do you ever worry about whether you can trust God? Many deny it, but their actions speak differently. Have you ever prayed for something and felt as though your prayers were going unanswered? After a while, it is easy to think that maybe it would be okay to help God out—give Him a little shove to start things off. But you may want to consider the following:

God is sovereign. He is both personal and loving. He has not forgotten you. Even though you may have to wait for the answer to your prayers, when it comes, it will be a wondrous blessing because you were willing to wait and trust the Lord for the answer.

God is infinitely wise. All knowledge about all things belongs to Him. He knows everything. Deep love and commitment toward those who have accepted His Son as their Savior are hallmarks of His personal care. Therefore, He has provided a way for sin to be eradicated from your life. In wisdom and mercy, He desires for you to live free of the bondage of sin and failure.

God loves perfectly and completely. He can meet all your needs. You may wonder how this can be, especially since you can't see or touch Him. Deep within the resources of His love, contentment and a sense of peace are waiting just for you. Nothing the world offers can duplicate these things.

Father God, You are sovereign and wise. You know everything about my life. You love me perfectly and completely and have the ability to meet all my needs. Thank You that You have not forgotten me!

FEBRUARY

Journey Out of Egypt

REPRESENTING: Proclaiming freedom from sin

KEY VERSE: Exodus 19:4

*You have seen what I did to the Egyptians, and how I bore you on
eagles' wings and brought you to Myself.*

For 430 years God's people were in slavery in Egypt until Moses came with
God's powerful declaration of deliverance: "Let my people go!"

Israel's dramatic journey out of Egypt is symbolic of our deliverance
from sin, and God's message to us today is the same as to Israel. He wants a
separated people: "Come out from among them and be separate, says the
Lord. Do not touch what is unclean, and I will receive you" (2 Cor. 6:17).

This month's destination on our spiritual journey is deliverance—
freedom from the power of sin. It is time to leave the bondage of spiritual
Egypt behind. It doesn't matter how many times in the past you tried and
failed. This time it will be different. The light of God's Word points the way,
and He will bear you up on eagles' wings.

So, wave good-bye to Egypt!

The Truth About Sin

SCRIPTURE READING: Romans 7:18–25   KEY VERSE: Romans 5:12

Just as through one man sin entered the world, and death through sin, and thus death spread to all men, because all sinned.

Man's natural state is one of sinfulness. It is a direct result of the Fall and the rebellion Adam and Eve demonstrated in the Garden of Eden. Our fallen nature is evident in feelings and emotions such as jealousy, anger, fear, resentment, lack of forgiveness, lust, and more.

When the apostle Paul became aware of the depth of his sin, he cried out, "Wretched man that I am! Who will set me free from the body of this death [death meaning a spiritual death]?" (Rom. 7:24 NASB).

Coming face-to-face with our sinfulness should bring the same response from us. If we were left on our own with no thought of God, sin would control our lives. Only by the grace of God and the mercy of Jesus Christ can we say with the apostle Paul, "Thanks be to God through Jesus Christ our Lord!" (Rom. 7:25 NASB).

Only Jesus Christ can save us from the clutches of sin. Only He can change the nature of our hearts and give us a new life. We can choose to live for Him and turn from evil, but first we must come to a point where we see our sin as He sees it. Nothing is glamorous about sin. It keeps us from experiencing all that God has for us.

Ask Him to surface anything in your life that reflects the old, sinful nature. Then pray to walk faithfully in the grace He provides through His Son, the Lord Jesus Christ.

Dear Lord, thank You for saving me from the clutches of sin, changing my nature, and giving me new life. I choose to live for You and turn from evil. Surface anything in my life that reflects the old, sinful nature. Then help me walk faithfully in the grace provided through Jesus.

How to Deal with Sin

SCRIPTURE READING: Romans 6:15–23   KEY VERSE: Romans 6:22

Now having been set free from sin, and having become slaves of God, you have your fruit to holiness, and the end, everlasting life.

You accepted Jesus Christ as your Lord and Savior, recognizing that He paid the penalty for your sins on the cross. You know that you're forgiven, cleansed, and righteous in God's eyes. But still, a particular sin plagues you. You think it's gone and the fight is over, but the temptation comes back. You cave in again at a moment of weakness or a time when your guard is down. Maybe you even wonder how God can still love you.

You're not alone. Paul expressed the same sentiment of frustration and exasperation. He said, "For the good that I wish, I do not do; but I practice the very evil that I do not wish" (Rom. 7:19 NASB). Paul knew that even though he was saved, the power of sin was still there, doing daily battle with his new nature.

What is the solution? First, you must see your sin, including recurring sin, for what it is—an offense against a holy God that can be removed only by the blood of Jesus. Confess the specific sin to Him, and refuse to become entangled by false guilt. You're forgiven freely.

Remember that you belong to Him completely; nothing else has the power to hold you captive. Turn to the One who frees you from sin when temptation strikes, and you will win every time.

Heavenly Father, I confess my recurring sins as offenses against You. Please cleanse them by the blood of Jesus. Remove my guilt, and let me realize I am forgiven and set free. Nothing has the power to hold me captive.

Confession and Forgiveness

SCRIPTURE READING: 1 John 1:5–2:2   KEY VERSES: Colossians 2:13–14

You, being dead in your trespasses and the uncircumcision of your flesh, He has made alive together with Him, having forgiven you all trespasses, having wiped out the handwriting of requirements that was against us, which was contrary to us. And He has taken it out of the way, having nailed it to the cross.

What role does confession of sin play in the life of a believer? The answer to this question often swings to one of two extremes. Some say since Jesus is sufficient atonement for all our sin when we accept Him as Savior, confession of specific sins isn't necessary at all. Others believe a detailed confession is needed each time we sin in order for God to be motivated to continue to forgive us.

Neither idea views forgiveness from God's perspective. Colossians 2:13–14 (NASB) explains an essential truth: "When you were dead in your transgressions . . . He made you alive together with Him, having forgiven us all our transgressions . . . and He has taken it out of the way, having nailed it to the cross."

Jesus' blood covers all of your sins—past, present, and future. The purpose of confession is not to catalog your sins or to gloss over sin with vague or general terms. In confession, you agree with God that what you have done is sin, that it is absolutely wrong and not in accord with His plans.

He wants you to tell Him straightforwardly what you've done so that you can experience the power of His forgiveness. To restore your sense of fellowship with the Lord, confess the things that strain your relationship with Him. One by one, lay your sins at His feet and you will feel the burden lift from your heart.

Father, thank You that the blood of Your Son, Jesus, covers all my sins— past, present, and future. One by one, I bring my sins to You. Lift their heavy burden from my heart.

A Done Deal!

SCRIPTURE READING: Psalm 25   KEY VERSE: Isaiah 43:25

I, even I, am He who blots out your transgressions for My own sake; and I will not remember your sins.

God never ridicules us or makes us feel unworthy. Instead, we read these words of Jesus:

Just as the Father has loved Me, I have also loved you; abide in My love. (John 15:9 NASB)

If you abide in My word, then you are truly disciples of Mine; and you shall know the truth, and the truth shall make you free. (John 8:31–32 NASB)

I have called you friends, for all things that I have heard from My Father I have made known to you. (John 15:15 NASB)

Love and truth. God is love and the source of all truth. The love He has for you is the same love He has for His Son, the Lord Jesus Christ. He gives you this love through His grace and mercy. It is a pure love, not tainted by guilt or obligation.

Regardless of how deep your past transgression may be, God is near to free you with the truth of His Word. Nothing is stronger than His love. When He forgives, He forgets (Ps. 103:12; Isa. 43:25). Once you have confessed sin, there is no need to beg or plead for His forgiveness. It is a done deal!

You can walk freely in the light of His love because He calls you His child. Your life is inscribed within the palm of His hand.

You are the apple of His eye; all of heaven rejoices at the sight of your name written in the Lamb's blood.

O God, thank You for freeing me from sin with the power of Your Word. As I journey down life's road, let me walk freely in the light of Your love. Make me secure in my relationship with You.

The Slave Market of Sin

SCRIPTURE READING: John 8:30–36   KEY VERSE: Galatians 5:13

You, brethren, have been called to liberty; only do not use liberty as an opportunity for the flesh, but through love serve one another.

Popular author Neil Anderson tells of a time when he was talking to a group about living a bondage-free life. One man spoke up and told how he had enjoyed a certain activity most of his life without feeling a trace of bondage to it.

"I paused for a second," said Anderson, "then I said, 'Well, congratulations, but can you stop?'

"I didn't hear another remark from him again until the end of the class when everybody left. He came up and said, 'So why would I want to stop?'

"I said, 'That's not what I asked; I asked if you could stop. What you think is freedom really isn't freedom at all. It's bondage.'

"Anybody who acts as his own God is in bondage to his sinful nature. We were sold into the slave market of sin. Jesus purchased us from the kingdom of darkness and saved us from ourselves. We are not our own; we were bought at a very high price, the precious blood of Christ. We are no longer slaves to sin but servants to Christ."

Many of us can relate to this story. Maybe your sin is gossiping. Or perhaps you have a difficult time telling the truth. You want people to think well of you, so you create stories that portray you in a heroic light.

Whatever the weakness, God can set you free. Ask Him to expose any sin in your life. Can you or are you willing to give it up in order to live free?

Lord, I want to live free! Take every bondage. Cleanse every sin. Expose every area of my life that needs change. I am willing to give up everything in order to live free.

"It Happened in the Spring"

SCRIPTURE READING: 2 Samuel 11:1–5   KEY VERSE: Psalm 28:8

The LORD is their strength, and He is the saving refuge of His anointed.

The following words remind us of the beginning to a beautiful novel: "It happened in the spring, at the time when kings go out to battle . . ." However, the poetic beauty quickly erodes to tragedy when we read how David yielded to temptation.

The danger that shouts to us is in thinking we are above reproach and could never fall as David did. No one is immune to sin. Only by keeping our spiritual walk before God pure are we given the strength to say no to temptation.

David could have turned and walked the other way. Instead, he stopped and allowed his eyes to gaze at something that would lead to ruin. The very fact that he had remained in Jerusalem when other kings were off at war lets us know that David had become soft and lazy. He sent his field commander into battle in his place, never stopping to think that the enemy was crouched at his side, waiting for a chance to strike.

If you are battling certain temptation, make a note of how David gave himself to sin. Ask God to show you how to avoid becoming lazy in your spiritual walk by taking advantage of the good things He provides—His Word, Christian music, and books written by godly men and women. David had a sincere love for the Lord. Once he realized his sin, he turned from it and God restored him.

Precious Lord, I am not immune to sin. Help me keep my spiritual walk pure before You so that I have the strength to say no to temptation.

Complete Redemption

SCRIPTURE READING: 2 Samuel 12:1–23   KEY VERSE: Psalm 32:1

Blessed is he whose transgression is forgiven, whose sin is covered.

Once his sin was exposed, David was filled with remorse. Over the years he had enjoyed a close, personal relationship with God. When he found out that his fellowship with God was in jeopardy, he cried out, "I have sinned against the LORD" (2 Sam. 12:13 NASB). God forgave David, yet the consequences of his sin remained, and the child who was born as a result of his adultery with Bathsheba died.

Sin corrupts. It's like rust on a new car; it eats into the finish and hides in hard-to-see places. Often when it is too late, the rust is exposed, but the car is ruined. David knew his only hope for restoration rested in God's forgiveness.

Psalm 32 is a beautiful testimony to God's cleansing touch in David's life. It also is a witness to us of God's mercy and unconditional forgiveness. No matter what you have done, God can and will forgive you. He promises to restore the years the locusts have eaten away—the years sin and disappointment devoured your purity (Joel 2:25).

In Isaiah 1:18, He tells us that He will make our sins as white as snow. Are you telling yourself that God can never use you because of something in your past? That is Satan's lie. God uses the broken and chipped things of this world to prove His redemption is complete and extended to all mankind. It is yours, and you can depend on His forgiveness when you come to Him as David did.

> *Dear heavenly Father, restore what the locusts have consumed—the years that sin and disappointment have devoured. You have a great plan for me, regardless of my past. I look with anticipation toward the future.*

Freedom from Sin

SCRIPTURE READING: 1 Samuel 15   KEY VERSES: Psalm 51:3–4

I acknowledge my transgressions, and my sin is always before me. Against You, You only, have I sinned, and done this evil in Your sight—that You may be found just when You speak, and blameless when You judge.

Saul deliberately disobeyed God, and even worse, he knowingly lied about it to the prophet Samuel. It was then that Samuel had to deliver the dreaded message that God had rejected Saul as king.

Was Saul sorry? Yes, but he never did accept full blame for his actions. You can hear the attempt at justification in his response: "I have sinned. I violated the LORD's command and your instructions. I was afraid of the people and so I gave in to them" (1 Sam. 15:24 NIV).

Now look at the words of King David, whom God appointed to be ruler after Saul. David had sinned grievously as well, but he said this: "I know my transgressions, and my sin is always before me. Against you, you only, have I sinned" (Ps. 51:3–4 NIV).

Can you tell the difference between these two confessions? Saul did not really repent because he refused to acknowledge the sin as his own. But David knew better. He fully acknowledged his sin, and he asked God for forgiveness.

That is the kind of repentance God wants from you. He knows your heart and your weaknesses, and He wants you to admit them. The Lord wants you to experience the relief and peace of being forgiven through Christ.

> *Master, I know my transgressions. My sin is always before me. Against You, and You only, have I sinned. I repent. Thank You for the blood of Jesus that cleanses my sin.*

The Divine Scapegoat

SCRIPTURE READING: Leviticus 16:1–22   KEY VERSE: Isaiah 53:6

All we like sheep have gone astray; we have turned, every one, to his own
way; and the LORD has laid on Him the iniquity of us all.

Through repeated usage, the term *scapegoat* has become quite familiar to
our secular culture. Its meaning—"an innocent party being blamed"—
has its roots, however, in an ancient Hebrew ritual known as the Day of
Atonement.

This holy day occurred once each year. The high priest took two male goats
as a sin offering for the iniquities of the people. One goat was slaughtered, and
its blood was sprinkled on the mercy seat. The remaining goat was sent into the
wilderness—after the high priest had placed his hands on the goat's head and
confessed the sins of the nation over it. Through this "scapegoat" observance,
God showed His mercy to the Israelites, allowing Him to continue His
covenant relationship with them.

In much the same way, Jesus became the divine scapegoat for the sins of
the world. He was and is the "Lamb of God who takes away the sin of the
world!" (John 1:29 NASB).

Our sins were placed on Him at Calvary. Indeed, our sins put Him there.

Jesus took the blame so that we could live. Have you trusted in His atonement? Have you come to Him for the forgiveness of your sins? Have you been
healed of your transgressions through His sacrifice?

> *Almighty God, thank You for the sacrifice of Your Son, Jesus, as the divine*
> *scapegoat for my sins. I praise You that He took the blame, so I could live. I*
> *rejoice in the liberating truth of His atonement for me.*

Sensitivity to Sin

SCRIPTURE READING: Numbers 22   KEY VERSE: Psalm 139:23

Search me, O God, and know my heart; try me, and know my anxieties.

In Numbers 22, we read how Balak, the Moabite king, sought to persuade Balaam to prophesy against Israel by offering the pagan prophet a significant sum of money to curse God's chosen people.

God warned Balaam not to accept the offer. However, when Balak's men showed up at his door with an extra-large sum of cash, temptation won out. Balaam went back to God to see if there was a chance He had changed His mind. The Lord gave Balaam permission to go, but was angry at him for not heeding His first command.

God knows the true motivation of our hearts. Balaam told the men he would go with them but could say only what God told him to say. Here's the catch: Balaam wanted the money more than he wanted to do what was right. He knew God did not want him to go, but he was willing to risk everything in order to cash in on the situation.

Balaam's donkey was the only thing that saved him from God's wrath. She saw a mighty angel blocking their path and stopped. However, Balaam became so angry that he beat her.

The Spirit of God always reveals sin. However, we can choose to go against God's warning by compromising our convictions. When this happens, we suffer in our disobedience. Ask the Lord to make you sensitive to sin. Pledge your devotion to Christ, and He will guard your life.

> *Dear God, make me sensitive to sin. Reveal the true motivations of my heart. I pledge my devotion to Christ. Let His power and truth guard me and direct my spiritual journey.*

Consequences of Compromise

SCRIPTURE READING: Judges 2   KEY VERSES: Judges 2:1–2

The Angel of the LORD came up from Gilgal to Bochim, and said: "I led you up from Egypt and brought you to the land of which I swore to your fathers; and I said, 'I will never break My covenant with you. And you shall make no covenant with the inhabitants of this land; you shall tear down their altars.' But you have not obeyed My voice. Why have you done this?"

Peter Marshall once said, "We are too Christian really to enjoy sinning, and too fond of sinning to enjoy Christianity. Most of us know perfectly well what we ought to do; our trouble is that we do not want to do it."

D. L. Moody wrote of a time when he had to stand for his personal convictions rather than be a part of compromise:

Once I got into a place where I had to get up and leave. I was invited to a home, and they had a later supper, and there were seven kinds of liquor on the table. I am ashamed to say they were Christian people. A deacon urged a young lady to drink until her face was flushed. I rose from the table and went out; I felt that it was no place for me. They considered me very rude. That was going against the custom; that was entering a protest against such an infernal thing. Let us go against custom when it leads us astray.

Some convictions are obvious because God outlines them in His Word. Others are personal between you and Him. Regardless, the principle remains the same. When God sets a warning in front of you, and you deliberately go against His command, you compromise your relationship with Him.

God cannot bless disobedience or compromise. If you want His best, tell Him that wherever He leads, you will follow—forsaking all that does not bring glory and honor to Him.

Lord, You cannot bless disobedience or compromise, so I want to follow where You lead, forsaking all that does not bring glory and honor to You.

The Remedy for Sin

SCRIPTURE READING: 2 Corinthians 5:14–21   KEY VERSE: Romans 8:1

There is therefore now no condemnation to those who are in Christ Jesus,
who do not walk according to the flesh, but according to the Spirit.

D. L. Moody once said, "Looking at the wound of sin will never save anyone.
What you must do is to look at the remedy."

Worrying about temptation and past sins only leads to episodes of guilt. If
you truly want to break the pattern of sin in your life, look to the cross of Jesus
Christ. This is your only remedy for sin. It was where God displayed His
unconditional love and forgiveness to all of mankind.

You may think what you have done in the past is too horrendous for God
to forgive. But nothing can separate you from the love of God. His forgiveness
and cleansing are for all who come to Him. You may be a believer who has
given in to temptation; God wants to free you from this bondage. However,
condemnation is not His way (Rom. 8:1).

He draws us to Himself through the gift of His love. You can scold a person
for doing wrong, and he may change his outward actions, but his heart remains
unchanged. God goes after the heart. The Word of God provides instruction on
how to live a godly life; to this He adds His unconditional love. God knows
once a person meets Jesus Christ, his life is eternally changed.

When dealing with people who have fallen, pray to have a Christlike attitude, one that is firm but loving. Let forgiveness be representative of your life,
and develop a willingness to help restore people who have sinned.

Precious heavenly Father, I look to the cross of Jesus Christ as the remedy for
my sin. You displayed Your unconditional forgiveness there. Thank You for
that precious sacrifice, the gift of Your love.

Sin Solution

SCRIPTURE READING: Galatians 6:4–9   KEY VERSE: Galatians 6:4

Let each one examine his own work, and then he will have rejoicing in himself alone, and not in another.

C an you get away with sin? You may cheat on a major school exam, pass the test and class, and do so without the teacher uncovering your deceit. You also may covertly engage in immoral behavior and falsely be perceived as morally upright.

The IRS may never catch your falsified income tax report. Your employer may never know you pilfered office supplies. But in each instance there are consequences for your actions. Even when others are unaware, God has established an inviolate moral law of sin and consequences. And although the consequences may be delayed, they will occur.

Paul applied the agrarian metaphor of sowing and reaping to our behavior. A crop is reaped much later than it is planted, but the harvest does come. Sooner or later, we experience the ramifications of our sin, since we are ultimately accountable to God.

Never underestimate the internal price you pay for sin. The weight of guilt is enormous. Bitterness and depression settle uncomfortably in your soul as you try to suppress the conviction of the Holy Spirit.

Confession and repentance are God's provisions—His solution—for dealing with transgression. Acknowledge yours to Him (and others when appropriate). Receive His forgiveness. You don't have to plead for it, just receive the gift of His pardon. Trust Him to help you handle the consequences.

Father God, thank You for Your provisions of confession and repentance to deal with my sin. I acknowledge my sins and receive the gift of Your pardon. I trust You to handle the consequences of any bad spiritual seed I have sown in the past.

Consequences and Punishment

SCRIPTURE READING: Hebrews 12:5–11   KEY VERSES: Hebrews 12:5–6

You have forgotten the exhortation which speaks to you as to sons: "My son, do not despise the chastening of the LORD, nor be discouraged when you are rebuked by Him; for whom the LORD loves He chastens, and scourges every son whom He receives."

One great misconception about the nexus between sin and consequences is a distorted notion of the character and nature of God.

Too many people view God as a celestial law enforcement officer, seeking to apply strict punitive measures to our misbehavior. Such a God is certainly not meant to be enjoyed. This tragic conclusion exists because of the confusion between consequences and punishment. God has established the moral law of sin and consequence in the spiritual realm as surely as He has fixed the law of gravity in the temporal realm.

God has designed consequences for our behavior as a means to teach us wise, profitable behavior. When we err, the often unpleasant results of our actions help to avoid reoccurrence. Consequences are not punishment. Punishment is retribution or revenge. God's punishment for sin was meted out on His Son at the cross, His justice and holiness both displayed and satisfied. He uses consequences as an expression of love to correct and keep us from evil.

Just as an earthly father uses consequences to teach his children, our heavenly Father allows the results of sin to instruct us in the ways of righteousness. His motivation is love, never punishment; and the consequences are always mingled with mercy.

Dear Lord, thank You for consequences that teach me to walk in the way of righteousness. How grateful I am that Your motivation is love instead of punishment and Your judgments are mingled with mercy.

Shearing Suckers

SCRIPTURE READING: John 15:1–8   KEY VERSE: John 15:5

I am the vine, you are the branches. He who abides in Me, and I in him, bears much fruit; for without Me you can do nothing.

Suckers are the small leafy offshoots on tomato plants. As harmless as they appear initially, they must be constantly pinched off from the main stems to produce healthy, abundant tomatoes. Permitted to grow, they divert the soil's nutrients into leaves and stems instead of fruit.

As Christ prunes your life, He carefully removes habits, addictions, misplaced priorities, and other extraneous matters that deplete your spiritual growth. Divinely schemed, the purging is executed so that the life of Christ might saturate your soul. The more God prunes, the more you experience the power of the Holy Spirit and bear His pleasant fruit.

Do you not want more of the life of Christ? More of His peace, joy, kindness, and patience? Do you not desire to be made like Him? Know that His pruning is for this sweeping purpose.

Never forget this fundamental factor—you have been placed into Christ by God, and He has been placed into your life through the habitation of the Holy Spirit. This is the significance of Christ's illustration of the Vine and the branches.

You are permanently and unalterably attached to the Vine. God's shears of loving care don't impair your fellowship with Christ. Instead, His using them is a sign of your vital union with the Vine, Jesus Christ. You belong to Him for eternity, and He has pledged Himself to constantly work for your good.

Heavenly Father, take the divine shears of Your Word and trim the suckers from my life. Strengthen my union with the Vine and make me more productive spiritually.

Saved by Grace

SCRIPTURE READING: 1 John 5:7–13   KEY VERSE: John 1:29

The next day John saw Jesus coming toward him, and said, "Behold! The Lamb of God who takes away the sin of the world!"

Have you ever wondered about your salvation? Many people do. They worry that they have done something to cause Jesus not to love them. They struggle with feelings of doubt, confusion, and fear. In 1 John 4:18 (NASB) we read, "There is no fear in love; but perfect love casts out fear, because fear involves punishment." The apostle John also reminded us that we are able to love God "because He first loved us."

Even before you were born, God knew what you would look like—the color of your hair, the sound of your voice, and the successes and failures you would face. In spite of all you have or have not done, God continues to love you with an everlasting love.

Jesus came to earth with a clear goal in mind, and that was to save those who are lost. He never said, "Be perfect and receive My salvation." Salvation comes to us one way, by the grace of God. When we accept His Son in faith, we receive eternal life.

You can work a lifetime to be good and perfect and not be any better off than when you first started. Salvation is based not on your works but on the finished work of Jesus Christ at Calvary. He is the One who bore your sins—past, present, and future.

Thank Him for the work He has done, confess any sin that comes to mind, and accept His forgiveness and unconditional love as a blessing.

O God, before I was born, You knew me. You knew my strengths and weaknesses, my successes and failures. Yet You love me with an unconditional, everlasting love. How I thank You!

The Precious Blood

SCRIPTURE READING: 1 Peter 1:17–21   KEY VERSE: Romans 3:23

All have sinned and fall short of the glory of God.

In Genesis we read about God performing the first animal sacrifice: "The LORD God made garments of skin for Adam and his wife, and clothed them" (Gen. 3:21 NASB).

Adam Clarke writes it is not likely that "sacrifice could have ever occurred to the mind of man without an express revelation from God." The slaying of the animals was His chosen way to atone for Adam and Eve's transgression. A blood sacrifice was the only payment that would suffice.

Many years later, God gave the Israelites specific commands concerning sacrifice for sins, from how to prepare the animal to what the priests should wear to what to do with the leftover portions from the altar. But the bottom-line requirement was still the same—blood.

When Jesus died on the cross, He literally took our place by becoming the ultimate and final sacrifice for mankind's sin. Once we accept Him as our Savior, our sins are covered by His precious, atoning blood.

Jesus submitted His life to the power of death for a time so that you can have life for all time. He satisfied once and for all God's requirement for forgiveness: "For the wages of sin is death, but the free gift of God is eternal life in Christ Jesus our Lord" (Rom. 6:23 NASB). The precious blood of Jesus is the only cleansing agent that works.

Lord, let the precious, cleansing blood of Your Son, Jesus, flow over my life today. O cleansing stream, cover me!

A Right View of Repentance

SCRIPTURE READING: Luke 3:3–6   KEY VERSE: Matthew 3:2

[John the Baptist said,] "Repent, for the kingdom of heaven is at hand!"

When John the Baptist called out, "Repent, for the kingdom of heaven is at hand," no one knew he was preparing the way for the coming of the Messiah.

John had been selected to preach repentance so that when Christ came, the hearts and minds of the people would be open to the truth of God. Many who heard his message repented and turned from evil. Others considered him foolish and extreme.

Repentance and sincere devotion to Christ separate a person from the natural ways of the world. Many people need God's forgiveness, but they resist any involvement with Him that disrupts their present lifestyle.

True repentance is a humble, quiet, life-changing experience between you and God. It involves a renewing of your mind and offers a new perspective on life—one of hope and lasting joy. Through repentance, we turn away from sin completely.

W. E. Vine defines this as "the adjustment of the moral and spiritual vision and thinking to that of the mind of God, which is designed to have a transforming effect upon the life."

Paul urged his readers, "Do not be conformed to this world, but be transformed by the renewing of your mind" (Rom. 12:2 NASB). That was the same type of call John issued right before Jesus began His public ministry, and it is God's call to you today.

Master, I answer Your call today. Adjust my moral and spiritual vision. Align my thinking with Yours. Renew my mind. Transform my life.

Division Among Believers

SCRIPTURE READING: Colossians 3:1–17   KEY VERSE: Colossians 3:10

[You] have put on the new man who is renewed in knowledge according to the image of Him who created him.

S in hurts and undercuts the body of Christ. Others feel the effects of a Christian's sin. The Christian worker who gossips at lunch and draws others into her conversation is guilty of slander. The sad result of her sin is that she tempts us to fall prey to her sin as well.

In an interview, evangelist E. V. Hill was asked what the greatest adversity is facing the body of Christ. Without hesitation, he replied that it is division among believers. The one group that has the knowledge to change the world for eternal good often ends up doing the most damage to its members.

Christians like to categorize sin; obvious things such as stealing, murder, and sexual misconduct are ranked high on the sin list. Yet "little" sins such as gossip and "white lies" are very seldom ranked. However, no sin escapes God's convicting hand, including feelings of unforgiveness, bitterness, anger, rage, malice, lying, slander, greed, idolatry, or immorality (Col. 3:5–10).

The apostle Paul told us to "put on the new self" and to be "renewed to a true knowledge according to the image of the One [Jesus Christ] who created [us]" (Col. 3:10 NASB). We are to be truthful about our attitude toward others. Christ called us to love one another (John 13:34). Ask the Lord to reveal any sin you have in this area, and then claim His forgiveness by faith.

> *Precious Lord, reveal any wrong attitudes I have toward others. Take any unforgiveness, bitterness, anger, rage, malice, lying, slander, greed, idolatry, or immorality out of my heart. Give me a pure love for others.*

The Way to Life

SCRIPTURE READING: Romans 14:7–12   KEY VERSE: Galatians 6:14

God forbid that I should boast except in the cross of our Lord Jesus Christ, by whom the world has been crucified to me, and I to the world.

Whenever we become tangled in sin, our first response should be one of grief and remorse, not just over what we have done but over whom we have hurt. When we say yes to sin, we grieve the heart of God.

When you are tempted to sin, ask yourself, Who is the boss of my life? If Jesus Christ is, then the desire to become involved with things that do not reflect God's nature usually fades and disappears over time.

Though each of us faces temptations periodically, saying no to sin should not be something we have to think over. Saying no is easy when you realize that saying yes hurts Someone whose love you can't live without.

Have you ever thought of God in this way—as Someone who loves you more than all the rest? Jesus came to demonstrate God's personal love to mankind. His death at Calvary said it all. He bore our sins out of love and eternal devotion.

Oswald Chambers spoke to this issue: "The Cross did not happen to Jesus: He came on purpose for it. He is 'the Lamb slain from the foundation of the world.' . . . The center of salvation is the Cross of Jesus, and the reason it is so easy to obtain salvation is because it cost God so much. The Cross is the point where God and sinful man merge with a crash and the way to life is opened—but the crash is on the heart of God."

Dear heavenly Father, You are the divine Boss of my life. I say a resounding no to sin and an eternal yes to You. I choose to walk the way of life.

The Transforming Grace of God

SCRIPTURE READING: 1 Timothy 1:8–17   KEY VERSE: Ephesians 1:7

In Him we have redemption through His blood, the forgiveness of sins, according to the riches of His grace.

Concerned about her salvation, the woman met with her pastor. "I don't know how Jesus can accept me," she cried. "I want to give my life to Him, but I'm not ready. You don't know what I've done. Jesus can't possibly forgive me."

Feeling guilty about past wrongs is understandable. Sin is ugly in God's eyes, but He took care of the problem on the cross. When you agree with God that your sin is wrong and accept Jesus' payment in your place, you are freed by His blood—clean and righteous in God's sight. No one is too wicked, too horrible, too unlovable, too vile for Jesus to love.

Paul, the missionary and apostle, said, "Christ Jesus came into the world to save sinners, among whom I am foremost of all. And yet for this reason I found mercy, in order that in me as the foremost, Jesus Christ might demonstrate His perfect patience" (1 Tim. 1:15–16 NASB). One of the greatest evangelists of all time was once a vicious persecutor of Christians.

No matter what you have said or done, you can hold fast to this promise: "In Him [Jesus] we have redemption through His blood, the forgiveness of our trespasses, according to the riches of His grace" (Eph. 1:7 NASB).

O God, I claim it! In Christ I have redemption—through His blood—the forgiveness of my trespasses, according to the riches of His grace.

Your Sin Is Forgiven

SCRIPTURE READING: Psalm 85   KEY VERSE: Psalm 85:2

You have forgiven the iniquity of Your people; You have covered all their sin.

The store manager listened as the little girl explained how her mom had told her she could have only one toy car. However, not being able to choose between two, she stole the second one.

At home she tried to act surprised when two cars popped out of the same box, but her mom saw through her folly. Once her dad was home from work, the truth came out, and they returned to the store.

Looking up at the manager with tears in her eyes, the little girl told him she was sorry. Her dad paid for the item and placed it in his pocket. On their way home, she touched her father's hand and said, "Daddy, I'm sorry. I don't ever want to do that again."

He held her tiny hand in his and said, "Honey, that was a hard lesson for you to learn. But I hope you realize what happens when you do something wrong. I also want you to know your mom and I love you very much and so does God."

Once they were back home, he reached inside his pocket and tossed the toy in the trash. The little girl blinked in confusion. "Dad, why did you do that?"

"Because you're forgiven. Once you tell God you are sorry and receive His forgiveness, He'll never bring that sin up again and neither will I."

Lord, I am so thankful that my sins are gone. You will never bring them up again. You have forgiven me; now help me to forgive myself.

A Casual View of Sin

Scripture Reading: Romans 6:1–7   Key Verse: Romans 6:7

He who has died has been freed from sin.

Most of us have heard how a frog can be boiled to death without any resistance. Placed in a cool pot of water on a cooking surface, the frog remains content and unsuspecting as the heat beneath is increased. His internal temperature rises with the temperature of the water until finally he is boiled alive!

Abraham and Lot were given a choice about the land they would occupy. Lot, seeing the lushness of the Jordan Valley, chose the richness of Sodom while Abraham settled in the land of Canaan.

Greed and lust fueled Lot's desires. F. B. Meyer wrote, "The younger man [Lot] chose according to the sight of his eyes. In his judgment he gained everything, but the world is full of Lots—shallow, impulsive, doomed to be revealed by their choice and end."

Lot never considered the character of the inhabitants of the land. He adopted a casual view of their sin. And in doing so he failed to realize the effect of their presence on his relationship with God.

Have you adopted God's perspective on sin, or do you have an indifferent attitude toward what is unholy before a holy God? Don't risk being lulled into deadly spiritual lethargy by the complacency of our society. God hates sin and calls us to do the same.

Father, I don't want to treat sin casually. Give me Your divine perspective on sin. Keep me from being lulled into spiritual lethargy by the complacency of the world in which I live. Let me understand—You hate sin, and You have called me to do the same.

Hazard of a Hard Heart

SCRIPTURE READING: Exodus 10   KEY VERSE: Exodus 8:19

The magicians said to Pharaoh, "This is the finger of God." But Pharaoh's heart grew hard, and he did not heed them, just as the LORD had said.

He had attended church since he was a small child. As an adult, he took careful notes on every sermon. When the pastor talked about specific sins, he recognized some of the problems in his own heart and said to himself, "That's me. I need to deal with these things." But like many, by the time he returned from church, he had forgotten about his plans to ask God to change his life.

The man has a hard heart. "How is that possible?" you may ask. "He's hearing what God says." When you hear God's Word and refuse to put it into practice, your heart is hardened against His truth. Eventually, if you continue to ignore His leading, He lets you follow your own slippery course.

God allowed Pharaoh to tell Moses no again and again. Pharaoh knew what he was supposed to do—release God's chosen people, the Israelites, from slavery and oppression. Because Pharaoh persisted in his disobedience, he learned painful lessons he could have avoided.

Ask God to sensitize your heart and make you aware of any tough spots of resistance. He will soften your spirit, renew your understanding, and set you on a course of true submission.

> *Precious Lord, sensitize my heart. Make me aware of any hard spots of resistance. Soften my spirit, renew my understanding, and set me on a course of true submission.*

Facing Failure

SCRIPTURE READING: Luke 15:1–10   KEY VERSE: Luke 15:7

I say to you that likewise there will be more joy in heaven over one sinner who repents than over ninety-nine just persons who need no repentance.

The agony of the Christian life is not just failing but trying and failing. Once we know Christ, we do want to please Him; we do want to live in the light of His truth; we do want to live victoriously. As a sage once said, "God didn't teach us how to swim in order to let us sink." God saved us so that we could enjoy and experience His abundant life. Yes, there are struggles, but we can win.

But how do we overcome the sins that constantly seem to overwhelm and subdue us? We first come to the point of absolute repentance. How serious have we become about the sin that besets us? Do we see how offensive it is to God? Have we literally, completely changed our minds about it?

Genuine repentance is a deep, profound act. Most of us have not reached that level; we flirt with our sins. If we have repented, however, then step two is still essential—to recognize our new identity in Christ. Jesus indwells us with all of His might and divinity. We overcome through Him because He is the Overcomer. No sin can stand before Him as by faith we claim His total conquest gained at Calvary. As we become serious about sin and recognize our new natures as believers, triumph is near.

> *Dear heavenly Father, I want to recognize and claim my new identity in You. Help me understand that Jesus dwells in me with all of His might and divinity. Let me realize that I can overcome through Him because He is the Overcomer.*

God's Answer to Sin

SCRIPTURE READING: John 3   KEY VERSE: John 3:3

Jesus answered and said to him, "Most assuredly, I say to you, unless one is born again, he cannot see the kingdom of God."

God's only answer to the problem of sin is Jesus Christ. No one can save himself; no person is "good" enough to get into heaven. One day each of us will stand before God and give an account of why He should allow us to enter His kingdom. What will your answer be?

Reasons such as being good and trying not to hurt anyone won't work. Jesus told Nicodemus, a man known for his extreme knowledge of the Jewish law and his sensitivity to spiritual matters, that he had to be born again to enter the kingdom of God (John 3:3). This "born again" phrase often evokes cynicism from nonbelievers, but God does not apologize for His Word.

The new birth Jesus talked about in John 3 is not physical but spiritual in nature. W. E. Vines explained, "Born again is used metaphorically in the writings of the Apostle John, of the gracious act of God in conferring upon those who believe the nature and disposition of 'children,' imparting to them spiritual life."

Only God's saving grace through a personal experience with Jesus Christ is the answer to mankind's sin. God does not want anyone to miss heaven's wonder and perfect love. His greatest desire is that you would experience the love and forgiveness of His Son, the Lord Jesus Christ, for eternity. Have you placed your trust in Him?

Father God, I come Your way, through Jesus Christ. Thank You for Your Answer to my sin. I place my eternal trust in Him.

Separated from Sin

SCRIPTURE READING: Psalm 103   KEY VERSE: Psalm 103:13

As a father pities his children, so the LORD pities those who fear Him.

We read in Psalm 103:8–13 (NASB):

> *The LORD is compassionate and gracious, slow to anger and abounding in lovingkindness. He will not always strive with us; nor will He keep His anger forever. He has not dealt with us according to our sins, nor rewarded us according to our iniquities. For as high as the heavens are above the earth, so great is His lovingkindness toward those who fear Him. As far as the east is from the west, so far has He removed our transgressions from us. Just as a father has compassion on his children, so the LORD has compassion on those who fear Him.*

Can you think of why it would be important to know that God has separated you from your sin? One answer is theologically based: since God can have nothing to do with sin, He must completely remove sin from you through the blood of Jesus Christ in order to have a relationship with you.

Another reason is more subtle. If you do not grasp the fact that your sins are truly gone, then psychologically your sins are still hanging around. What happens when sin remains? You feel guilty, convicted, and unrighteous.

Positionally in Christ, your sin is gone; but this truth must be absorbed by you emotionally to be experientially real. That is why God says your sins are removed from you "as far as the east is from the west." How far is that? It is immeasurably and inexpressibly far.

> *Father, thank You for separating me from my sin. It is not hanging around. It is not hiding. It is gone—removed as far as the east is from the west. Thank You!*

Behavior to Match Your Identity

SCRIPTURE READING: 2 Corinthians 6:14–7:1 KEY VERSE: 2 Corinthians 7:1

Therefore, having these promises, beloved, let us cleanse ourselves from all filthiness of the flesh and spirit, perfecting holiness in the fear of God.

An American on business in the Far East is not very likely to assimilate Asian culture. Quite the contrary. The food is different; there is a language barrier; the wardrobes are distinct. He is constantly reminded of the dissimilarities. His identity as an American is well established. He acts and thinks like an American precisely because he is one. Understanding your identity in Christ is a pivotal principle for success in combating the world's influence.

A dramatic transformation occurred when you were saved. You became a "new creature" in Christ (2 Cor. 5:17 NASB). You became a citizen of God's kingdom. You still live in your indigenous culture, with all of its allures, trials, temptations, and charms; but you are no longer the same man or woman.

Living holy or separately from the impulses of the world is possible only as you realize the amazing metamorphosis that has transpired within. You are quite obviously still "in the world," but you are now not "of the world."

The rationale for rejecting the waywardness of the world is that it doesn't fit your new identity anymore. You don't act like an unregenerate person because you are a new person in Christ.

Learning who you are in Christ takes time, complete with failure, for your behavior to match your identity; but you have a lifelong, resident Teacher, the Holy Spirit, to help you along the way.

Precious heavenly Father, You brought me out of the "Egypt" of sin and set my feet on the road to Your promised land. As I continue on this spiritual journey, help me match my behavior with my new identity.

Binding Behaviors

SCRIPTURE READING: 1 Peter 1:13–16   KEY VERSE: 1 Peter 1:13

Therefore gird up the loins of your mind, be sober, and rest your hope fully upon the grace that is to be brought to you at the revelation of Jesus Christ.

Here's how to handle binding behaviors. First, identify the problem behavior. Be honest with yourself, or ask a trusted friend to be honest with you. Denying that you have a problem prevents you from experiencing true victory and hope.

Second, take responsibility for your behavior. No matter how small or large the behavior may seem, admit that it exists and that you are responsible for its continued presence.

Third, trace the behavior to the source. Ask God to help you remember when you were programmed to feel or act a certain way. Low self-esteem, feelings of rejection, or helplessness all have beginning points. And these behaviors lead to other habits that weaken our self-concept.

Fourth, forgive yourself, and forgive others who have hurt you. Forgiveness does not mean the person who hurt you can walk away without being punished. Forgiveness is something you do for yourself so that you can experience freedom from bitterness and resentment. Harboring angry feelings can lead to physical and emotional health problems. God tells us that vengeance belongs to Him. Let the Lord have your hurt and pain, and He will take care of the situation.

Fifth, renew your mind with the truth of God's Word. When you do this, you will discover that God loves you more than you can imagine. You also will receive needed strength and hope.

Lord, I want to take responsibility for my own behavior. Reveal to me the reasons behind my negative responses, and then help me forgive myself and others. Heal my hurt and pain.

MARCH

Journey to the Promised Land

REPRESENTING: Claiming God's promises

KEY VERSE: Philippians 4:19

My God shall supply all your need according to His riches in glory by Christ Jesus.

The nation of Israel had crossed the searing desert, battled numerous enemies, and wandered in the wilderness for forty years. Now—at last—they stood poised at the border of their promised land.

But there was a major problem. Jericho. A formidable walled city, it was a seemingly insurmountable obstacle that blocked their way.

Jericho was a divinely planned obstacle in the life of Israel. The outcome of the battle would bring glory to God and provide conclusive evidence to Israel that He was doing exactly what He had promised He would do.

This month you will learn to recognize obstacles in your journey of faith as opportunities to discover your true identity in Christ and to tap into His sufficiency. Joy, peace, wisdom, security, grace, power, unconditional love, an eternal inheritance—all these blessings are God's promises to you.

The promised land waits just beyond the Battle of Jericho. I don't know about you, but I'm ready to go!

Obstacles or Opportunities?

SCRIPTURE READING: Deuteronomy 11:18–28   KEY VERSE: Deuteronomy 11:26

Behold, I set before you today a blessing and a curse.

Joshua and the nation of Israel were preparing to enter the promised land. Moses would not go with them. His last responsibility as their leader would be to issue a charge concerning the land they were about to enter. He explained that if they would keep the commandments of the Law, then God would drive out their enemies before them.

Often we find ourselves wondering why God does not remove all the obstacles after He blesses us. The excitement of a new job turns sour the moment we find out the boss has a dark side. The dream house becomes a nightmare when we find out the roof leaks and the water heater needs replacing.

Many times God places obstacles in our lives to keep us humble and dependent on Him. The very name God gave the promised land—Canaan—means "a place of humility." The Israelites longed to enter the land of promise, yet they realized that along with the promise came the tests and trials of life.

There will be times when you feel as though you have run into a brick wall. The obstacle facing you may seem overwhelming, but take heart. These are the times God wants you to turn to Him and trust Him to remove the obstacle blocking your path.

> *Dear Lord, when it seems that a brick wall looms ahead, let me turn to You. Help me realize that obstacles keep me dependent on Your power. I trust You to remove every barrier from my path in Your perfect timing.*

Facing the Jerichos of Life

SCRIPTURE READING: Joshua 6   KEY VERSE: Joshua 1:6

Be strong and of good courage, for to this people you shall divide as an inheritance the land which I swore to their fathers to give them.

No military officer worth his stripes would go into conflict unprepared, without a clear and cogent plan of attack. The risk would be too great, and the chances of winning slim. Yet that was exactly what God wanted Joshua to do—approach the awesome, fortified city of Jericho without the first conventional military procedure. Literally all God gave to Joshua was his marching orders and the promise that the Israelites would be the winners.

How could Joshua hold his head high and approach the battlefield with confidence? He knew who was in charge. He did not have to worry about defeat or loss. Any momentary feelings of weakness came crashing down with the walls and were forgotten in the glory of taking the city for the Lord.

When you face a Jericho in your life—a problem you cannot solve, the seemingly impenetrable fortress of a broken relationship—trust God for the conquest. Obey His Word and apply His principles to each situation.

You may not understand how the sequence of events will unfold, and you may not feel the emotions of triumph while you wait for the outcome. But in the Lord you cannot lose; the victory is yours.

Heavenly Father, as I face the Jerichos of life, give me assurance that victory is mine. I want to respond to Your marching orders and not worry about the seemingly impenetrable fortresses ahead.

Characteristics of True Believers

SCRIPTURE READING: Ephesians 1:1–14   KEY VERSE: Ephesians 1:11

In Him also we have obtained an inheritance, being predestined according to the purpose of Him who works all things according to the counsel of His will.

A life of enduring holiness (reflecting the mind and character of God) is possible only when we first are convinced of our identity in Christ. The Scriptures attribute these remarkable characteristics to believers:

- We are the salt of the earth.
- We are saints.
- We are joint heirs with Jesus.
- We are justified by faith.
- We are ambassadors for Christ.
- We are eternally secure in Christ.
- We are triumphant in Christ.
- We are accepted in the Beloved.

- We are children of God.
- We have peace with God.
- We are free from condemnation.
- We are the temple of God.
- We are blessed with every spiritual blessing.
- We are citizens of heaven.
- We are complete in Christ.

Many other features are already yours through faith in Christ. They are gifts from the Father, bestowed upon every disciple for effective service.

Knowing who you are in Christ is the starting point for abundant living. You can live a holy life because you are holy in Christ. Today agree with God concerning your new identity in Christ.

O God, I declare my new identity in Christ: I am the salt of the earth, a child of God, a saint who has peace with You. I am joint heir with Jesus, free from condemnation, and justified by faith. I am the temple of God, an ambassador for Christ, eternally secure, triumphant, complete, and accepted in Christ. I am a citizen of heaven and blessed with every spiritual blessing!

The Sufficiency of Christ

SCRIPTURE READING: Ephesians 1:15–23   KEY VERSE: Colossians 1:18

He is the head of the body, the church, who is the beginning, the firstborn from the dead, that in all things He may have the preeminence.

As Paul addressed the deity and power of Christ in the first chapter of Colossians, he continually stressed the preeminence of Christ. Paul said He is "the first-born of all creation," "the first-born from the dead," and the One who is "to have first place in everything" (vv. 15, 18 NASB).

Paul's use of the term *first place* was not, however, the comparative term we sometimes imagine. He was not saying that Jesus is prominent—that is, Christ is first, my family second, the church third, my job fourth, and so on. That wasn't Paul's or God's intention.

What Paul—and the Spirit who inspired him—was attempting to communicate was that Jesus is preeminent. Jesus is above and beyond anyone and anything. Jesus is to be first in our homes, first in our finances, first in our relationships, first in our jobs, first in our leisure time, first and foremost in every conceivable aspect of life. Nothing can compare to Christ. He came not to be on the top of a priority list but to fill all with His fullness.

Is Christ the undisputed Lord over all of your life, reigning supreme? Have you allowed Him "to have first place in everything"?

Jesus, You are above and beyond anyone or anything in my life. You are first in my home, my finances, my relationships, my leisure time, and my work. You are undisputed Lord over my life.

Unchanging Joy

SCRIPTURE READING: John 6:32–40   KEY VERSE: John 6:40

This is the will of Him who sent Me, that everyone who sees the Son and believes in Him may have everlasting life; and I will raise him up at the last day.

Although the Christian life is most certainly a fight of faith, it is not endless striving and straining. There is a monumental difference between abiding in Christ and striving, and understanding the discrepancy can make a major change in the joy, peace, and contentment we experience as we serve Christ.

J. Hudson Taylor, the founder of China Inland Mission, wrestled with the distinction until one day, at age thirty-seven, he saw the total sufficiency of Christ for every need. The catalyst for this liberating discovery was a personal letter from a missionary friend, John McCarthy, who wrote,

To let my loving Savior work in me His will, my sanctification is what I would live for by His grace. Abiding, not striving nor struggling; looking unto Him to subdue all inward corruption; resting in the love of an Almighty Savior. This is not new and yet 'tis new to me. I feel as though the first dawning of a glorious day had risen upon me. I hail it with trembling and yet with trust.

I seem to have got to the edge only, but of a sea which is boundless; to have sipped only, but of that which fully satisfies.

Christ literally seems to me now the power, the only power for service; the only ground for unchanging joy.

Lord, help me abide in You and not struggle or strive. You are my power for service, my only ground for unchanging joy.

Christ in You

SCRIPTURE READING: John 14:15–27   KEY VERSE: John 16:14

He will glorify Me, for He will take of what is Mine and declare it to you.

How does God Himself, whose immensity cannot be measured, reside in such frail bodies as ours? How does the transcendent Christ live in finite human temples?

We may not comprehend the vastness of this principle, yet the method by which God imparts His presence is plain and clear in the Scriptures: Christ lives in us through His indwelling Holy Spirit. The Holy Spirit supernaturally brings the reality of Christ into our earthly frames.

As the third person of the Trinity, the Holy Spirit is just as much deity as the Father and the Son. He imparts the life of Christ to us through His residence in our lives.

The Holy Spirit reveals and shares with us all that Christ is. By making His home in us, He assures us of the presence and power of the risen Christ.

Because the Holy Spirit possesses all the attributes of deity and because He inhabits our mortal bodies, He is infinitely adequate to meet any of our needs. He is not a God far off but a God who is near.

The resurrected Christ is your sure and steadfast hope for all of life, a hope that is every believer's to claim because of the indwelling ministry of the Holy Spirit.

> *Come, Holy Spirit, and do Your work. Reveal all that Christ is and wants to be to me. Give me assurance of His presence and power. Let the same Spirit who raised Christ from the dead work abundantly in me.*

The Wisdom of God

SCRIPTURE READING: Proverbs 1:1–7   KEY VERSE: Proverbs 1:7

The fear of the LORD is the beginning of knowledge, but fools despise wisdom and instruction.

The apostle Paul made a clear distinction between the learned wisdom of his time and the wisdom of God. Such a difference still exists in this so-called intellectual age. As we send men into space and harness the atom, we still must be sure to lock our doors at night.

The wisdom of God is as superior to the wisdom of men as a star is to a sixty-watt bulb. Man's wisdom is knowledge and utilization of data. God's wisdom is strength, right thinking, guidance, and a right course for every man in every age in every circumstance.

Perhaps the best definition of *wisdom* is "viewing life from God's perspective." That means sifting our ambitions, challenges, problems, and tasks through the filter of God's eternal truth—the Scriptures.

God's wisdom can never be achieved through a mechanical formula. If that were the case, then any person—wicked or righteous—could enjoy its benefits. Receiving God's wisdom involves developing a growing, intimate relationship with Jesus Christ who is our wisdom (1 Cor. 1:30).

That's what Solomon meant when he said, "The fear of the LORD is the beginning of knowledge" (Prov. 1:7). As we seek and worship God and submit to His will, we increasingly become the repository of His wisdom.

Precious Lord, let me view life from Your perspective. Help me sift my ambitions, challenges, problems, and tasks through the filter of Your truth. Give me divine wisdom through an intimate relationship with Your Son, Jesus.

Prevailing Peace

SCRIPTURE READING: John 15:18–25   KEY VERSE: 2 Thessalonians 3:16

Now may the Lord of peace Himself give you peace always in every way. The Lord be with you all.

Europe trembled. Hitler's menacing armies were poised for a strike against Poland. Attempting to appease the dreaded dictator, England's Prime Minister Neville Chamberlain traveled to Germany and, on September 29, 1938, signed the infamous Munich Pact. Upon his return Chamberlain triumphantly announced, "I believe it is peace for our time." A short time later Germany invaded Poland, and World War II began.

Was Jesus' talk of peace like Chamberlain's optimistic boast? After all, why talk of such when war, violence, greed, and ill will still abound? Although Jesus talked much about peace and promised the disciples (and us) that He would leave us His peace, He did not ignore the reality of the world's conflict.

That's why His Passover message concerning peace was immediately followed by this clarification: "In the world you will have tribulation" (John 16:33). Jesus was a realist. There is nothing of evasiveness or idealism in His ministry. How, then, could He promise peace?

Christ Himself is our peace. His presence, strength, and comfort are ours in every gale—for He is always with us.

Dear heavenly Father, thank You that despite the tribulation in this world, I can have peace. I claim Christ as my peace right now. I accept His presence, strength, and comfort as I face the storms of life.

Genuine Security

SCRIPTURE READING: James 4:13–14   KEY VERSE: Proverbs 27:1

Do not boast about tomorrow, for you do not know what a day may bring forth.

The older we grow, the more security conscious we become. The prospects of putting kids through college and providing for retirement, savings, and investments take on disproportionate significance.

In reality, however, our sense of well-being is never assured. Economic collapse, sickness, political or environmental fluctuations, or any number of unknown factors could seriously jeopardize our best-laid plans.

That is possible at any stage of life. That is the disquieting point of Proverbs 27:1: "Do not boast about tomorrow, for you do not know what a day may bring forth."

Our only genuine security lies in our relationship with Jesus Christ. That is universally applicable because God is sovereign, which means that God is in control. He "guides and governs all events, circumstances, and free acts of angels and men and directs everything to its appointed goal for His own glory" (*The New Bible Dictionary*). Your security lies in His power to work everything for your good and His glory.

That is also eternally relevant because God is immutable. That means God is always the same and operates on unchanging principles.

> *Almighty God, I praise You that every detail of my life is directed by Your sovereign hand. I rest in the assurance that You govern each event and circumstance. I am secure in the knowledge that Your power weaves the dark and rough threads of life into a pattern for my good and Your glory.*

Amazing Grace

SCRIPTURE READING: Ephesians 2:1–10   KEY VERSE: Ephesians 2:13

Now in Christ Jesus you who once were far off have been brought near by the blood of Christ.

I t is little wonder that the hymn "Amazing Grace" is sung so resoundingly in churches across the world. Its vivid imagery reminds us of the preeminence of grace and its indispensable role in our salvation and sanctification. But what makes grace so amazing?

God's grace is amazing because it is free. No currency exists that can ever purchase grace. We are usually suspicious of anything free, but God's offer is without any hidden strings. He bore the cost for our sins (therefore, it is not cheap grace) so that He could extend it freely to any man on the basis of faith— not intellect, status, or prestige.

God's grace is amazing because it is limitless. His grace can never be exhausted. Regardless of the vileness or number of our sins, God's grace is always sufficient. It can never be depleted; it can never be measured. He always gives His grace in fullness.

God's grace is amazing because it is always applicable. Do you need wisdom? God's grace provides it through His Word. Do you need strength or guidance? God's grace sustains you by His Spirit. Do you need security? God's grace supplies it through His sovereignty.

The amazing grace of God! Full and free! Without measure! Pertinent for your every need!

It's free! It's limitless! It is applicable to my every need today! O Lord, thank You for Your amazing grace. I praise You that it flows full and free in my life.

Supernatural Strength

SCRIPTURE READING: Hebrews 12:1–3   KEY VERSE: 1 Peter 5:7

Casting all your care upon Him, for He cares for you.

Spiritual fatigue hits everyone. In the race to know and serve Christ, our bodies, minds, and hearts can reach an overload point, causing us to drop back. If severe enough, spiritual fatigue can discourage us from future participation.

God's strength to endure is ours when we "lay aside every encumbrance, and the sin which so easily entangles us" (Heb. 12:1 NASB). Cast your burdens on the Lord (1 Peter 5:7). Keep short accounts with God daily concerning your sin.

God's strength comes when we recognize that "in due time we shall reap if we do not grow weary" (Gal. 6:9 NASB). Your efforts will pay off. Harvesttime will come. Your toil will be rewarded. God promises it.

God's strength comes to finish the race when we are not "anxious for tomorrow; for tomorrow will care for itself" (Matt. 6:34 NASB). Live one day at a time. Do not be unduly concerned about tomorrow. The race is run step-by-step.

God's strength comes when we let Him turn our weaknesses into His strengths: "He gives strength to the weary, and to him who lacks might He increases power" (Isa. 40:29 NASB).

When you are weary, draw from almighty God's unlimited power supply. Faint not. Fear not. Fret not. He gives supernatural strength to finish the race.

> *Dear God, transform my human weakness into supernatural strength. Let me faint not, fear not, and fret not. Give me supernatural strength to finish the race.*

The Cycle of Blessing

SCRIPTURE READING: Psalm 145   KEY VERSE: Proverbs 10:22

The blessing of the LORD makes one rich, and He adds no sorrow with it.

Nature's cyclical pattern marks God's scheme of blessing. All blessings come from above (Gen. 49:25; Eph. 1:3). As Creator of all, the Lord is the Giver of life along with what sustains us (Ps. 145:15–16).

Heat from the sun, moisture from the rains, and oxygen in the atmosphere originated in His mind and exist through His wisdom and power (Gen. 1:1–2:3). He is the Designer of our bodies— organs, bones, tissues, muscles, nerves.

Our Father is also the Originator of our spiritual blessings. We can know God only because He first chose to reveal Himself through His creation; His Son, our Lord Jesus Christ; and the Bible (1 John 4:19).

When we receive the blessings of God through faith, the cycle continues as we share His presence in our conversation and our deeds. God told Abraham: "I will bless you . . . and so you shall be a blessing" (Gen. 12:2 NASB).

The Lord favors us with His encouragement, hope, and joy. In turn we encourage the fainthearted, revive the sagging soul, and bring cheer to the afflicted.

Are you participating in God's cycle of blessing? Look to Him as your Resource; then look to help others.

> *Precious heavenly Father, You are the Originator of all my spiritual bless-ings. Help me to plug into Your divine cycle of blessing. Let me look to You as my divine Resource in every situation, and then reveal ways I can bless others.*

How to Count Your Blessings

SCRIPTURE READING: Psalm 34   KEY VERSE: Psalm 34:8

Oh, taste and see that the LORD is good; blessed is the man who trusts in Him!

When you are asked to count your blessings, your list may not be overwhelming. You struggle to make ends meet; your days are hard. You are grateful for much, but weariness clouds your vision.

Pause to think of this: when you have the Lord Jesus Christ, you have the greatest blessing possible. That is not spiritualizing; it is the bedrock of your existence now on earth and one day in heaven.

In Christ you have the guarantee of eternal life. Life may be unsettling, but a place of unparalleled beauty and joy awaits the one who knows Christ as Savior, Lord, and Life. Heaven is real, and its blessings are sure.

In Christ Jesus you have the Source of true life. He gives love, joy, peace, strength, comfort, hope, and patience. He nourishes your soul and energizes your spirit. Possessions are nice, but they cannot impart life—only Jesus can.

In Christ you have a Friend for all seasons. He understands your disappointments, rejoices in your triumphs, and stands with you in your trials. You can confide in Him, weep before Him, and celebrate with Him.

Begin with all you have in Jesus Christ when you count your blessings. Then you will lose count.

Jesus, You are my greatest Source of blessing. You are my life. You give love, joy, peace, strength, comfort, and hope. You nourish my soul and energize my spirit. Thank You, Lord!

Clothed with Power

SCRIPTURE READING: Luke 24:44–49   KEY VERSE: John 6:63

It is the Spirit who gives life; the flesh profits nothing. The words that I speak to you are spirit, and they are life.

After Jesus rose from the dead and ascended to the Father, His disciples were zealous to spread His message of salvation. Yet Christ commanded them to wait until they were "clothed with power from on high" (Luke 24:49 NASB) on pentecost when the Holy Spirit would come for a new, indwelling ministry.

Think seriously about this fact: If the Holy Spirit was necessary for the apostles to live and minister effectively, do we not need His power as well? The Christian life is started by the Holy Spirit in the new birth experience and continued by the same Holy Spirit.

We need God's Holy Spirit to enable us to live in victory over our circumstances. Only He gives us His hope, strength, and peace in the midst of crises. Only He supplies the mind and life of Christ when our emotions and situations are unpredictable and unstable.

We need the Holy Spirit to carry out the commands of Scripture through us. We can love our enemies, give thanks in heartache, deny ourselves, and turn the other cheek when we are ridiculed—only as He expresses Christ's life through us.

The Lord gives you His all-sufficient Holy Spirit to glorify Himself through you. Let Him complete what He started in you at salvation by yielding to His reign daily.

Dear Lord, I yield to Your reign in my life so that You can complete what You started in me at salvation. Enable me to live in victory over my circumstances. Give me the mind of Christ when my emotions and situations are unstable.

A Changed Life

SCRIPTURE READING: John 3:1–17   KEY VERSE: Psalm 62:1

Truly my soul silently waits for God; from Him comes my salvation.

After we are saved, the constant pressure to conform to the world's standards can give us spiritual amnesia. We have to pay the electric bill on time, fight the rush-hour traffic, mow the yard, and wash the dishes just as everyone else does. The danger is that the familiar routine can cause us to lose sight of the radical transformation that occurred when we were born again.

At salvation, we received a new spirit, the Holy Spirit, who works through our ordinary experiences to accomplish the supernatural goal of conforming us to the image of Christ. In our bill paying, we can depend on His provision. In the irritating traffic snarls, we can meditate on Scripture. (Try it, it works!) In the yard work, we can enjoy His creation. In the kitchen, we can give thanks for His many gifts to us.

As new creatures with a new spirit, we have a new purpose—to honor God in all we do: working, eating, drinking, driving, playing, and thinking.

If your Christian experience borders on boring, remember the monumental change that occurred when you were saved and the divine dimension that is now yours to enjoy by faith and obedience.

> *Heavenly Father, thank You for the tremendous change that occurred when I was saved. Thank You for the divine dimension that is mine to enjoy in every area of my life. I want to honor You in all I do.*

God's Workmanship

SCRIPTURE READING: Matthew 22:34–40   KEY VERSE: Matthew 22:40

On these two commandments hang all the Law and the Prophets.

Some evangelicals espouse the warped view that loving ourselves is selfish and wrong.

While Christians obviously are called to love God and others, loving ourselves in a biblical, nonnarcissistic fashion fosters a healthy spiritual balance. We love ourselves properly when we see ourselves as God sees us.

God declares His children to be His workmanship. He views us as men and women of inestimable worth—valuable enough to execute His own Son on our behalf.

Your clothes, home, car, work, and friends do not determine your worth. God does. He values you so much that He desires to spend eternity with you.

We also love ourselves rightly when we treat ourselves properly. As God's masterpieces, we should take care of ourselves. Our bodies need balanced nutrition and exercise. Our personal grooming should be neat. We polish our furniture and wax our cars because they are objects of worth to us. Are we not worth more than they?

You are God's good and lovely creation. The more you affirm God's evaluation of yourself, the more you will adore Him and love others.

O God, You have declared me to be of inestimable worth. Help me view myself as You see me—valuable enough to execute Your own Son on my behalf.

Your True Identity

SCRIPTURE READING: Ephesians 4:17–24   KEY VERSE: Ephesians 4:24

You put on the new man which was created according to God, in true righteousness and holiness.

Determining identity is a lifelong struggle for many people. Teenagers look to peers and parents trying to discover their unique identity. Possessions and status are the criteria for the majority of their conclusions.

Adults tend to define their identity by their vocation, financial bracket, or social strata. Determining our identity greatly affects our behavior. We act like who we think we are.

One of the greatest assets of the Christian is that his identity is rooted in the person of Jesus Christ. Because he is a child of God—an heir of God, a citizen of heaven as well as earth, a saint, and God's workmanship—he can act accordingly.

Do you know who you are in Christ?

Your marriage, career, relationships, and ambitions all hinge upon your new relationship with God's Son, Christ Jesus.

Your values, priorities, and perspectives are determined by this new relationship with Jesus. You are secure in Him. You are complete in Him. Your past, present, and future are bound up in the person of Jesus Christ.

Father, I am thankful that I am complete in Your Son, Jesus Christ. My past, present, and future are bound up in Him. Let my values, priorities, and perspectives always reflect this divine relationship.

Measuring Your Wealth

SCRIPTURE READING: Romans 10:8–13   KEY VERSE: Romans 10:13

Whoever calls on the name of the LORD shall be saved.

I f someone asked you if you are wealthy, you probably would respond negatively.

"I pay my bills and have a little left over. I do better than some, but I am
certainly not wealthy."

But did you know that in Christ Jesus you are immensely wealthy?

"I do not feel wealthy. From all indications, primarily my pocketbook, I
definitely am not affluent."

You are using the wrong standard. The things that man honors, God
despises. By God's measuring stick, you possess extraordinary riches. As a
believer, you have the riches of God's grace bestowed upon you through the gift
of His Son, Christ Jesus.

There is no circumstance, no problem, no obstacle, that you face apart
from the lavish grace of God. He gives wisdom, strength, guidance, patience,
and love without limit. You are a wealthy saint because you have all the
resources you need for life on earth, and in heaven, in the person of Jesus
Christ.

God's help is available whenever you need it. Eternal life is yours forever.
His undeserved blessings overflow into your heart daily.

You are a wealthy saint. The treasures of a new life in Christ are completely
yours.

*Master, thank You for bestowing Your riches on me. Thank You for the
treasures of my new life in Christ. Eternal life. Blessings of wisdom,
strength, guidance, and patience. Love without limit.*

Claiming Your New Position

SCRIPTURE READING: Colossians 3:1–17   KEY VERSE: Colossians 3:3

You died, and your life is hidden with Christ in God.

Although financial poverty can occur through uncontrollable events, spiritual poverty is inexcusable for any born-again Christian.

Because we have been placed in Christ by God, we have constant, unlimited access to the Source of all spiritual blessings.

Why, then, do some walk well beneath the high calling of Scripture? Why do too many Christians suffer spiritual lack—living in perpetual defeat and disobedience?

The primary culprits that cause spiritual malnourishment are ignorance and unbelief. Our ignorance is of our resources in Christ. We fail to realize we are no longer habitual sinners, but justified saints.

But we must believe. Unbelief will always keep Christians mired in spiritual poverty. As long as you think of yourself in nonbiblical terms, suffering from self-condemnation and self-pity, you will not experience the joy, peace, and power that come from faith in Jesus Christ. You are a wealthy saint. God has a high calling for you.

By faith and a scriptural confession of what God's Word says about you, claim your extravagant, new position in Christ.

Lord, on the basis of Your Word and by faith, I claim my new position in Christ. I am wealthy. You have a high and noble calling for me. I rejoice in my spiritual riches!

Chosen by God

SCRIPTURE READING: 1 Peter 1:3–12   KEY VERSE: 1 Peter 1:3

Blessed be the God and Father of our Lord Jesus Christ, who according to His abundant mercy has begotten us again to a living hope through the resurrection of Jesus Christ from the dead.

C an you remember the rejection you felt when you were not chosen for one of these?

- The basketball team
- The cheerleading squad
- The promotion at work
- The college of your choice

Now, think of the thrill when you

- made the basketball team. • were selected for the cheerleading squad.
- received the promotion.   • were accepted by the college you desired to attend.

You experienced great joy and gladness in being chosen.

Did you know that God chose you for salvation before the foundation of the world? Did you know that He was working out the miracle of your new birth in His mind before there was yet one evidence of creation?

Such undeserved love should stagger you, humble you, and drive you to profound adoration for the goodness, mercy, and grace of our Lord Jesus Christ.

God chose you. Think of the value that places on your life. It does not matter where you live, what you look like, what kind of car you drive, or your level of income.

Rejoice. You have been chosen by God and are forever His.

Dear heavenly Father, I often feel rejected by others. Thank You that You selected me for salvation before the foundation of the world. I am accepted. I am chosen. Thank You!

A Child Of God

SCRIPTURE READING: 1 Peter 1:13–21   KEY VERSE: Romans 9:23

He might make known the riches of His glory on the vessels of mercy, which He had prepared beforehand for glory.

All of us must respond individually to God's offer of salvation (Eph. 1:13). Once we make a positive response of faith, the marvelous truth of God's sovereign working has just begun. We as believers are predestined for something far beyond our wildest imagination: "He predestined us to adoption as sons" (Eph. 1:5 NASB).

God did not save you just to escape the torment of hell and the condemnation of holy punishment. He saved you so that He might draw you into His household. You are a son or daughter of Jehovah God. As a child of God, you have the exhilarating prospect of fellowshipping intimately with your heavenly Father while depending on His loving provision. Forever, you will be a son or daughter of the Father.

You are also "predestined to become conformed to the image of His Son" (Rom. 8:29 NASB). The process of becoming like Christ begins at salvation. It continues through your life on earth. It will be consummated in heaven. God is at work irrevocably to make you like His very own Son. Can you think of anything more glorious?

Almighty God, please continue to conform me to the image of Your Son. I praise You that You are at work irrevocably in my life.

Heir to an Immeasurable Fortune

SCRIPTURE READING: Psalm 19   KEY VERSE: Acts 20:32

So now, brethren, I commend you to God and to the word of His grace, which is able to build you up and give you an inheritance among all those who are sanctified.

"I f only I were a Rockefeller or a Vanderbilt, my future would be secure." Most of us have probably dreamed what our lives would be like if we were heirs to such massive fortunes.

How would your thinking and living change if today you understood that you are the heir of treasures beside which even the wealthiest earthly estates pale?

The amazing truth is that God has named you an heir of His holdings: "And now I commend you to God and to the word of His grace, which is able . . . to give you the inheritance among all those who are sanctified" (Acts 20:32 NASB).

What does He own? He owns it all. As Creator of heaven and earth and all that is in them, God is the sole proprietor of the universe. It is in His hands to bestow His unspeakable wealth upon you.

God is your Father. You are His son or daughter. All that is His belongs to you. You have an inheritance that will never fade or tarnish because you are an heir of the Father's immeasurable fortune.

O God, You are my Father. I am Your child. All You have belongs to me. Thank You for an inheritance that will never fade.

Eternal Life

SCRIPTURE READING: Psalm 103   KEY VERSE: Psalm 103:4

Who redeems your life from destruction, who crowns you with lovingkind-
ness and tender mercies.

Whether on the deserted streets of Bombay or in a plush oceanfront home, whether clothed in tattered jeans or a fine suit, you can enjoy the good life that Jesus Christ imparts to all who believe and abide in Him. The good life is eternal life received as a gift through faith in Christ's sacrifice for our sins.

Eternal life is as good as it gets. It is the everlasting, unending, unceasing presence of the eternal God, lavishing all of His goodness upon you in His limitless mercy and grace. It is a permanent possession, unaffected by the rise and fall of money, men, or nations. It is guaranteed by Christ's death, burial, and resurrection.

But you can experience the reality of eternal life here and now. A new quality of life is available to all who have become one with the Savior. It is the abundant sufficiency of Christ for every circumstance.

Each day is an opportunity to draw from the divine well of peace, joy, love, faithfulness, gentleness, goodness, patience, and self-control without diminishing the supply by one ounce. Do not ever be deceived. Real life is in Jesus, and Jesus is in you. Inexhaustible, boundless life for you forever.

Precious heavenly Father, thank You for the inexhaustible, boundless life
that is in Your Son, Jesus. Let me continually draw from Your divine
resources.

Abundant Life

SCRIPTURE READING: Isaiah 43   KEY VERSES: Isaiah 43:18–19

Do not remember the former things, nor consider the things of old. Behold, I will do a new thing, now it shall spring forth; shall you not know it? I will even make a road in the wilderness and rivers in the desert.

In *The Root of the Righteous,* A. W. Tozer urged readers, "Keep your feet on the ground, but let your heart soar as high as it will. Refuse to be average or to surrender to the chill of your spiritual environment."

As believers, we must live out the truth given to us in Hebrews 11. Our citizenship is registered in heaven where we have an eternal destiny. When we view life with this perspective, our outlook is positive and hope filled.

We are fully alive through Jesus Christ, who lives in us by the power of His Spirit. In fact, we are much more alive now that we have received God's Son as our Savior than when we walked this earth in physical form only. We are alive eternally to spiritual things that were once beyond our ability to understand.

The Old Testament saints could only imagine what was to come. They lived and died in their faith. However, they were not disappointed. Their devotion to God—and His to them—was sufficient for all their needs.

Are you living as Tozer suggested, keeping your feet firmly planted in the truth of God's Word, all the while dreaming and thinking of what God has for you in the not-so-distant future? This is the faith that draws you even closer to the reality of God's precious love. Jesus came so that we might have abundant life now—a tiny foretaste of what is yet to be.

Almighty God, I want to keep my feet on the ground while my heart soars to heights unlimited. Help me not to surrender to the chill of my spiritual environment. Plant my feet firmly in Your Word as I dream of the unlimited future You have planned for me.

The Temple Of God

SCRIPTURE READING: 1 Corinthians 3:9–17   KEY VERSE: 1 Corinthians 3:16

Do you not know that you are the temple of God and that the Spirit of God dwells in you?

Before you were saved, you were a reflection of this godless age. Your thoughts and habits, though perhaps good ones, were more benevolent than godly. Once Christ came to live in your heart, your life was changed. Your body, even in its fallen state, has become His place of residence. We know that while God resides in heaven, His Spirit lives within the lives of those who believe in Him.

Rather than living among the trees or in the wind, God who is personal and intimate in nature seeks a dwelling place where He can express Himself. He actually desires to live with His creation and has chosen the lives of those who love Him as His home.

In Old Testament times the Jews worshiped God in the temple. But Jesus' coming abolished the need for a man-made habitat. Just as our Lord walked and talked with the people of His day, He is doing the same with those who belong to Him through the indwelling power of the Holy Spirit.

What happens if we, as temples of God, become dirty and dark through our association with the sinfulness of this world? The gravest result is the loss of intimate fellowship with Christ. Nothing equals that. Filling your life with things that sadden God brings tearful consequences.

Don't darken the light that God has placed inside you. You are His temple, His home this side of heaven.

Father, thank You for coming and living inside me. Continually cleanse every corner of my spiritual temple. Make it a fit habitation for a King.

Unconditional Love

SCRIPTURE READING: 1 John 4:7–11   KEY VERSE: 1 John 4:7

Beloved, let us love one another, for love is of God; and everyone who loves is born of God and knows God.

God's love for you stands unmatched by anything this world has to offer. Only His love can

- calm the restlessness of your soul.
- heal any hatred you have experienced.
- change worry and doubt to hope and security.
- resolve the anger and bitterness that come from disappointment.
- give you a sense of purpose, self-worth, and hope.

God never grows tired of you. He sees the span of your life. His eye is on the potential that your life holds.

He spends each moment completely absorbed in thoughts of you—developing you, molding you, and blessing you.

So often we miss His blessings because we worry about what we should or should not do. Questions fill our minds: *Did I do it right? Is God pleased with me?*

God loves you, and His love will never change. He has a plan for your life, and you will succeed. The key is to remain focused on Him and not on who you think you should be.

Don't waste time comparing yourself to others. Many who are single wonder why God has not answered their prayers for a husband or wife. He has. He has given you Himself, and in His timing He will satisfy the longing of your heart in the way that is best for you.

Dear Lord, calm my restless soul. Heal my hurt, and resolve my anger and bitterness. Replace my worries and doubts with hope and security. Give me new purpose for living.

A Marvelous Creation of God

SCRIPTURE READING: Psalm 71   KEY VERSE: Psalm 71:5

You are my hope, O Lord GOD; You are my trust from my youth.

Most of us know hope when it appears. We start our day with the anticipation that something good is just around the corner, but then it happens—disappointment steals our hope, and we wonder if the excitement and joy we felt were from God or our imagination.

Hope stealers are at work twenty-four hours a day. They include the criticism of others, difficult circumstances, trials, feelings of rejection and self-doubt, and more. What can you do to safeguard yourself against such thought patterns?

First, tell yourself the truth about your situation. Don't beat yourself down. God never does (Rom. 8:1).

Second, remember that God is the God of possibilities. In *The Attributes of God*, A. W. Tozer maintained,

> God is kindhearted, gracious, good-natured and benevolent in intention . . . We only think we believe, really. We are believers in a sense, and I trust that we believe sufficiently to be saved and justified before His grace. But we don't believe as intensely and as intimately as we should. If we did, we would believe that God is . . . gracious and that His intentions are kind and benevolent. We would believe that God never thinks any bad thoughts about anybody, and He never had any bad thoughts about anybody.

What does God think about you? Marvelous. Wonderful. His creation. You are His child, and He is proud of you.

> *Father, as I face criticism, difficult circumstances, trials, and rejection today, help me remember Your declaration concerning me: I am marvelous, wonderful, Your creation. I accept Your evaluation and reject the negative opinions of others.*

Contentment

Scripture Reading: Philippians 4:6–13   Key Verse: Philippians 4:12

I know how to be abased, and I know how to abound. Everywhere and in all things I have learned both to be full and to be hungry, both to abound and to suffer need.

We struggle enough over the issue of contentment, and most of us live in fairly good conditions with enough to eat and clothes to wear. Imagine Paul in prison, without some of the basic necessities and without personal freedom, and read his words carefully: "Not that I speak from want; for I have learned to be content in whatever circumstances I am. I know how to get along with humble means, and I also know how to live in prosperity; in any and every circumstance I have learned the secret of being filled and going hungry, both of having abundance and suffering need. I can do all things through Him who strengthens me" (Phil. 4:11–13 NASB).

Paul was not a blind and foolhardy optimist who denied reality. He had already endured much physical hardship, yet he could still look at his bleak prospects, humanly speaking, and say he was truly content. When he said that Christ was his strength for everything, he meant everything. He did not try to count his "haves" and "have-nots" in a spirit of worry or fear.

Paul knew that God's best for him was found by abiding in Christ daily, trusting Him to furnish what he needed. More important, Paul knew that looking around in envy at other believers would lead only to attitudes of defeat and discouragement. And that is not God's best for anyone.

Thank You, God, for what You have graciously given me: food, shelter, friends, and family. I trust You to furnish any lack in my life. Teach me to be content.

Complete in Christ

SCRIPTURE READING: Colossians 2:6–10   KEY VERSE: Colossians 2:10

You are complete in Him, who is the head of all principality and power.

On a scale of one to ten, how complete would you say your life is? What person, job, object, or achievement would make your life more fulfilling? Most of us would have probably scored moderately high on the first question and added a few names or items to the second.

Did you know, though, that the apostle Paul insisted that once we place our trust in Christ as Savior, at that instant we become "complete in Him"? The word *complete* in the original Greek meant "full." When a person is full, he has no room for anything more. Think about this: if Christ is in you, your life is a "ten." In Jesus Christ is "the fulness of Deity" (Col. 2:9 NASB). That is, Christ is the sum of all perfection—without blemish or want.

That same Christ resides in you and supplies all your needs. Therefore, when you have Christ, you have it all. You lack nothing. You possess eternal and abundant life. In Him are all of the wisdom, love, patience, kindness, and comfort you will ever need. No demand is unmet through the limitless resources of the indwelling Christ. Since you are complete in Him, your search for meaning is over. Christ is your life, and that is enough.

Almighty Lord, thank You that I am complete in You. My life is a "ten." All my needs are supplied. I have it all. I lack nothing!

Your Future Reward

SCRIPTURE READING: 1 Corinthians 3:1–14   KEY VERSE: Revelation 22:12

Behold, I am coming quickly, and My reward is with Me, to give to every one according to his work.

When the sixteenth-century Polish astronomer Nicolas Copernicus first proposed that the earth revolves around the sun, not vice versa, he was met with scorn and ridicule. It was years later that his theory was found to be entirely accurate. Life often seems that way. Evil men are treated as kings, while good men are ignored.

The psalmist contemplated this seeming discrepancy in Psalm 73: "Behold, these are the wicked; and always at ease, they have increased in wealth. Surely in vain I have kept my heart pure" (vv. 12–13 NASB).

In the Sermon on the Mount, Jesus indicated that His followers would be persecuted on earth. He went on to say, however, that they should rejoice in such treatment because their "reward in heaven is great" (Matt. 5:12 NASB).

Believers are justly recompensed in heaven for their conduct and works on earth—as they trust the Lord to do His works through them. All inequities and injustices are more than compensated by the rewards that Christ will distribute to His followers.

Whether or not you are now recognized at work or home, whether or not you are treated with due respect, remember that God will honor your obedience for all eternity.

Dear heavenly Father, I rejoice in the knowledge that all inequities and injustices will be compensated in eternity. Until that time, help me continue to do Your work Your way.

You Have It All!

SCRIPTURE READING: John 1:1–18   KEY VERSE: John 1:4

In Him was life, and the life was the light of men.

Every individual who has trusted Jesus for his salvation has received the Source for his most compelling needs in the person of the indwelling Christ.

Christ is the Bread of Life. He is the Sustenance who nourishes our innermost being. Our hunger for meaning and purpose in life is fully satisfied in Christ. He is meaning; He is purpose. We want not for significance in life when we have Christ as our life.

Christ is the Water of Life. He channels His all-sufficient life through our earthen vessels—drenching us with His joy, peace, love, hope, contentment, strength, and steadfastness. He quenches our thirst for self-worth, assuring us of our inestimable value to Him. He freely gives us His abundant life.

Christ is the Light of Life. He enlightens us with eternal truth, bequeathing us wisdom for the journey. He sheds His light upon what is truly valuable so that we can pursue the things that are profitable, not foolishly chasing empty dreams or false, deceiving philosophies.

When you have Christ, you have it all—meaning, purpose, life in its fullest sense, truth, and wisdom. You belong to the Creator, Sustainer, and End of all things.

Jesus, You are my Bread of Life. You are my Sustenance. You are the Water of Life, channeling Your sufficiency through me. You are the Light of Life, giving wisdom for the journey ahead. In You, dear Lord, I have it all!

APRIL

Journey to the Cross

REPRESENTING: Trusting Jesus

KEY VERSES: Colossians 2:6–7

As you therefore have received Christ Jesus the Lord, so walk in Him, rooted and built up in Him and established in the faith, as you have been taught, abounding in it with thanksgiving.

The trip that Jesus took was planned from the foundation of the world. He was the first to make the trip: "Now it came to pass, when the time had come for Him to be received up, that He steadfastly set His face to go to Jerusalem" (Luke 9:51). Since then, hundreds of thousands of people down through the centuries have followed in His footsteps.

Our spiritual journey this month takes us to the cross. I invite you to come and stand once again at the foot of Golgotha. Let the cleansing blood from Calvary flow over you anew. Hear the cry from the cross: "It is finished!" Witness love in action.

Like Jesus, you must steadfastly set your face toward Jerusalem. Don't let anything prevent you from this journey of a lifetime. We have a divine destination. We're going to the cross.

The Wonder of the Cross

SCRIPTURE READING: Colossians 2:6–15   KEY VERSE: Acts 26:18

To open their eyes, in order to turn them from darkness to light, and from the power of Satan to God, that they may receive forgiveness of sins and an inheritance among those who are sanctified by faith in Me.

The wonder of the Cross is that it displayed both the love and the holiness of God. In one moment in time, God's hatred of sin and His unfailing compassion for sinners blended together in the blood of His Son, Jesus Christ.

The Cross was necessary because man could not save himself from sin, and holy God could not condone sin. God's holiness, however, was matched by His love, which sent Christ to die in our stead, bearing our guilt, dying our death.

In his book *The Cross of Christ,* John R. W. Stott discussed the significance of sin's gravity and God's amazing love:

> All inadequate doctrines of the atonement are due to the inadequate doctrines of God and man. If we bring God down to our level and raise ourselves to His, then, of course, we see no need for a radical salvation, let alone for a radical atonement to secure it.
>
> When on the one hand, we have glimpsed the blinding glory of the holiness of God and have been so convicted of our sin by the Holy Spirit that we tremble before God and acknowledge what we are, namely "hell-deserving sinners," then—and only then—does the necessity of the cross appear so obvious.

Dear heavenly Father, as I journey to the cross during this coming month, reveal its true meaning. Help me understand its wonder. Make it real to me.

Eternal Benefits of the Cross

SCRIPTURE READING: Romans 3   KEY VERSE: Romans 5:1

Having been justified by faith, we have peace with God through our Lord Jesus Christ.

The self-substitution of Christ for man's sin is the heart of the Cross. Because of His death at Calvary, Christ allows believers to enjoy the eternal benefits of these central truths:

Propitiation. The wrath of God against sin was fully vented on His own Son at the cross. Christians never need to fear angering God. Our sin is forgiven, and even God's chastisement for sinful behavior is motivated by compassion.

Redemption. Christ's death purchased us out of the slavery of sin. His shed blood paid the penalty of death and ransomed us from sin and evil. We have been delivered from the kingdom of Satan and placed into the kingdom of God's Son.

Justification. By God's grace we no longer are guilty before God. Christ's death secured our verdict, releasing us from the sentence of death. He declares us righteous and credits His righteousness to our account.

Reconciliation. Once enemies, God and man are now friends. The Cross made a permanent change possible between formerly alienated man and God. The right Man is now on our side, and we are on His.

> *Dear Lord, thank You for the eternal benefits of the Cross—that my sin is forgiven, I am redeemed from the slavery and penalty of sin, justified and reconciled with You.*

The Cry of the Cross

SCRIPTURE READING: 1 Corinthians 2   KEY VERSE: 1 Corinthians 2:2

I determined not to know anything among you except Jesus Christ and Him crucified.

To some, a cross might seem an odd symbol for a religious faith. It does, after all, carry the same meaning as an electric chair or a hangman's noose—death.

Yet this gruesome form of Roman torture stands at the heart of Christianity. An emblem such as the sign of the fish is a legitimate New Testament expression, but the cross of Jesus Christ is the authentic badge of Christianity.

You see, God so loved you that Christ died for you. There was no way around it. Sin—the state and condition into which all men are born—had carved an abyss between God and man that nothing but the Cross could traverse. The message of the Cross is love, God's immeasurable, amazing love for man. The holy love of God sent His Son to earth in human form and placed Him on two pieces of timber.

When you think upon the cross and its painful accoutrements—nails, thorns, jeers, whips, and ridicule—think of the overwhelming love of God. God loves you. He died for you. He was raised for you. He saves all who trust Him for forgiveness of sin. He reserves eternity in your name. That is the love of God and the consummate cry of the cross.

Lord, thank You for Your overwhelming love demonstrated at Calvary. You died for me. You were raised for me. You saved me and have reserved eternity in my name. Thank You that I have heard the cry of the cross.

A Living Savior

SCRIPTURE READING: Mark 15–16   KEY VERSE: Luke 24:6

He is not here, but is risen! Remember how He spoke to you when He was still in Galilee.

One cannot diminish the torture or agony of the Cross. Christ suffered and died for our sin, willingly laying down His life for the transgressions of men. Yet there can likewise be no diluting the supernatural power of the Resurrection.

None of the benefits of the Cross—forgiveness of sin, justification of sinners—could be ours today without a living Savior. The resurrection of Christ attested more than any other event to His full and absolute deity. Jesus met and conquered death, Satan, and sin, proclaiming His divine nature and displaying His divine power.

Today, the believer can enjoy the exquisite delight of union with the resurrected Christ. At work, in the store, in the house, or on the road, you have Jesus Christ in you, and God has placed Him in you.

The resurrected Christ lives in you so that you may partake of His life and sup with Him. He helps you, comforts you, guides you, loves you, and pours His life out through you. Jesus does more than just live. He lives in you, makes His abode in your heart, and infuses your ordinary life with supernatural meaning, strength, and hope. He arose just as He said He would, and He lives to give you the abundant life He promised.

Jesus, You live in me! I am partaker of Your life. I can fellowship with You. Come and comfort, guide, and pour Your life through me. Infuse my ordinary life with supernatural meaning.

Grace Plus Nothing

SCRIPTURE READING: 1 Corinthians 15:1–28   KEY VERSE: Hebrews 10:12

This Man, after He had offered one sacrifice for sins forever, sat down at the right hand of God.

Many Christians lack joy because they are not sure of their relationship with Christ. The Jews of Jesus' day believed the only way they could be sure of their standing with God was by keeping the law. It provided measurable evidence of their devotion.

However, Jesus offered a new theology, one based on God's unconditional love and acceptance. The Jewish leaders were bound by the law and refused to accept salvation as being a gift of grace. Imagine their dismay when Jesus told them that He was the fulfillment of the law. Through Christ, we have personal access to God the Father without bearing the burden of the law and its consequences. Only grace secures our position with God.

Jesus told Nicodemus, "You must be born again" (John 3:7). His words indicated a need for a spiritual rebirth or regeneration. It is something human hands cannot achieve. There is nothing we can do to earn salvation. Salvation equals grace plus nothing.

The next time you are tempted to doubt your salvation, think of the Cross where grace paid the eternal price for all of our sins. We are saved and sure by the power of His grace—nothing more, nothing less.

Father, I am saved by grace—nothing more, nothing less. I accept it. Thank You!

Secured by Christ

SCRIPTURE READING: Galatians 6:13–15   KEY VERSE: Ephesians 2:14

He Himself is our peace, who has made both one, and has broken down the middle wall of separation.

God calls us to serve Him out of love and devotion, not out of work or obligation. The Pharisees prided themselves in the fact that they kept the whole law. They believed that would please God and secure their salvation.

The sad point is that whenever you base anything—a marriage, a friendship, a job, or more important, your relationship with God—on works, you never know where you stand. There is always a degree of doubt involved because you are driven to achieve standards set by yourself and others.

Jesus set a new standard for your relationship with God: "For the law was given through Moses, but grace and truth came through Jesus Christ" (John 1:17). God never meant for the Jews to view the law as a pathway to salvation. Instead, it was given as preparation for the coming of Christ.

We can be sure of our salvation because we are secured by Christ and not by our performance. Some people say salvation by grace alone is "cheap talk." But nothing is cheap about the Cross. Jesus Christ, the most valuable person who has ever lived, loves you so much that He willingly laid down His life that you might experience eternal life with Him. It is His gift of love to you.

Lord, thank You for laying down Your life so that I can experience eternal life with You. Thank You for Your gift of love. Help me realize Your grace is not cheap.

Eternal Changes

SCRIPTURE READING: 1 Corinthians 2:1–5   KEY VERSE: John 18:37

Pilate therefore said to Him, "Are You a king then?" Jesus answered, "You say rightly that I am a king. For this cause I was born, and for this cause I have come into the world, that I should bear witness to the truth. Everyone who is of the truth hears My voice."

Each of us must come to a point where we respond to the cross of Christ. There is no escaping it. Those who followed Jesus were faced with this fact, as were those who refrained from acknowledging His public ministry. Nicodemus approached Jesus under the cover of darkness.

At that time, the focus of Nicodemus's heart was not on eternal but on temporal issues. However, by the time of Christ's death, all of that had changed dramatically. Joseph of Arimathea, along with Nicodemus, requested permission to bury the body of Christ. Once Pilate placed his seal on the document granting their request, their lives were changed forever.

Hurrying to the site of the Crucifixion, they fought frantic, fearful thoughts, but their minds were made up. Jesus would have a proper burial, and they didn't care who among their peers found out that they were responsible for this last act of devotion. Joseph donated his own tomb. Nicodemus gave all the spices he had gathered in preparation for his own death and burial.

Nicodemus had never publicly acknowledged Jesus; neither had Joseph (John 19:38). But with each handful of myrrh and aloe packed around the Lord's body, the commitment of their hearts was made sure. The wonder of the Cross is not in death but in the eternal changes it brings.

Master, thank You for the eternal change that has occurred in me. My sins are forgiven, my destiny assured, my life changed forever.

The Great Decision

SCRIPTURE READING: Romans 6:1–14   KEY VERSE: Romans 6:11

Likewise you also, reckon yourselves to be dead indeed to sin, but alive to God in Christ Jesus our Lord.

All day long he had barked orders at his detachment of soldiers. If there was a job lower than this one, he couldn't name it. No one volunteered for this detail; they were sentenced to it. A cold rain washed over the centurion's face as an intense storm swept over Jerusalem. The earth rolled and shook in response to each bolt of lightning. There amid the wind and rain, he found himself face-to-face with the cross of Jesus Christ.

Earlier he had witnessed the jeers of the crowd and the hate that had poured out of their mouths. And though he didn't show it, his heart mourned for the crucified man's family. How helpless and vulnerable they appeared. Then in a loud outcry, begging God to forgive those who had harmed Him, Jesus died.

The centurion knew what anger looked like. He had seen it often among his fellow soldiers. He also knew the contempt of betrayal and what it felt like to be rejected. But he saw none of that on Christ's face. There were only love and forgiveness.

Looking up to the cross, the centurion proclaimed in a loud voice: "Truly this was the Son of God!" (Matt. 27:54 NASB). Whether or not he understood all that had happened, he recognized the identity of the Man on the cross.

The greatest decision you will ever make has to do with the cross of Christ, where the Son of God gave Himself for you. Acknowledge Him and receive eternal life.

Precious Lord, I acknowledge the Cross and what You did for me there. You gave Your life for me. Thank You for Your love.

God Never Gives Up

SCRIPTURE READING: Colossians 3:1–17   KEY VERSE: Colossians 1:13

He has delivered us from the power of darkness and conveyed us into the kingdom of the Son of His love.

When Christ told Peter of his coming denial, Peter stiffened and protested, "Even though all may fall away because of You, I will never fall away" (Matt. 26:33 NASB). But Jesus knew the truth. Peter would deny Him, not once but three times.

Peter's robust personality vowed never to leave Jesus' side. But within a matter of hours he was reduced to fear and hiding from Jewish and Roman officials. The encouraging message of the Resurrection is that God never gives up on us.

Among Christ's last words to Peter before His death were words of restoration: "But I have prayed for you, Simon, that your faith may not fail. And when you have turned back, strengthen your brothers" (Luke 22:32 NIV). Jesus knew Peter would fall, and He loved him anyway. He gave His zealous disciple hope of future service when He said, "Strengthen your brothers."

God takes our weaknesses and turns them into points of strength and honor for Himself. Jesus was totally committed to Peter. He knew Peter would suffer a bitter defeat, but there was an event coming that would revolutionize his thinking—the Resurrection.

Imagine Peter's amazement as Jesus stepped into the Upper Room the night of His resurrection. The joy Peter experienced was there because of the love and acceptance Christ portrayed. This same love is yours today.

Dear heavenly Father, let the message of the Resurrection revolutionize my life, as it did Peter's. Through the power of the Resurrection, take my weaknesses and turn them into strengths that will bring glory and honor to You.

God's Gift to You

SCRIPTURE READING: 1 Corinthians 1:18–25   KEY VERSE: Colossians 1:20

By Him to reconcile all things to Himself, by Him, whether things on earth or things in heaven, having made peace through the blood of His cross.

From the disciples' point of view the Cross seemed ridiculous. In fact, no one understood why Jesus submitted to such treatment. They could not comprehend what He was doing for them. For years, they prayed for Messiah to come. However, their idea of a Savior was something far from what they saw in Jesus. The man they had hoped would come was one of military might. He would put to rest once and for all the nagging pursuit of the Roman government and, for that matter, everyone else who troubled God's chosen people.

But God's purposes seldom revolve around human strength and ability. Instead, He tells us to deny ourselves, to take up His cross, and to follow Him. This inherently leads to the crucified life—a life where Christ reigns. It also is a life that mirrors our Lord's example while teaching us to focus the attitude of our hearts on God and His will alone.

Christ's only focus was to do the will of the Father. You cannot save yourself. Any human effort or striving to reach some point of holiness outside acknowledging what Christ did for you at Calvary is done in vain.

The Cross is God's gift to you. It was something Jesus did out of love. His greatest desire is to have you beside Him for all eternity. This Easter allow the cross of Christ to find its place deep within your life as you celebrate His resurrection.

Almighty God, thank You for the gift of the Cross. Let the cross of Christ find its place deep within my life as I celebrate the Resurrection this season.

The Blood of the Lamb

SCRIPTURE READING: Luke 22:7–20   KEY VERSE: Luke 22:20

He also took the cup after supper, saying, "This cup is the new covenant in My blood, which is shed for you."

For hundreds upon hundreds of years, the Jews had met together to celebrate that dreadful and exciting night in Egypt when the Lord's destroyer passed over the Israelites' homes and spared their firstborn (Ex. 11–12).

Why should this Passover night be any different? Yet the disciples sensed Jesus' intense mood and listened attentively as He spoke: "I have earnestly desired to eat this Passover with you before I suffer; for I say to you, I shall never again eat it until it is fulfilled in the kingdom of God" (Luke 22:15–16 NASB).

Their minds reeled under the weight of Jesus' words. He had talked about His mission before, but what did He mean now? The disciples watched His hands closely as He lifted the cup and told them to drink together: "This cup which is poured out for you is the new covenant in My blood" (Luke 22:20 NASB). Then Jesus called the bread His body, to be broken and given for them.

In one moment, Jesus changed the significance of Passover and the entire sacrificial system forever. The disciples didn't comprehend the full importance of Jesus' message. It was late, and there was so much to understand. But later when He appeared to them after the Resurrection, the truth became clear.

The blood of the Passover lamb was the blood of the one eternal Lamb, sufficient to cover the sins of all for all time (Heb. 9:11–14).

O Lord, standing at the foot of the cross, I come to receive forgiveness from You. Your blood is sufficient for my sins. Cleanse me now.

No Wonder They Call Him Savior

SCRIPTURE READING: John 19   KEY VERSE: Philippians 2:8

Being found in appearance as a man, He humbled Himself and became obedient to the point of death, even the death of the cross.

O f all forms of execution devised by man through the millennia, crucifixion ranks among the cruelest and most abhorrent. Although crucifixion was first practiced by the Phoenicians and Carthaginians, the Roman Empire adopted the notorious practice as a universal form of death among its enslaved states. Even secular writers of the time shrank from giving detailed accounts of the cruel and degrading punishment.

Jesus, our Savior, died in such a manner, impaled on crude timber, in full view of a mostly hate-satiated crowd. It was an excruciatingly painful way to die. Yet Christ's physical agony on the cross, as horrid as it was, should never obscure the reason Jesus hung on display. He died for our sins so that we could receive His gift of eternal life.

There God the Son experienced spiritual death—separation from God the Father. Christ's forlorn cry, "My God, My God, why hast Thou forsaken Me?" (Matt. 27:46 NASB), was the most dreadful utterance of history. For an awful moment in time, God the Father forsook His Only begotten Son.

Jesus "humbled Himself by becoming obedient to the point of death, even death on a cross" (Phil. 2:8 NASB) so that we could enjoy the splendor of resurrection life and everlasting communion with God the Father. Author Max Lucado writes, "No wonder they call Him Savior."

> *Jesus, thank You for Your sacrifice on the cross of Calvary. Because of You, I can enjoy resurrection life and everlasting communion with God. No wonder they call You Savior!*

The Foundation of Forgiveness

SCRIPTURE READING: 1 John 1:8–2:2   KEY VERSE: Romans 6:6

Knowing this, that our old man was crucified with Him, that the body of sin might be done away with, that we should no longer be slaves of sin.

Firemen ran, shouted, hauled hoses, and sprayed countless gallons of water. But within minutes the building was engulfed in flames. Just when they thought everyone was safely out, they heard another voice yelling for help.

One fireman chose to go inside. He knew the odds. The ceiling was ready to collapse at any second, but without hesitation he answered the call. Moments later, a man was pushed from a window into the net below. But the fireman never came out.

Moving stories like this one about heroism in the face of death are examples of the kind of compassion Jesus talked about when He said, "Greater love has no one than this, that one lay down his life for his friends" (John 15:13 NASB). When Jesus said that, He wasn't referring to an abstract ideal that sounds good only on paper.

Jesus knew the cost. Long before you were even born, at the time of creation, God laid down the penalty for sin: death and separation from Him forever. And although God loves you dearly, He cannot overlook His own law; someone has to pay the price for your sin. Christ came to trade places with you, His innocent life taking the place of your guilty one.

Have you accepted the gracious offer of your Rescuer, or have you pushed Him away? He is the only One who can truly save you.

You laid down Your life for me, Jesus. You paid the penalty for my sin. You took my place. How I praise You!

The Record Book of Sin

SCRIPTURE READING: Romans 6:15–23   KEY VERSE: 2 Corinthians 5:21

He made Him who knew no sin to be sin for us, that we might become the righteousness of God in Him.

At a strict private school, the administration used a demerit system of discipline. Whenever students broke a rule or failed to carry out instructions, they were given demerits worth a certain number of points. Punishments were handed out according to the points, which were tallied each week in a black register.

One day, the principal called a special assembly. In several swift motions, he tore the book apart and scattered the pieces on the floor. The students stared in astonishment as he explained his actions: "All of you are completely pardoned. There's no more record of your past wrongs. You don't deserve this forgiveness; your behavior was still wrong. I did this out of my love for you to show you a picture of what Jesus does when you accept His forgiveness."

On the cross, Jesus tore up the record book of your sin and took the punishment for you. His blood covers your sin forever. Jesus sees you as absolutely spotless and righteous, washed of all guilt.

Is your slate clean? It can be today. Receive Christ as your Savior, and He erases all your sin. That's what His love is all about.

Dear Lord, how I praise You that there is no record of my sin. It is cleansed by the blood of Calvary. Thank You for Your forgiveness that makes me spotless, righteous, and cleansed from all guilt.

The Sin Bearer

SCRIPTURE READING: 1 Peter 2:21–25   KEY VERSE: Isaiah 53:6

All we like sheep have gone astray; we have turned, every one, to his own way; and the LORD has laid on Him the iniquity of us all.

A teammate of a partially paralyzed football player tearfully told a national television audience that he would gladly take his injured friend's place. What a noble gesture! Of course, it could only be a well-intentioned desire, for despite his empathy, he could not assume his friend's painful condition.

Yet the miracle of the Incarnation was not just that infinite God became finite flesh, but that He did so to bear all our sin on the cross. In God's magnificent mercy, our sin was heaped onto Jesus' sinless deity at Calvary's holy tree. Jesus did not merely sympathize with our helpless plight; He bore the penalty of our sin—spiritual and physical death—so we might be unshackled from death's horrible irons.

God did that through the substitutionary sacrifice of His Son. Jesus was punished in your place and died for your sins, bearing the full wrath of the Father. Your sin debt has been paid. Jesus became sin for you so you might be restored to a right relationship with Him by faith in His glorious work.

The Sin Bearer has finished His task. Have you trusted Him for the gift of eternal life? Have you thanked Him for going to the tree on your behalf and dying your death?

> *Father God, my debt is paid! I rejoice! The Sin Bearer has finished His task. Thank You that I am restored to a right relationship with You by faith in the work of Your Son, Jesus.*

Christ Is What His Cross Is

SCRIPTURE READING: John 1:19–29   KEY VERSE: Revelation 5:9

They sang a new song, saying: "You are worthy to take the scroll, and to open its seals; for You were slain, and have redeemed us to God by Your blood out of every tribe and tongue and people and nation."

Something about the sight of blood strikes a sober chord in man. Whether it's media images of bloodstained clothing or an accident with badly wounded victims, the visual aspect of spilled blood graphically reminds us of death's reality.

When the Bible speaks of Christ's poured-out blood, it is invariably linked with His sacrificial death on Calvary for our sins. The writer of Hebrews went to great lengths to portray Christ as God's all-sufficient sacrifice. Apart from Christ's shed blood, there is no gospel, no forgiveness, no justification, no sanctification. The blood of Christ, His death, satisfies God's justice and provides the means for reconciliation between sinful man and holy God.

P. T. Forsyth, a Scottish clergyman, wrote in the *Cruciality of the Cross:* "Christ is to us just what His cross is. All that Christ was in heaven or on earth was put into what He did there. Christ, I repeat, is to us just what His cross is. You do not understand Christ till you understand His cross."

The cross of Christ is His death. His death is His shed blood. His shed blood is the only acceptable payment for sin and the only way of access to holy God.

Lord Jesus, Your blood is the only acceptable payment for sin. It is the only access I have to a holy God. I come Your way.

A Symbol of Life

SCRIPTURE READING: Isaiah 1:18–21   KEY VERSE: 1 Peter 3:18

Christ also suffered once for sins, the just for the unjust, that He might bring us to God, being put to death in the flesh but made alive by the Spirit.

Blood is not a pleasant topic for most people, and most of us are happy if we go a long time without seeing any. Unless you are in the medical profession or a related occupation, you probably do not deal with blood very often.

But in Jesus' day, the presence of blood was a real part of daily life; in fact, it was a part of sacrificial worship in the temple. According to Mosaic Law, God required the blood of an unblemished animal as the atonement, or payment, for a person's sin. The rules for slaying the animal and handling the blood were extremely complex, and only members of the priesthood were allowed to perform the ceremonies. Since the death of one animal did not pay for all sins, the system of sacrifice was continual.

What Jesus did on the cross, however, was a once-and-for-all blood sacrifice (1 Peter 3:18). No doubt that was a new and difficult concept for the disciples to grasp, and Jesus' words at their last Passover meal together were critical for their understanding of what was about to happen.

Jesus shed physical blood for you. He was in agony, His flesh was torn for you, and He experienced temporary separation from the Father because of your sin. The next time you take Communion, think about His blood—not as a symbol of death but as a symbol of the new life that you have through His sacrifice.

Heavenly Father, thank You for the blood of Jesus, which is the symbol of life. Thank You for the new life I have because of Calvary.

The High Cost of God's Grace

SCRIPTURE READING: Romans 5:17–21   KEY VERSES: 1 Peter 1:18–19

Knowing that you were not redeemed with corruptible things, like silver or gold, from your aimless conduct received by tradition from your fathers, but with the precious blood of Christ, as of a lamb without blemish and without spot.

Think of the things in life that are most important to you. Because you are a believer, your thoughts may immediately go to your relationship with Jesus Christ. This is very important. Think of what life would be if you did not know the love of God. Certainly it would be hopeless and dark.

Your thoughts probably turn next to family and friends or some provision God has given. All of these are very important to who you are. Most of us have heard that man has three basic needs: to be loved, to belong, and to know that he is worthy—that his life counts for something.

Rarely do we think of what Jesus gave up to accomplish the Father's will. More often the mind sees Him cast in heaven's glory and power. However, Jesus gave up everything to come to earth. He yielded His position at the right hand of the Father, a place of extreme power and intense love.

He abandoned His personhood and the need to belong to heaven's glory. He also laid down His possessions and rights. He cast aside everything that was His so that He could come to you. This is the high cost of grace.

Jesus was still God's beloved and all-powerful Son. His quest for obedience to the Father's plan superseded His own needs. He became poor so that we might become eternally rich. This is the high cost of grace.

Jesus, thank You for abandoning the glory of heaven to come to this sinful earth. You gave up glory, power, and Your position at the Father's side—all for me. How I praise You!

Your Precious Passport

SCRIPTURE READING: Hebrews 9:11–15   KEY VERSE: Psalm 85:2

You have forgiven the iniquity of Your people; You have covered all their sin.

T he message of the Cross goes far beyond the salvation of your soul. It is
entwined in everything you do and all that you are.
Theologian Henry Thiessen writes,

Not only is the believer justified by [God's] grace, but also by the blood of
Christ. Paul wrote, "Having now been justified by His blood, we shall be saved
from the wrath of God through Him" (Romans 5:9). The Bible further says,
"According to the Law, one may almost say, all things are cleansed with blood,
and without shedding of blood there is no forgiveness" (Hebrews 9:22).

   This sets the ground of our justification. Because Christ has borne the
punishment of our sins in his own body, God is able to remit the penalty and
to restore us to His favor. In justification, sins are not excused but punished
in the person of Christ, the substitute. The resurrection of Christ is one proof
that His death on the cross has satisfied God's claims against us (Romans 4:25;
1 John 2:2).

Christ's death took away your sin. When God views your life, He sees the
saving work of His Son. This is your precious passport into His throne room,
where love and mercy flow everlasting. Jesus made a wondrous way for you to
stand cleansed and forgiven before His altar. Let this be your song of praise
today and forever more!

> *Father, thank You for the passport into Your throne room. How I praise You*
> *that I stand cleansed and forgiven in Your presence. This is my song of*
> *praise today and forever more!*

A Definition of Love

SCRIPTURE READING: Ephesians 2:1–10   KEY VERSES: Ephesians 2:4–5

God, who is rich in mercy, because of His great love with which He loved us,
even when we were dead in trespasses, made us alive together with Christ (by
grace you have been saved).

I n his book *The Cross of Christ,* John R. W. Stott talked about why Christ's
death at Calvary is God's greatest revelation of divine love:

> It is not only the justice of God which seems to be incompatible with the pre-
> vailing injustices of the world, but also His love.
>
> Personal tragedies, floods, and earthquakes, accidents which cost hun-
> dreds of lives, hunger and poverty on a global scale, the cold vastness of the
> universe, the ferocities of nature, tyranny and torture, disease and death, and
> the sum total of the misery of the centuries—how can these horrors be rec-
> onciled with a God of love?
>
> Christianity offers no glib answers to these agonized questions. But it does
> offer evidence of God's love, just as historical and objective as the evidence
> which seems to deny it, in the light by which the world's calamities need to be
> viewed. The evidence is the cross.
>
> Only one act of pure love, unsullied by any taint of ulterior motive, has
> ever been performed in the history of the world, namely the self-giving of
> God in Christ on the cross for undeserving sinners.
>
> That is why if we are looking for a definition of love, we should look not
> in a dictionary, but at Calvary.

Calvary defines Your love for me, dear Lord. I receive it with thanksgiving
and praise. Let me share its reality with others.

The Ultimate Victory

SCRIPTURE READING: Colossians 2:13–15   KEY VERSE: Romans 8:11

If the Spirit of Him who raised Jesus from the dead dwells in you, He who raised Christ from the dead will also give life to your mortal bodies through His Spirit who dwells in you.

The cross of Jesus Christ satisfied God's holy justice by paying the price of sin—death—and it also was the cosmic battleground where Christ won the ultimate victory.

Nineteenth-century Scottish commentator John Eadie wrote, "Our redemption is a work at once of price and of power—of expiation and of conquest. On the cross was the purchase made, and on the cross was the victory gained. The blood which wipes out the sentence against us was there shed, and the death which was the death blow of Satan's kingdom was there endured."

Theologian F. F. Bruce added, "As He was suspended there, bound hand and foot to the wood in apparent weakness, they imagined they had Him at their mercy, and flung themselves upon Him with hostile intent . . . But He grappled with them and mastered them."

The Christian life is a victorious one. We are triumphant over the power of death, sin, the law, hell, and Satan because the Conqueror, Jesus Christ, has defeated and humiliated them all. Jesus won at Calvary. At the very moment He appeared to lose to the cruelty and prejudice of men, He vanquished every foe.

Master, thank You for victory over death, sin, the law, hell, and Satan. Jesus defeated and humiliated them all. He won the victory for me at Calvary. I praise You!

Eternally Secure

SCRIPTURE READING: 1 John 5:10–13   KEY VERSE: Ephesians 1:13

In Him you also trusted, after you heard the word of truth, the gospel of your salvation; in whom also, having believed, you were sealed with the Holy Spirit of promise.

Perhaps more than ever, our age is security conscious. We like the reassurance of a healthy savings account. We like the benefits that come from working for a supposedly solid company. We treasure the comfort and strength of a good marriage. Yet we must admit that even the biggest savings account can run dry, the best company can go under, and the healthiest marriage can fragment.

God wants us to look to Him for our security. He alone is the cornerstone, the rock, the stronghold, the fortress, the shelter in whom we can find safety, peace, and protection.

You are secure in your position in Him. You are "in Christ," placed there by God Himself. He will keep you forever. Because you are a joint heir with Christ, all the blessings of heaven are yours.

Your eternal destination is fixed. Heaven is your home; no sin can change that once you place your faith in Christ.

Your past sins and mistakes have been thoroughly forgiven through Christ's shed blood. You are a new creature in Christ. The old things have passed away.

You can carry your present problems and challenges to Him in prayer, and He promises to help and sustain you. He upholds you with His eternal grip of love. If you are looking for security, look to Christ. He never changes.

Precious Lord, I am secure in You; my eternal destination is fixed; my sins and mistakes are forgiven. I can take my problems and challenges to You, and You uphold me with the eternal grip of Your love. Thank You, Father.

Love Displayed

SCRIPTURE READING: John 8:1–11   KEY VERSE: Romans 8:34

Who is he who condemns? It is Christ who died, and furthermore is also risen,
who is even at the right hand of God, who also makes intercession for us.

I n his book *The Cross of Christ*, John R. W. Stott explained how God's love is
consummately displayed in the death of His Son:

> First, God gave His Son for us . . . In sending His own Son, eternally begotten
> from His own Being, He was not sending a creature, a third party, but giving
> Himself. The logic of this is inescapable. How could the Father's love have been
> demonstrated if He had sent somebody else to us?
>
> Secondly, God gave His Son to die for us . . . His was to give Himself to the
> uttermost, to the torture of crucifixion and to the horror of sin-bearing and
> God forsakenness . . . For the Sinless One to be made sin, for the Immortal
> One to die—we have no means of imagining the terror or the pain involved
> in such experiences.
>
> Thirdly, God gave His Son to die for us, that is to say, for undeserving sinners
> like us . . . But God demonstrated His own righteousness for us—His unique
> love—in this, that He died for sinful, godless, rebellious, and helpless people
> like us (Romans 5:8).

Never doubt God's love for you. The pierced hands and feet and speared
side are His everlasting display of perfect love.

> *Dear heavenly Father, thank You for giving Your Son to die for me. Give me*
> *a fresh glimpse of the pierced hands and feet, the speared side, that display*
> *Your everlasting love.*

Validated by God

SCRIPTURE READING: Matthew 28:1–10   KEY VERSES: Romans 1:3–4

Concerning His Son Jesus Christ our Lord, who was born of the seed of David according to the flesh, and declared to be the Son of God with power according to the Spirit of holiness, by the resurrection from the dead.

You have just finished eating in a nice restaurant. Before exiting, you make sure your parking ticket is validated so that the parking attendant will allow you to leave without a charge. The validation is the key to verify your visit. The dictionary defines *validation* as "to give legal force to; to legalize; authoritative; sustainable in law."

The resurrection of Jesus Christ is the binding validation, or proof, of Jesus' deity. The bodily resurrection of Christ testifies beyond doubt that Christ was "the Son of God with power" (Rom. 1:4). He can no longer be thought of as a mere prophet, a deluded evangelist, a wise teacher, or just the son of Mary and Joseph.

His resurrection also validates the truthfulness of all that Jesus said. Throughout His ministry, Christ foretold His death and resurrection. The angel at the vacant tomb announced, "He has risen, just as He said" (Matt. 28:6 NASB).

Jesus said that He would conquer death, and He did. Because He fulfilled that bold claim, we can rely on every word He uttered and every deed He accomplished. If you are looking for compelling evidence of Jesus' deity and authority, the Resurrection is sufficient.

O Lord, I believe! You have conquered death. You have risen, just as You said. Let me live in the power of Your resurrection and share its message with others.

Forever Is Guaranteed

SCRIPTURE READING: 1 Corinthians 15   KEY VERSE: 1 Corinthians 15:26

The last enemy that will be destroyed is death.

It's a cold winter day. The canvas awning under which you sit flaps roughly. The people behind you cry silently. Those gathered around the sides are red-eyed and somber.

In front of you a preacher stands next to the casket of your loved one—the one with whom you ate, laughed, walked, and communed for all these years.

Long minutes pass. It is over. Friends hug you; the preacher consoles you; and you return to your car for the lonely trip home.

In this setting of grim, undeniable reality lie the profound and majestic hope, comfort, and assurance of the Christian faith—forever set in the scriptural jewel of John 11:25 (NASB): "I am the resurrection and the life; he who believes in Me shall live even if he dies."

Death isn't the final act. It isn't the ultimate farewell scene.

Because Jesus confronted death and emerged the Victor, we who believe in Him also will live—even though we die. Because of Christ's resurrection, our forever is guaranteed. Our faith is valid; our hope is sure; our expectations are fulfilled. Christ, the Death Slayer, has won the ultimate battle and invites all who believe in Him to experience the delightful fruit of His victory—eternal life.

> *Dear God, I praise You that my forever is guaranteed. My spiritual journey will not end with death. It will continue for eternity.*

The Offer of God's Grace

SCRIPTURE READING: Romans 7:5–25   KEY VERSE: Romans 5:6

When we were still without strength, in due time Christ died for the ungodly.

It wasn't long ago that a Texas toddler named Baby Jessica captured the hearts of Americans. Her plight dominated the media for days as she was trapped in a narrow, abandoned well shaft. Offers to help rescue the little girl poured in from across the nation, which celebrated her subsequent deliverance.

In a striking way, all of mankind, apart from God, is in a similar predicament. Paul put it this way: "While we were still helpless, at the right time Christ died for the ungodly" (Rom. 5:6 NASB).

Baby Jessica, tightly wedged in the shaft, was utterly helpless to save herself. Left to her own devices, she would have perished. Her only hope was an able rescuer.

Hopelessly trapped in sin, man can receive salvation only through the grace of God. We are as helpless as Baby Jessica to extricate ourselves from our spiritual pit of death. It is tough to admit that we are powerless, but that is our condition before a holy God.

Either we must embrace the offer of His grace through Jesus Christ, or we shall die in our sins. Have you received the offer of God's grace, the forgiveness of your sins through His death on the cross? Only His grace can save you.

Precious heavenly Father, I embrace the offer of Your grace through Jesus Christ. I accept its liberating truth to free me from the deep well of my sin. Thank You for rescuing me.

A New Beginning

SCRIPTURE READING: Romans 5:6–11   KEY VERSE: Hebrews 13:5

Let your conduct be without covetousness; be content with such things as you have. For He Himself has said, "I will never leave you nor forsake you."

D o you ever wish for a new beginning? We can make such a mess of our lives that we may think: *I wish I could start all over again. It would be different this time.* Perhaps that would happen, but we might find ourselves in the same dilemma.

The good news of the gospel is that we can have a new start. When we receive Jesus Christ as Savior and commit our lives to Him, Christ fully forgives our sins. Our guilt is removed; our stains are washed by the blood of Christ. Though we may still reap the consequences of our past behavior, we are no longer under God's condemnation or in sin's captivity.

We also have the power of God to guide and help us in the present. We can be different because the Holy Spirit of God indwells us. He is our daily Companion; He is greater than our emotional or physical habits; He can deliver us.

Also, our future is secured. We have everything to look forward to since Christ will never leave us or forsake us. We may face many difficult situations, but we have Christ. We are bound for heaven through His guarantee; we cannot slip or fall from His grip. His love and grace continually surround and enfold us.

You can have a new start that never ends when you receive Christ as your Savior, Lord, and Life. He will never fail you (Heb. 13:5).

Father God, today is a new beginning for me. The past is forgiven. My future is assured. This is the day You have made. I will rejoice and be glad in it!

A New Look at the Cross

SCRIPTURE READING: Luke 23:26–46   KEY VERSES: John 10:29–30

My Father, who has given them to Me, is greater than all; and no one is able to snatch them out of My Father's hand. I and My Father are one.

A believer who is unsure if his actions adversely affect his security in Christ lives on a spiritual tightrope, fearing doom with every misstep. Thinking that his salvation is in limbo is a poor foundation for confident Christian living.

The Christian who is unsure that he is secure in his relationship with the Lord Jesus Christ will live in confusion. He is not quite sure whether God accepts him or not. He is perplexed at which decisions and actions endanger his security and which do not. How does he keep a list? He is also anxious and fearful. He cannot wake up each morning with confidence that a loving, forgiving God has him perfectly in His eternal grip. He is dependent on his performance:

- Is it good enough?
- Have I done enough?
- Have I overlooked anything?

A new look at the Cross will remove all doubt:

There is therefore now no condemnation for those who are in Christ Jesus. For the law of the Spirit of life in Christ Jesus has set you free from the law of sin and of death. (Rom. 8:1–2 NASB)

My Father, who has given them to Me, is greater than all; and no one is able to snatch them out of the Father's hand. I and the Father are one. (John 10:29–30 NASB)

Dear Lord, help me realize that my security rests in the Cross, not in my performance. No one—no person or circumstance—is able to snatch me out of Your hand.

Saved and Sure

SCRIPTURE READING: Hebrews 9:23–28   KEY VERSE: Hebrews 9:28

Christ was offered once to bear the sins of many. To those who eagerly wait for Him He will appear a second time, apart from sin, for salvation.

Believers who look to obedience or disobedience to secure salvation will rise and fall like the ocean tides. Only when our gaze is fixed on the cross can our doubts and fears dissipate.

At the cross Christ died for all of our sins—past, present, and future. As surely as yesterday, tomorrow is covered by the blood of Christ. Christ's sacrifice is all-sufficient:

> *Otherwise, He would have needed to suffer often since the foundation of the world; but now once at the consummation of the ages He has been manifested to put away sin by the sacrifice of Himself. And inasmuch as it is appointed for men to die once and after this comes judgment, so Christ also, having been offered once to bear the sins of many, shall appear a second time for salvation without reference to sin, to those who eagerly await Him. (Heb. 9:26–28 NASB)*

At the cross we were justified by God. That means God credited us with right standing before Him, absolving us of all guilt and enabling us to fellowship with Him.

Once we receive Christ by faith, all of the merit of the Cross is enforced by God on our behalf. Nothing we do or do not do can ever bring us under condemnation again. We are saved and sure.

> *Dear heavenly Father, I fix my gaze upon the cross. I rejoice that yesterday, today, and tomorrow are covered. Thank You that I am saved and sure.*

It Is Finished

SCRIPTURE READING: Isaiah 61:1–3   KEY VERSE: Hebrews 12:2

Looking unto Jesus, the author and finisher of our faith, who for the joy that was set before Him endured the cross, despising the shame, and has sat down at the right hand of the throne of God.

The dominant, swelling theme of the Cross is triumph. The almighty shout of "It is finished" declared the victory of God over the power of sin and the devil.

Make no mistake; Christ fought and won the cosmic battle of the ages on a small patch of Jewish ground. The substitutionary death of Christ atoned for our sins. Jesus Himself canceled and paid our sin debt.

The devil and his demons were likewise crushed by Christ at the cross. Satan's hold on man was shattered, so that we who place our faith in the Savior are released from his dark domain and transferred into the kingdom of God.

Theologian Lewis Chafer wrote, "Christ clearly won a victory over Satan on the cross. In offering salvation to men, Christ fulfilled what was anticipated in Isaiah 61:1, where He is said to have provided freedom for those who were captives."

The author of Hebrews exclaimed that Jesus "for the joy set before Him endured the cross, despising the shame, and has sat down at the right hand of the throne of God" (Heb. 12:2 NASB).

The anguish of Christ on the cross—the nails, the taunts, the pain, the shame—is part and parcel of eternal conquest.

Be amazed at what God did with hands and feet nailed to a tree.

O God, I am amazed at what You did with hands and feet nailed to a tree. The anguish of Your Son became eternal conquest. Thank You that Satan was defeated at the cross and I am released from his dark domain and transferred into Your kingdom. It is finished!

MAY

Journey to the Battlefield

REPRESENTING: Having confidence to face enemies

KEY VERSE: 2 Chronicles 20:15

Thus says the LORD to you: "Do not be afraid nor dismayed because of this great multitude, for the battle is not yours, but God's."

Anytime a man chooses God's way, it won't be long until that commitment is challenged, and that was exactly what happened to Jehoshaphat. In 2 Chronicles 20 we find a great and formidable enemy advancing toward this godly King of Judah to destroy the kingdom. Jehoshaphat had no battle plan. No strategy. No secret weapons. But God promised victory.

Like that of Jehoshaphat, your commitment to God will be continually challenged. When conflicts arise, you must face a spiritual enemy with spiritual strategies. This month, we will journey to the spiritual battlefield and learn how to confront the enemy. We will learn to use our spiritual weapons. We will discover how to be victorious in the face of the temptations and pressures of life. We will learn strategies for casting down vain imaginations, controlling the mind, and winning the victory. Most important—we will learn to never give up!

Are you ready? God's army is moving out for the battlefield. Forward march!

A Quick Response

SCRIPTURE READING: 2 Chronicles 20:1–4   KEY VERSE: 2 Chronicles 20:3

Jehoshaphat feared, and set himself to seek the LORD, and proclaimed a fast throughout all Judah.

Jehoshaphat received devastating news. Judah was about to be invaded: "A great multitude is coming against you." The first thing the king did was go to God in prayer: "[He] turned his attention to seek the LORD; and proclaimed a fast throughout all Judah" (2 Chron. 20:2, 3 NASB).

When trials or tragedies come, let your quick response be one of petition and prayer. The people realized there was nothing they could do to save themselves from the approaching army. Only God could intervene. In prayer we must be willing for Him to do whatever it takes to bring about a victory.

Second, we must humble ourselves before God, confessing our need of His wisdom and deliverance. When adversity strikes, many people try to work out their circumstances on their own. But God told Jehoshaphat the battle was not his. It was God's.

Judah was delivered, but not by conventional means. God instructed the choir to go before the army and sing songs of praise to Him. As the battle cry rose, the Lord delivered His people from the hand of the enemy, and He will do the same for you.

Prayer, praise, and trust are key elements to victory. Are you trusting the Lord for the solution to the problem facing you? If not, you can begin right now. Give your burdens to Him in prayer, and praise Him for the victory.

Dear God, I trust You to work out every problem I face today. I give my burdens to You and ask You to reign as Lord over each circumstance.

When the Odds Are Against You

SCRIPTURE READING: 2 Chronicles 20:5–12   KEY VERSE: 2 Chronicles 20:12

O our God, will You not judge them? For we have no power against this great multitude that is coming against us; nor do we know what to do, but our eyes are upon You.

The odds were certainly against Jehoshaphat and his men. Surrounding them were the hordes of three armies—vastly outnumbering the Israelites. Jehoshaphat's response provides all of us whose backs are against the proverbial wall with a godly game plan:

First, Jehoshaphat acknowledged God's unequaled power: "Power and might are in Thy hand so that no one can stand against Thee" (2 Chron. 20:6 NASB). Whatever your circumstances, God is greater. His power is sufficient. His grace is adequate. His mercy is abundant.

Second, Jehoshaphat admitted his helplessness: "We are powerless before this great multitude who are coming against us" (2 Chron. 20:12 NASB). Your strength is limited. God's might is unsurpassed.

Third, Jehoshaphat focused on God's presence: "Our eyes are on Thee" (2 Chron. 20:12 NASB). Don't dwell on your problem. Concentrate on God's active presence and participation in the midst of your difficulty.

The battle is His to win as you daily trust Him. He will fight for you if you let Him. He has yet to lose.

Heavenly Father, power and might are in Your hand. No one can stand against You. I am powerless in the face of my circumstances, but my eyes are on You.

Pour Out Your Heart

SCRIPTURE READING: 2 Chronicles 20:13–17   KEY VERSE: 2 Chronicles 20:17

"You will not need to fight in this battle. Position yourselves, stand still and see the salvation of the LORD, who is with you, O Judah and Jerusalem!" Do not fear or be dismayed; tomorrow go out against them, for the LORD is with you.

Jehoshaphat had a huge problem. The armies of the Moabites and Ammonites and Meunites were about to march on him and his people (2 Chron. 20:1 NASB). It was a time of national emergency, and most leaders would have called their advisers or mustered the army—but not King Jehoshaphat.

"Jehoshaphat was afraid and turned his attention to seek the LORD" (2 Chron. 20:3 NASB). He didn't falter, complain, or waste time in pessimistic thinking. Instead, he immediately called the people together for a time of prayer with fasting.

Notice the attributes of God he named at the beginning of his prayer: "O LORD, the God of our fathers, art Thou not God in the heavens? And art Thou not ruler over all the kingdoms of the nations? Power and might are in Thy hand so that no one can stand against Thee" (2 Chron. 20:6 NASB).

The king recognized God's ultimate power and authority, and therefore he was not afraid of what mere men might do to him. Furthermore, he showed that he was willing to be involved in the process of God's answer. The king didn't mouth a halfhearted, unemotional statement; he prayed with interest and passion and sincerity.

Have you ever poured forth your heart to the Lord? He wants you to cry out to Him and actively seek His deliverance.

O God, You handle the strategy. Provide the resources for my battles. I know that even while I am praying, my deliverance is on the way.

A God-Centered Prayer

SCRIPTURE READING: 2 Chronicles 20:18–24   KEY VERSE: 2 Chronicles 20:6

O LORD God of our fathers, are You not God in heaven, and do You not rule over all the kingdoms of the nations, and in Your hand is there not power and might, so that no one is able to withstand You?

Jehoshaphat's prayer was God centered. He didn't indulge in negativism by dwelling on the details of the difficulty. God wants you to be specific about a problem, but His desire is to move your focus onto His power. Name your concern, and begin with praise for His action and blessing in the past; then express the truth of His omnipotence.

The king was no novice in rulership, and that wasn't the first kingdom problem. He had learned the value of coming to God in absolute humility, acknowledging his utter dependence. So complete was his trust that he never lapsed into self-reliance.

In other words, he could have quickly thanked God and then spread out the battle maps to make plans with his commanders. In your situation, the temptation to figure it out yourself may be the same, but God wants you to let Him handle the strategy.

What is even more awesome is that while the king prayed, God already had their deliverance under way. By the time the army of Judah arrived on the scene, they beheld a field of corpses. Not one foe was left standing. God not only provided what they needed, but He supplied them with gracious abundance.

Trusting Him to provide the resources for every demand makes you a God-centered person.

O Lord, the God of our fathers, are You not God in the heavens? And are You not ruler over all the kingdoms of the nations? Power and might are in Your hand so that no one can stand against You. Deliver me from the hand of my enemy.

Your Enemy

SCRIPTURE READING: 2 Chronicles 20:25–30   KEY VERSE: 1 Peter 5:8

Be sober, be vigilant; because your adversary the devil walks about like a roaring lion, seeking whom he may devour.

Just as Jehoshaphat faced the enemy, you have a formidable enemy. His name is Satan. He was created full of wisdom and beauty (Ezek. 28:12–17). He was given a place on God's holy mountain. He was created a holy and righteous being. However, pride was the beginning of his fall; in the end it led him to exalt himself to the position of God. In his vanity he declared, "I will be like God."

He is our fiercest adversary (Zech. 3:1; 1 Peter 5:8); accuser (Rev. 12:10); Lucifer, or light bearer (Isa. 14:12), which means "to deceive"; dragon (Rev. 12:7); slanderer (1 Peter 5:8); murderer and liar (John 8:44); deceiver (Rev. 20:10); prince of this world (John 12:31); prince of the power of the air (Eph. 2:2); destroyer (Rev. 9:11); tempter (Matt. 13:38); and god of this age (2 Cor. 4:4).

Never take Satan's ability or evil intent lightly. He was created with tremendous power. However, the Lord also equipped us with "divinely powerful" spiritual weapons that, when used correctly, can overthrow Satan's work against us (2 Cor. 10:3–5 NASB).

Satan's future is one of eternal death (Isa. 14:15; Rev. 12:7–10), yet he remains a force that needs to be reckoned with. Our only effective course of action is through the power and blood of the Lord Jesus Christ. Never battle the enemy on your own. Even the angels use the mighty name of Jesus when warring against his evil (Jude 9).

Lord, Your power is my defense against the adversary. Your blood secures my victory. Let Your name, Your power, and the blood of Jesus reign over the circumstances of my life.

Resisting the Devil

SCRIPTURE READING: Ezekiel 28:12–17   KEY VERSE: John 8:44

You are of your father the devil, and the desires of your father you want to do. He was a murderer from the beginning, and does not stand in the truth, because there is no truth in him. When he speaks a lie, he speaks from his own resources, for he is a liar and the father of it.

The United States did not win the Persian Gulf War on sheer military strength alone. The commanders, the president's advisers, and even the president himself spent a great deal of time learning about the enemy. No war is won by brute force. Tactical strategy and in-depth knowledge are always necessary.

If we are going to win the war against Satan and his forces, we must know something about him. For one, he is our adversary, a fallen angel, the prince of this age, and the father of lies. But foremost, he is a defeated foe.

He deceives the body of Christ by coming as an angel of light. He strategically interjects error into our thinking with the purpose of confusing and derailing us in our spiritual walk. Satan's chief goal is to cause us to doubt God.

The way to oppose him is with the truth of God's Word and by the power of the Holy Spirit. If you want to win spiritually in this life, begin by memorizing Scripture. Even a single verse can make a big difference when it comes to spiritual warfare. Ask God to reveal any sin in your life. Confess it, and then pray for His strength to turn from it. Dedicate your life to glorifying Him and not the ways of the world.

The enemy will always remind you of times of defeat, but Jesus Christ speaks only of His love and power and victory. You can place your complete hope in Him because He will never fail you.

Master, let Your Word dwell in me richly. Reveal any sin in my life, then give me the strength to turn from it. I dedicate my life to glorifying You and not the ways of the world.

God's Protective Clothing

SCRIPTURE READING: Ephesians 6:10–18   KEY VERSE: Ephesians 6:12

We do not wrestle against flesh and blood, but against principalities, against powers, against the rulers of the darkness of this age, against spiritual hosts of wickedness in the heavenly places.

A t some point, you will be tempted to compromise your walk with the Lord. It may come in a way that is obvious, and immediately you will say no.

More than likely, the enemy's deception will wear a subtle face. Once you accept Christ as your Savior, Satan's goal shifts. Your name is written in the Lamb's Book of Life, and God owns the deed. However, the enemy remains committed to your spiritual and emotional destruction.

"Our struggle is not against flesh and blood," wrote Paul, "but against the rulers, against the powers, against the world forces of this darkness, against the spiritual forces of wickedness in the heavenly places" (Eph. 6:12 NASB).

Therefore, clad yourself each day with God's protective covering—the belt of truth, the breastplate of righteousness, the readiness of the gospel of peace on your feet, the helmet of salvation, the shield of faith, and the sword of the Spirit.

Prayer is the cement that seals the armor to our lives. In teaching His disciples this principle, Jesus prayed, "And do not lead us into temptation, but deliver us from the evil one" (Luke 11:4).

Jesus understood how deadly the enemy's darts could be. But He didn't leave us hopeless. He lives within our hearts. Therefore, He wants us to take our stand against the enemy by faith through constant prayer.

Father, do not lead me into temptation, but deliver me from the evil one. Protect me from his deadly darts. Help me take my stand against the enemy by faith through constant prayer.

Dressed for the Battle

SCRIPTURE READING: 2 Corinthians 10:3–4   KEY VERSE: 1 Timothy 6:12

Fight the good fight of faith, lay hold on eternal life, to which you were also called and have confessed the good confession in the presence of many witnesses.

It is not surprising that the evil we face today is so intense: "For our struggle is not against flesh and blood, but against the rulers, against the powers, against the world forces of this darkness, against the spiritual forces of wickedness in the heavenly places" (Eph. 6:12 NASB).

When the enemy attacks, make sure you are dressed for the battle by claiming God's armor daily:

The belt of truth. When you claim God's truth, you are victoriously empowered to stand against the falsehood of the enemy.

The breastplate of righteousness. Satan's accusations are groundless because you are righteous through Christ.

The shoes of peace. Whatever you face, Jesus faces it with you. You can rest in His peace because He is in control.

The shield of faith. God is your complete and perfect shield against the fiery darts of the enemy. He will protect you.

The helmet of salvation. When your mind is focused on Christ, you will not be led astray.

The sword of the Spirit. Nothing is more powerful than the Word of God. It's your offensive weapon against Satan's assaults. Claim a verse of Scripture that pertains to your need, and steadfastly cling to it.

Precious Lord, I clothe myself in my spiritual armor today. I take the belt of truth, the breastplate of righteousness, the shoes of peace, the shield of faith, the helmet of salvation, and the sword of the Spirit. I am ready for battle.

A Damaging Influence

SCRIPTURE READING: 1 Corinthians 10:14–22   KEY VERSE: 1 Corinthians 10:21

You cannot drink the cup of the Lord and the cup of demons; you cannot partake of the Lord's table and of the table of demons.

The believer is firmly—if reluctantly—engaged in spiritual warfare with Satan and his demons. Although you are no longer under the devil's mastery, you are not immune to his plots and schemes.

The battle is not one of possession, for you belong to Christ alone, but for control. It is not one of destiny, for your future with Christ in heaven is secure, but for daily victory.

The adversary seeks an opening from which he can build a spiritual stronghold and influence your thoughts and actions for evil. You can give demonic forces unnecessary inroads into your life by participating in questionable activities—watching movies overloaded with sensuality or horror, reading materials laced with raucous references to a carnal lifestyle, listening to music with lyrics promoting lewdness and rebellion.

This is not an attempt to be legalistic. Anything that usurps Christ's role as Lord in your life, competing for your devotion and time, can be fodder for demonic activity. The important issue is to examine your life, asking God to reveal any area of thought or deed that could give Satan and his powers opportunity for a damaging influence.

Dear heavenly Father, I know I am not immune to the plots and schemes of the enemy. Please reveal any area of thought or deed that could give Satan and his powers opportunity to influence my life.

The Real War

SCRIPTURE READING: Romans 8:35–39   KEY VERSE: Galatians 5:17

The flesh lusts against the Spirit, and the Spirit against the flesh; and these are contrary to one another, so that you do not do the things that you wish.

War changes the tenor of men and nations. During the Persian Gulf War, residents of the countries represented by the coalition forces were transfixed for weeks. Both citizens and soldiers were alert to the slightest developments, keenly aware that the next maneuver could mean victory or defeat, life or death. When the conflict concluded, concern gradually diminished, and life returned to the ordinary routine for most.

Every believer in Jesus Christ is involved in a fierce spiritual struggle. Unlike soldiers in wars that begin and end, we face an incessant foe in the devil who never relaxes his evil desires. Thus, we can never let down our guard against Satan's weapons of doubt and deception. He cannot affect our eternal destiny, for that has been secured by Christ's death and resurrection; but he certainly can disrupt our present state of affairs with his rebellious scheming.

Be alert. Be vigilant. Be disciplined. You are in a fight of faith, a real war with casualties of great proportions. Wake up each morning with your game face on, and engage the enemy with confident faith.

Almighty God, I realize I am in an ongoing fight of faith. Help me be alert, vigilant, and disciplined—ready to engage the enemy with confident faith.

Controlling Your Thoughts

SCRIPTURE READING: Colossians 3:1–17   KEY VERSE: 1 Corinthians 2:16

"Who has known the mind of the LORD that he may instruct Him?" But we have the mind of Christ.

The computer age is here to stay and, along with it, a new dictionary of technological terms. One that we should be familiar with by now is *software,* which is the operational basis for all computer systems. Impressive computer hardware is displayed in ads and on desks; but the compact, hidden software makes the system functional.

In a sense a person receives an entirely new software package when he receives Christ as Savior, Lord, and Life. He is taken out of Adam (his old way of living) and placed into Christ (his new way of living). Through the indwelling Holy Spirit, he now has "the mind of Christ" (1 Cor. 2:16), which allows him to align his thoughts with those of Christ and to view life from God's perspective.

Such thoughts do not automatically register, however. Our old software package of selfishly oriented, independent thinking has made deep inroads into our personalities. We are presented daily with the mind-set of a godless world and the darts of our constant adversary, the devil.

Experiencing the benefits of your new nature and your new mind depends upon the daily introduction of spiritual programming provided by the Father for your new life in Christ.

Dear God, thank You for reprogramming me—taking out the old, pouring in the new. I praise You that I now have the mind of Christ, which allows me to align my thoughts to view life from Your perspective.

When Facing Temptation

SCRIPTURE READING: Luke 4:1–14   KEY VERSE: 2 Timothy 2:22

Flee also youthful lusts; but pursue righteousness, faith, love, peace with those who call on the Lord out of a pure heart.

It is a matter not of *whether* temptation will confront Christians but of *when*. As long as we live in a world where Satan and sin are at work, temptation will knock at the door of our hearts and minds. But with Christ indwelling us, we need not open the door. We can resist the temptation.

You can take preventive measures in many instances. If gossip is a problem, avoid gatherings where idle talk will run rampant. If immoral thoughts are a problem, stay away from questionable relationships or enticing activities.

Paul told Timothy to "flee from youthful lusts" (2 Tim. 2:22 NASB). If you are thrust into a tempting situation or if you battle a particular ungodly attraction, then you must deal firmly with temptation.

Realize who is behind your temptation. The devil is always ultimately the crafty perpetrator of temptation's schemes. He seeks to wreak havoc in your life, veiling his tactics in the light of pleasure.

Then by an act of your will, think through the consequences of surrendering to temptation. What will be the outcome of this? Will it help your relationship with Christ? Who will be affected if you succumb? Contemplating the aftermath should alert you to the danger.

O Lord, help me to be vigilant to guard against temptation in my life. Give me the ability to see behind the immediate pleasures of sin to recognize Satan at work to wreak havoc in my life.

A Way of Escape

SCRIPTURE READING: James 4:1–8   KEY VERSE: 1 Corinthians 10:13

No temptation has overtaken you except such as is common to man; but God is faithful, who will not allow you to be tempted beyond what you are able, but with the temptation will also make the way of escape, that you may be able to bear it.

Helen Lemmel's song, "Turn Your Eyes Upon Jesus," strikes a comforting chord when facing the temptation to give up. It asks the questions, "O soul, are you weary and troubled? No light in the darkness you see?" and then it directs the anguished soul to look to the Savior for abundant life. As your eyes are turned upon Jesus and you look into His face, the things of earth grow dim in the light of His glory.

The enemy of our souls sends temptation for the purpose of discouraging us and causing us to give up. God allows temptation. Without its fierce and mighty blows against our lives, we cannot fully develop the courage that accompanies faith.

The Lord knows you will make mistakes. In facing temptation, train yourself to say no to the tempter. There is Someone stronger within you, and He calls you to remain faithful to the One who can save you from the physical and emotional sorrow temptation brings.

Jesus understands the turmoil that comes as a result of fiery trials. Therefore, He has provided a plan of escape from Satan's angry grasp (1 Cor. 10:13). However, you must first say no to the enemy's enticement. Jesus used Scripture when He was tempted to turn from God. The Word of God is your sure defense. Hide it in your heart, and call out to the Lord of your soul.

Precious heavenly Father, I turn my eyes upon You for strength for my journey. Enable me to say no to the enemy's enticements along the way. I cry out to You for help!

Something Worth Thinking About

SCRIPTURE READING: Ephesians 2:1–7   KEY VERSE: Matthew 26:41

Watch and pray, lest you enter into temptation. The spirit indeed is willing, but the flesh is weak.

Controlling your thoughts can be difficult, especially if you open the door to thoughts that are not in keeping with the thoughts of Christ. Many people say, "Well, that's not my problem. I don't think about sinful material or things that would compromise my relationship with God." But they overlook their negative thoughts and feelings toward themselves and others.

Hidden within the vast resources of our minds is a tremendous ability to store and retrieve data. The brain is so complex that scientists still do not know all its capabilities. However, one thing is clear: we view ourselves in light of what we believe to be true. If we construct a negative belief system concerning who we are, then we will act negatively. Thus, the old adage, "Winners never lose and losers never win," is true. Not because winners win and losers lose, but because of how each group views itself.

For the next week refuse to react to any negative thought about yourself or others. If your inner self says you are ugly, look in the mirror and tell yourself, "I am a child of God, and He loves me just the way I am"—end of discussion!

God will never belittle or embarrass you. He leads you to His altar of forgiveness so that you can experience His glorious love and care on a personal basis. It is there that He gives you a totally new beginning. Now that's worth thinking about!

Father God, I praise You that I am Your child and You love me just the way I am. I am a winner!

The Peak of Pressure

SCRIPTURE READING: Matthew 4:4–11   KEY VERSE: 2 Corinthians 2:11

Lest Satan should take advantage of us; for we are not ignorant of his devices.

M ost temptation comes when we are at the peak of pressure. Immediately following Jesus' baptism, the devil came to Him and began tempting Him to rely upon His own ability and not the strength and faithfulness of God. This is the same type of temptation the enemy sets in front of us on a regular basis. He is consistently afoot, trying to get us to rely on our own abilities and knowledge.

God calls us to surrender to His will, while Satan whispers that we can do anything we want to do on our own apart from God. Another lie that Satan uses to trick us is the thought that God has forgotten us. For example, those who have never married may find themselves doubting God's ability to provide a mate. Instead of continuing to seek Him and His contentment, they rush into a marriage that is not in keeping with His will.

Commit yourself to waiting for God's best. If you do, you will never be disappointed. Jesus stood firm when tried by Satan. The focus of His heart was not on His personal needs but on the will of the Father. Christ gained victory in the temptation because He was more concerned about pleasing God than satisfying His physical needs.

If you are in a trying situation, make it your goal to seek the wisdom of Christ. Pray for His strength to resist the enemy, and trust Him for the outpouring of His blessings in your life.

Dear Lord, change my focus from my own will to Your divine plan. I commit myself to wait for Your best. Give me strength to resist the enemy and trust You for blessings in my life.

Your Best Defense

SCRIPTURE READING: 2 Corinthians 12:7–10   KEY VERSE: 2 Corinthians 12:10

I take pleasure in infirmities, in reproaches, in needs, in persecutions, in distresses, for Christ's sake. For when I am weak, then I am strong.

One of the saddest accounts of temptation's fury is Peter's denial. He denied the notion that he would desert the Lord, but that was exactly what happened (Matt. 26:33).

Peter was accustomed to taking charge of a situation. In many ways, he was fearless, especially out on the open Sea of Galilee with the sails of his fishing boat flailing in the wind and the bow crashing through the waves. But that was a familiar environment for Peter, not like what he experienced the night of Christ's arrest.

In fact, none of the disciples were ready for what happened. They were even less prepared to witness the Crucifixion. Peter ended up denying the Lord three times, just as Jesus predicted. What did the temptation involve, and why did Peter yield to the enemy's snare?

Somehow Peter forgot the principle of godly strength. The apostle Paul later recorded this principle in 2 Corinthians 12:10: "When I am weak, then I am strong." Jesus is your only sure strength. When temptation comes, your best defense is not to fight it in your own ability but to go to God in prayer. Claim your position as His child, stand firm in your faith, and acknowledge His strength as yours.

Though Peter fell, Jesus encouraged him not to give up. When temptation traps you, know that Christ will forgive and restore you, just as He did Peter.

Heavenly Father, You are my strength and defense against temptation. I am Your child. I stand firm in my faith and acknowledge that when I am weak, then I am strong!

Where the Battle Is Won

SCRIPTURE READING: Matthew 26:36–46   KEY VERSE: Luke 5:16

He Himself often withdrew into the wilderness and prayed.

Jesus must have felt that the world was closing in. He knew what lay ahead, and in the fullness of godhood and the fullness of manhood, Jesus understood what death on a cross involved. The physical humiliation and agony of crucifixion would only be compounded by the horror of experiencing God's wrath for the sins of the world. There was only one solution for dealing with the feelings welling up inside Him—prayer. So Jesus went to the Garden of Gethsemane to pour out His heart to the Father in private prayer.

Where do you go when life seems unbearable, when stress is stretching every fiber of your being to the maximum? Jesus identifies with your pain and trial. He knows how it feels to be overwhelmed with conflicting emotions. But think about this: the worst problem you will ever face is nothing compared to what Jesus went through. And Jesus, who is God Himself, handled His ordeal on earth by going to the Father in private prayer.

You need time alone with your heavenly Father. You need solitude to read His Word, to communicate your deepest thoughts, and to discover His answers. Yes, prayer time with others is important to spiritual growth as well, but sometimes just you and the Lord need to be together. Seek a place where you can spend time with Him, and you will discover an intimacy beyond comparison.

I want to spend more time with You alone, Father. Help me find moments of solitude where I can come into Your presence to be renewed and empowered for the battles of life.

Snared by the Schemer

SCRIPTURE READING: Psalm 25   KEY VERSE: 1 Peter 4:7

The end of all things is at hand; therefore be serious and watchful in your prayers.

Warren Wiersbe commented on our struggles with the enemy: "The word *warfare* in 2 Corinthians 10:4 means campaign. Paul was not simply fighting a little skirmish in Corinth; the attack of the enemy there was part of a large satanic campaign. The powers of hell are still trying to destroy the work of God (Matthew 16:18), and it is important that we not yield any ground to the enemy."

Many believers fail to realize that they are in spiritual warfare on a daily basis. The enemy fights a relentless battle for our minds, thoughts, and beliefs. Our values are under constant attack as we are challenged to "get in step" with a society that has long since left its spiritual foundation far behind.

Don't be rocked to sleep mentally by thinking that because you are a member of a certain church with a certain denomination as its backbone, there is no way you will fall to Satan's deceptive temptations. In 1 Peter 4:7, we are told to be "serious and watchful."

Even believers can fall prey to the enemy, so stand strong in Christ. Every thought, every issue that is raised up against God must be taken "captive to the obedience of Christ" (2 Cor. 10:5 NASB). You are the only one who can assume responsibility for your life.

Don't be snared by the enemy into thinking that you don't need Jesus Christ. Life is given to every fiber of your being.

O God, give me sound judgment and a sober spirit. Help me take captive every thought that is raised against You. Pour life into every fiber of my being.

Those Trying Times

SCRIPTURE READING: James 1:1–8   KEY VERSE: Isaiah 10:15

Shall the ax boast itself against him who chops with it? Or shall the saw exalt itself against him who saws with it? As if a rod could wield itself against those who lift it up, or as if a staff could lift up, as if it were not wood!

Your nine o'clock meeting is scheduled to begin in thirty minutes, and you are late to work. Traffic reports warn commuters to take an alternate route. The interstate is blocked with a stalled car.

Pulling out into the roadway, you tell yourself to relax. But a red sports car decides you are occupying his lane of traffic and cuts in front of you. The damage from the collision is minor, but you'll have to wait for the police to arrive and then make a report.

You arrive at work only to learn the meeting was canceled due to your absence, and the boss wants to see you in his office immediately.

Trials and hardships are a part of life. Each of us experiences them. Many times they arrive without warning and leave us feeling out of control. But God has a design for troubled times. He uses each trial to draw us into a greater dependence on Him.

Hannah Whitall Smith wrote, "In order really to know God, inward stillness is absolutely necessary." When God is the anchor of your soul, His faithfulness and strength always overshadow life's pressures. Stillness and trust in Him are our strength (Isa. 30:15). Draw close to Jesus Christ, and He will calm the winds of adversity in your life.

> *Lord, still my spirit. Relieve my anxieties. Calm the winds of adversity in my life.*

Renewing Your Mind

SCRIPTURE READING: Romans 12:1–2   KEY VERSE: Colossians 2:15

Having disarmed principalities and powers, He made a public spectacle of them, triumphing over them in it.

In his letter to the Romans, Paul addressed believers from diverse backgrounds. Many had been involved in pagan cults. They had accepted Christ as their Savior, but they still fought intense battles within their minds.

Satan's number one target is your mind. He wants you to think negatively, feel insecure, and run from where God has placed you.

Studies show morality and hope are at an all-time low in our age. But it should be just the opposite for believers. We have everything to live for, not because of who we are, but because of whom we contain—Jesus Christ.

You renew your mind by committing yourself to thinking and viewing life from God's perspective. More than likely, you will have to ask God to help you make this change. It may also mean cutting off Satan's access to certain areas of your life. Run a check on all that you read, listen to, and watch on television.

Ask God to show you what needs to go. Anything that conflicts with His truth is Satan's ploy to sidetrack you. However, the real battle for the mind is fought in the will. God will renew your thinking, but you must be willing. Choose purity over evil, truth over a lie.

Master, help me change my thinking. I want to think Your thoughts and view things from Your perspective. Reveal any area of my life where I need to cut off Satan's access.

The Warfare of Prayer

SCRIPTURE READING: Matthew 12:22–30   KEY VERSE: Psalm 143:8

Cause me to hear Your lovingkindness in the morning, for in You do I trust; cause me to know the way in which I should walk, for I lift up my soul to You.

Why do we so easily neglect prayer? Why do we so often seek solutions in our own strength and resources instead of quickly turning to God in prayer?

True, our flesh is weak; but there is another reason why our prayer life can be ineffective or sporadic: we have an archenemy, the devil, who constantly works to keep us off our knees. Why? Our adversary—and he is exactly that—knows that victory comes as we seek and trust God in personal prayer.

Satan craftily gets us too busy to pray. He deceives us into thinking that life is lived only on the physical plane. As a believer, you are preeminently a spiritual being, indwelt by the Spirit of God. Therefore, you have a spiritual enemy—Satan—and to defeat him, you must employ spiritual weapons.

No weapon is mightier than prayer. That is where the battle is fought and won. When we turn to God and trust Him, we have placed the matter squarely in the hands of the One who has soundly defeated the devil and who leads in His sure triumph.

Your enemy is too strong for you, but not for your risen and ascended Lord. Come to Him in prayer, and watch Him win the battles that you could not achieve in your own strength.

Precious Lord, the enemy is too strong for me, but You are greater than all his powers. Please fight my battles. I cannot win in my own strength.

Your Family's Defense

SCRIPTURE READING: Psalm 140:1–8   KEY VERSE: 1 Thessalonians 5:17

Pray without ceasing.

You don't fight real wars with popguns, and you don't fight the devil with mere determination or resolve. God provides our families' defense against Satan. If we are to succeed, we must take up His weapons.

Pray for each member of your family every day. Ask God to surround each one with His supernatural hedge of protection against the tactics of the evil one. Call out their names before God, thanking Him that they are inscribed on the palm of His hand.

Especially pray the Word of God. Find Scriptures that pertain to your particular problems, and pray those Scriptures to God. It is the truth of God, and the truth always defeats the lies of Satan.

Resist the devil in the name of Jesus. Through your union with Christ, you have been given victory over the enemy. Jesus defeated Satan through His sinless life, His atoning death, and His triumphant resurrection. Satan is a vanquished foe. Though he still puts up a vicious fight, you can overcome him through the power of Jesus Christ.

Rebuke the devil in Christ's name, command him to flee, and stand firm. Ask the Holy Spirit to fill your family members and leave no room for the devil to set up shop.

> *Dear heavenly Father, in the name of Jesus, I rebuke the power of the enemy over my family and command him to flee! Holy Spirit, fill each member of my family so that there is no room for Satan to operate.*

Overcoming Power

SCRIPTURE READING: Luke 24:14–32   KEY VERSE: John 14:16

I will pray the Father, and He will give you another Helper, that He may abide with you forever.

L uke told the story of two people on their way to Emmaus after the Crucifixion. They were greatly dismayed and discouraged by what seemed to be the end of their dreams. They had thought Jesus would free Israel from Roman rule. Now that He was dead, all hope appeared lost until their eyes were dramatically opened by the risen Savior.

All of us have known the crushing feeling of disappointment, especially when we think God is leading us a certain way and things turn out differently. However, the death of Jesus Christ was not an ending but a wondrous beginning. His disciples as yet had not been empowered with the Spirit of God. Therefore, their spiritual perspective was limited.

No one, including the disciples, could grasp the power available to them until after pentecost had come. Only then were Christ's followers fully clothed with power from on high.

The powerful message of the Resurrection is that God now inhabits the hearts of His people through the indwelling presence of His Holy Spirit. The next time you feel doubtful or discouraged, remember the power God gave to you through His Son. It is overcoming power from on high—over all the power of the enemy—and it is given to every person who places faith in Jesus Christ.

Almighty God, thank You for the power of pentecost, which surges through my spirit today. I praise You for overcoming power from on high that triumphs over all the forces of the enemy.

The Ups and Downs of Life

SCRIPTURE READING: John 14:25–31   KEY VERSE: John 16:33

These things I have spoken to you, that in Me you may have peace. In the world you will have tribulation; but be of good cheer, I have overcome the world.

A new believer bemoaned her inconsistent lifestyle only weeks following her rather dramatic salvation.

"If I am a believer, why do I still have so many problems?" she honestly wondered. Whether new or mature believers, we will encounter spiritual cycles—times when we are up and times when we are down.

Jesus was a realist when He described the type of upsetting experience His disciples (that includes us) would face: "These things I have spoken to you, that in Me you may have peace. In the world you have tribulation, but take courage; I have overcome the world" (John 16:33 NASB).

If you are in the midst of unsettling circumstances, take courage; the rest of us are too. In such times, we maintain contentment and stability through our constant, unchanging, permanent relationship with Jesus Christ.

Cling to Christ through consistent, personal communion, bringing Him all your needs and fears. He is the Helmsman of your soul in disturbing times, and your safety and peace lie in His steady hands. He will keep you on course.

O Lord, in the world I have tribulation, but You have overcome the world, and I can overcome through You. You are the Helmsman of my soul in disturbing times. My safety and peace are in Your hands. I rejoice that You will keep me on course with my destiny.

Resolute Trust

SCRIPTURE READING: Hebrews 2:14–18   KEY VERSE: Isaiah 26:3

You will keep him in perfect peace, whose mind is stayed on You, because he trusts in You.

S tock markets rise and fall. Farm prices soar and plummet. Personal health peaks and dips.

Such is the nature of our unstable environment: ever changing, altering, moving, shifting. But believers have a firm anchor in such fluctuation, a sure faith in an unchanging God who promises to never leave us helpless.

God is sovereign. God is always at work in every detail of our lives, using each setback and victory for His primary purpose: to glorify Himself by conforming us to Christ's image. No event or person is outside the power and rule of God.

God is wise. His wisdom is yours as you humbly ask and expectantly receive. His Word and Spirit will light your path to fulfill His will for your life.

God is loving. Whatever comes you are kept secure in the love of God. His love ensures He will provide for, guide, and sustain you. He tenderly cares for your innermost needs. Nothing can keep you outside His love.

Because God is sovereign, wise, and loving, you can trust Him without reservation. Resolute trust will quell your fears, calm your quivers, and stabilize your emotions. He holds you fast and will not let go.

Precious heavenly Father, You are an unchanging God who never leaves me helpless. You are sovereign and at work in every detail of my life. Use each setback and victory to accomplish Your purpose of conforming me to Christ's image.

When in Need

SCRIPTURE READING: Hebrews 4:12–16   KEY VERSE: 2 Timothy 2:26

They may come to their senses and escape the snare of the devil, having been taken captive by him to do his will.

We are likely to think of the obvious—hatred, lust, immorality—as Satan's primary weapons of temptation and defeat. But our accuser possesses a far more deadly and cleverly disguised agent of spiritual destruction—discouragement.

In times of need, he causes us to dwell on our mistakes, our repeated failures, our constant confession of sins, and our general lack of holiness and unrighteousness. It doesn't take much on the devil's part to disillusion us. We are all too well acquainted with our infirmities. Allowed to linger, discouragement breeds despair, which engulfs any sense of godly hope and confidence. Like a battle tank out of gas, we are neutralized on the spiritual battlefield.

If you have experienced this bewildered state, you can disarm the deceiver with this unchanging Bible truth: God's grace will never fail you.

Christ's grace saved you. His face smiles upon you even when you stumble. His grace has reserved a place in heaven for every believer that no sin or sins can alter.

His throne is adorned with grace and mercy. As the Son of man, Christ understands your plight. He will never turn you away. The instant you call on Him and thank Him for His forgiveness, discouragement has no room to stand. Go boldly to Him.

Father God, I take authority over the enemy's tool of discouragement in my life. I give You all my mistakes, failures, and recurring sins. Thank You for grace that will never fail.

Standing Strong in His Grace

SCRIPTURE READING: Psalm 46   KEY VERSE: Psalm 46:1

God is our refuge and strength, a very present help in trouble.

What is grace?
Grace is help.

We all need God's help. Apart from the gift of His Son, we couldn't be saved from sin. Apart from the gift of the Holy Spirit, we couldn't experience His divine provision.

Never be too proud to ask for God's help. Refusing His aid is like a starving man rejecting a sumptuous feast. The psalmist wrote, "God is our refuge and strength, a very present help in trouble" (Ps. 46:1).

Grace is acceptance. If you have received Jesus as your Savior, you never have to earn God's approval. You already have it. While He does discipline His children, God never rejects us for performance. The love of God is abundantly yours through Christ. His acceptance of you as a member of His family is irrevocable.

Grace is compassion. Jesus sympathizes with us. He identifies with our weaknesses, our fears, our anxieties. God is not distant, cold, detached. When Christ became flesh, He took on all the infirmities of mankind. Though sinless, our God weeps with us in sorrow, is grieved by our sin, and is exhilarated by our obedience.

Stand strong in His grace. Receive His help. Relax in His acceptance. Bask in His compassion. The God of grace is with you.

Dear Lord, You are my refuge and strength, a present help in time of trouble. Thank You for unconditional acceptance and unlimited compassion. Help me stand strong in Your grace.

The Ground of Victory

SCRIPTURE READING: Psalm 96   KEY VERSE: Psalm 96:4

The LORD is great and greatly to be praised; He is to be feared above all gods.

General Norman Schwarzkopf revealed after the Persian Gulf War that the one-hundred-hour battle was decided in the very first minutes when Allied planes savaged Iraqi air defenses.

"When I saw our planes knock out their radar, I knew at that very moment we had them," Schwarzkopf said.

There is a very distinct parallel for Christians. Although we are in a very real war, with enticements to sin and an adversary who harasses us, the outcome of the conflict has been decided.

That occurred at Calvary when Jesus "disarmed the rulers and authorities, [making] a public display of them, having triumphed over them through Him" (Col. 2:15 NASB). Jesus defeated Satan on the cross. He took away the sting of death by bearing our sins, making reconciliation between God and man possible.

The man or woman who has believed in Him and received His forgiveness of sins is on the winning side. But we deal with our foe on the ground of victory. We are not helpless, frightened little children but sons and daughters of God who triumph over Satan "through Him."

Don't shrink from the battle. It was won at Golgotha, and you share in its victory through your union with the Victor, Jesus Christ.

> *O God, thank You that the battle was already won at Golgotha. I share in its triumph through my union with Christ. I praise You that I deal with the enemy on victory ground!*

The Worth of Weakness

SCRIPTURE READING: Psalm 103 KEY VERSE: John 10:10

The thief does not come except to steal, and to kill, and to destroy. I have come that they may have life, and that they may have it more abundantly.

The late Traian Dorz was an influential Christian leader in Communist Romania following the Second World War.

As such, he was beaten on many occasions by Communist authorities seeking to weaken his faith. After each beating by one particular guard, he would look into the guard's menacing face and say, "I want you to know that God loves you very much, and I love you very much too."

The guard returned one evening for what Dorz thought was yet another pummeling. Instead, the guard reported he had found Jesus as his Savior.

Traian Dorz modeled the biblical idea of weakness. Contrary to the world's definition, weakness is not fear, cowardliness, or defeat. Weakness is a rational appraisal of our strength versus God's strength. We are finite; He is infinite. We are erratic; God is unchanging.

In view of this truth, it is foolish not to trust in God for help and guidance, to come to Him in solid anticipation that He can and will handle our problems.

Draw on the inexhaustible reservoir of God's wisdom, grace, and mercy. In your limitations, you have the power of an unlimited God to sustain you.

Almighty God, I receive by faith Your wisdom, grace, and mercy. Thank You that in my limitations, I have Your unlimited power to sustain me.

Defend Against Deception

SCRIPTURE READING: Jude 1–4   KEY VERSE: John 14:6

Jesus said to him, "I am the way, the truth, and the life. No one comes to the Father except through Me."

Heresy always contains enough truth to be attractive. However, Satan, the author of heresy, never offers us the complete truth. He always offers counterfeits. Any teaching that leads people away from God and causes them to question the validity of the Scriptures is deadly.

The false teachers of Peter's day taught that Jesus was a good man, an acclaimed teacher, and a prophet from God. They even imitated His teaching but stopped seriously short of professing His deity.

Today's false teachers have much more than a foot in the doorway to our churches, educational institutions, and businesses. They are allowed to openly profess their beliefs as truth. They teach belief in a god, but not the God of the Bible. They teach that we can become godlike if we will practice self-discipline and search within ourselves to find truth.

Nothing could be more steeped in deception. Jesus said, "I am the way, and the truth, and the life; no one comes to the Father, but through Me" (John 14:6 NASB).

The best defense to the enemy's deception is personal knowledge of God and His truth. Set your heart on knowing the true God, and He will expose the false teaching of those around you.

Father, I come to You through the way, Jesus Christ. Help me guard against the deception of the enemy. Expose all that is false. Reveal to me the truth of Your Word. I set my heart to know You.

Never Give Up!

SCRIPTURE READING: Revelation 3:20–22   KEY VERSE: Matthew 16:18

I also say to you that you are Peter, and on this rock I will build My church, and the gates of Hades shall not prevail against it.

The title of today's devotion—"Never Give Up!"—brings to mind a stirring memory of the people who fought in World War II. On the brink of destruction, Churchill's call to arms rallied his troops. The result was a shift in the way England fought the rest of the war.

Setting its focus on one thing—victory—England refused to be dominated by any outside force. It rose from the charred ruins of wartime to become once again a great and mighty nation. Looking back to that defining moment in history brings a sense of pride. Here is a group of people who said, "No, we will not go down in defeat. We believe there is a future for us, and we will step forward through the darkness to find a candle of hope."

When you are tempted to give up, think back to this point in history. What would have happened if England had given in to the evil of Hitler's rule? Oppression and a sense of loss would have swept through the nation with such vengeance that recovery would have been hard, if not impossible.

England had made its choice even before the Allies joined the war. The inner strength of the nation was the motivating factor. Are you facing what appears to be a sure defeat? Are air-raid sirens sounding all around you? Stand firm in your faith in God. Cling to Him, and declare that with His help, you will never give up. The victory you long to receive is yours.

Dear heavenly Father, I declare it: I won't ever give up! As I travel the rough pathways of this world—in the face of danger or defeat—I will stand firm in You. The victory is mine!

JUNE

Journey into the Wilderness

REPRESENTING: Withstanding adversity

KEY VERSE: Psalm 145:18

The LORD is near to all who call upon Him, to all who call upon Him in truth.

It was a divinely ordained journey—Jesus was "led up by the Spirit into the wilderness to be tempted by the devil" (Matt. 4:1). The wilderness speaks of testing, adversity, difficulty, and brokenness. Jesus traveled there, and so will we. It is not possible to get through life without it. There is no bypass. There are no detours.

But as it was for Jesus, the wilderness can be a place of strengthening and spiritual preparation if we learn to respond properly.

This month's devotions focus on the wilderness experiences—adversity, storms of life, and brokenness. *Not a pleasant destination,* you may be thinking. No—but a necessary one, for if you do not learn to deal with the difficulties of life, then you may respond as many of Christ's disciples who deserted Him when He talked of suffering (John 6:60, 66).

When your spiritual journey takes you through the wilderness of adversity, remember that you don't travel alone. Jesus Christ, the Son of the living God, walks with you. To whom else will you go?

When Storms Come

SCRIPTURE READING: Matthew 8:23–27   KEY VERSE: Matthew 20:28

The Son of Man did not come to be served, but to serve, and to give His life a ransom for many.

Jesus came to earth as God in the flesh. He didn't have to take on the form of humanity, but He did. He momentarily laid aside His eternal glory to identify with the needs of sinful man.

No one knows the personal loss or the private pain that Jesus suffered. Wherever He traveled, storm clouds gathered. Wherever He spoke, political unrest ensued. For every person who joined His band of disciples, hundreds more turned against Him.

Christ could have focused on the storms that tore at His mind and heart. Instead, He chose to calm the stormy lives of others—a Roman centurion whose servant was dying, a young man bound by demonic oppression, a woman caught in adultery, a disabled beggar, a man born blind, and a Pharisee who came to Him hidden by night's cover.

Even when the storms grew to overwhelming proportions, Jesus did not waver in His faith. He never lost sight of His eternal purpose. Dying on the cross, He offered salvation to the thief being crucified beside Him.

When the storm clouds gather in your life, remember that Jesus personally understands your pain and suffering. And there is never a time when you are beyond His loving grasp.

Dear Lord, You are not a stranger to adversity. When storm clouds gather, help me remember that You understand my pain and suffering. There is never a time when I am beyond Your loving grasp.

Nothing Happens by Chance

SCRIPTURE READING: Romans 8:28–29   KEY VERSE: Isaiah 55:8

"For My thoughts are not your thoughts, nor are your ways My ways," says the LORD.

An earthen dam breaks, sending thousands of gallons of water rushing down a rocky ravine. In the wake of the flood lies a sleeping Bible college community. After the waters recede, thirty-nine people are reported dead and countless others injured. Can God possibly be in this senseless tragedy?

God is indeed in everything. If anything is beyond His reach, then He cannot be God. Everything abides under His control, and He promised to work all things together in such a fashion that good comes out of them.

Almost fifteen years later, the tiny Bible school is now a thriving Christian college with twice the enrollment as before the tragedy. The trial that had the potential to devastate God's plan became a pathway to stronger faith.

Pain and suffering are a natural part of life. In times of intense testing we learn of God's undivided love and devotion toward us.

Nothing happens by chance with God. He always has a purpose in mind when He allows us to be tested. Sometimes it is to refine us. Sometimes it is to draw us to a closer walk with Him.

Whatever you are facing today, God knows the extent of your sorrow. Place your trust completely in Him, and He will help you bear the weight of your adversity.

Thank You, Lord, that nothing happens by chance. You always have a divine purpose in mind when You allow me to be tested. Let my adversities refine me and draw me closer to You.

Why?

SCRIPTURE READING: Genesis 50:15–21   KEY VERSE: Deuteronomy 29:29

The secret things belong to the LORD our God, but those things which are revealed belong to us and to our children forever, that we may do all the words of this law.

We may never know the reason why some things happen. A friend is killed in a senseless auto accident; a loved one suffers with a terminal illness; a child dies from a rare, incurable disease. We wonder how any good could possibly come from such heartache.

There are times when God reveals the purpose for our suffering. Other times He doesn't. In those hidden times our faith is tested and stretched.

Jesus knew the will of the Father. He understood that pain and suffering were part of the plan. Yet He cried from the cross: "My God, My God, why have You forsaken Me?" (Matt. 27:46). For one brief moment in time, Jesus felt all the emotions that we feel in tragedy—loneliness, fear, confusion, abandonment.

That is why He tells us to come to Him when our hearts are breaking, when fear has absorbed us, when we don't know how we will face tomorrow, when all within us wants to question His judgment. He understands our hurt; He personally knows our pain.

There is a mystery to tragedy, but it is not mysterious to Jesus. He knows the plan. He may not always provide all the answers you want to hear, but He promises never to leave you alone in the midst of the trial. Call out to Him, my friend; He is listening.

> *Heavenly Father, when I feel lonely, fearful, confused, or abandoned, help me remember that You are no stranger to these emotions. You personally know my pain. I am so thankful that I am never alone in the midst of my trials.*

Keys to Triumph

SCRIPTURE READING: James 1:1–8   KEY VERSE: James 1:2

My brethren, count it all joy when you fall into various trials.

Problems, heartaches, and pressures have always been a part of the Christian life. The early church suffered greatly at the hands of Roman and Jewish leaders. Early church members often worshiped in secret to avoid arrest and persecution.

How could the early church handle such extreme pressure? The people learned to turn their trials into triumphs by praising and worshiping God. In fact, historians say if one word could be used to characterize the early church, it would be *joy*.

Throughout the ages, God has always moved in response to the praise and worship of His people. The power of praise and joy opened the doors to Paul and Silas's jail cell. A shout of praise to God brought down the walls of Jericho. Praise led Hezekiah's army into victorious battle.

The heartbeat of James's message to the early church was simple—don't allow your trials to overcome you. Instead, turn your trials into triumphs.

The keys to triumph are a joyful heart, a willingness to understand God's ways, a surrendered life, and an attitude of faith. No matter how fierce the trial, how strong the temptation, you can experience victory today by expressing your praises to God.

O God, I don't want to let my trials overcome me. Give me the ability to turn them into triumphs by understanding Your ways and rejoicing in You. Give me a joyful heart of praise.

Anchor Your Roots

SCRIPTURE READING: Acts 16:22–34   KEY VERSE: Acts 16:25

At midnight Paul and Silas were praying and singing hymns to God, and the prisoners were listening to them.

Mount Mitchell, located just north of Asheville, North Carolina, on the Blue Ridge Parkway, is a favorite spot for tourists. People come to experience the beauty of the terrain and the excitement of the volatile climate on the summit.

Storms often gather quickly. Temperatures can drop dramatically, even during the summer. By mid-November the Park Service usually closes all roads near the peak because of snow. The rugged spirit of the mountain draws many people. The untamed attitude seems to capture the imagination.

Yet the stamina of the fir trees gains the most attention. Tightly compacted, they have learned to weather the storms of life. Gnarled from the constant winds that sweep across the mountain, they anchor their roots around large rocks. Instead of resisting the gales of winter, they lean with the wind while releasing a sweet mountain fragrance.

When trials come, we can respond in one of four ways: (1) resist, (2) run, (3) retreat, or (4) reap the rewards of going through the difficulty.

How do you respond to the windy trials that suddenly overtake your life? Anchor your roots in Jesus, and He will be your joy and strength.

Father, I do not want to resist, run, or retreat. I want to reap the benefits of my adversities. I anchor my roots in You so that I can stand strong against the gales of life.

He Will Come to Help

SCRIPTURE READING: Matthew 14:22–32   KEY VERSE: Matthew 14:27

Immediately Jesus spoke to them, saying, "Be of good cheer! It is I; do not be afraid."

Jesus knew a storm was coming. Yet He watched passively as His disciples pushed away from the shoreline and began rowing into deeper water. Finally the sails caught the wind, and the oars were pulled inside the boat.

From a Galilean hillside, Christ continued to study their obedient journey. Perhaps Peter was manning the rudder; John and Bartholomew, in deep conversation, rested against the bow; and Matthew, serious in thought, appeared caught up in Thomas's animated words.

By the evening's fourth watch, the scene was dramatically different. The sea had turned into a fierce enemy, and fear filled the hearts of the disciples. Swamped by elevating waves, the tiny boat listed in its struggle to stay afloat. There was no mistake—Jesus had deliberately sent the disciples into the path of the storm.

Some of life's stormiest moments are found at the heart of obedience. While the storms of life are not easy, they are necessary. Jesus used this one as a catalyst to refine the disciples' faith. He did not leave them alone. The moment all hope in human help had faded, Jesus went to them.

Whatever you're facing today, Christ is in it with you. And just as He rescued His disciples, He will help you.

Thank You, Lord, that You are always available to help me. As I travel the pathway of obedience, whatever I encounter on my journey, You are there.

How to Handle Your Burdens

SCRIPTURE READING: Matthew 11:28–30   KEY VERSE: Psalm 55:22

Cast your burden on the LORD, and He shall sustain you; He shall never permit the righteous to be moved.

W hen our burdens become unbearable, we can seek to dump them in several places. Perhaps we have a friend who will listen to our problems. Perhaps we can find relief in a brief getaway where we can be refreshed and strengthened. We might even have access to a Christian counselor who can give us solid advice.

But nothing or no one can provide the rest and relief that Jesus can when we come to Him with our burdens. Our Savior has broad shoulders, sturdy hands, and a compassionate heart. He bids us to give Him every grievous or weighty matter.

If you are carrying a burden that has you at the breaking point, come to Jesus in prayer. Don't worry about the right words; just cry out to God. Tell Him how you feel. Prayer is simply talking with God, and that is what you do to shift your burden to Christ.

Come in childlike faith. Jesus said that He would give His light and easy load in return for your heaviness. Does He lie? Is He being too simplistic?

No. God can sustain you as you trust Him. Focus on His power, and receive His all-sufficient help. He will not let you down. He will not let you fall. Jesus hears your plea. He will lighten your load so that you may persevere.

Master, sometimes it seems as if my burdens are unbearable. Thank You for Your broad shoulders, sturdy hands, and compassionate heart. You exchange my heavy load for Your light and easy burden.

When Your World Turns Upside Down

SCRIPTURE READING: John 11:17–22   KEY VERSE: John 11:22

Even now I know that whatever You ask of God, God will give You.

F ew of us are prepared for the worst when it comes. Often tragedy strikes without notice—the sudden death of a loved one, a layoff at work, or a medical report confirming a terminal illness.

These events and many more have the potential to turn our world upside down. How do we handle circumstances that leave us suddenly feeling out of control and frightened?

At the death of her brother, Martha longed for Jesus to return to Bethany. The pain was too great for her to bear alone. She knew He was the Christ, the Son of God; and yet she was torn emotionally by her human feelings. Had Jesus been present when Lazarus became ill, she reasoned, he never would have died.

Faith versus human reasoning—in this case faith won out. Fighting back tears, Martha said, "Even now I know that whatever You ask of God, God will give You" (John 11:22). She believed Jesus had complete control over the situation. No matter how upside down her world appeared, Christ's presence restored order and hope.

God may not completely remove the painfulness of your circumstances. But He will bring order and peace if you will turn to Him. He is your present help in troubled times.

Precious Lord, when it seems my world is upside down and all is out of control, help me have faith in You. Although You may not remove the pain of my circumstances, You will be my Guide in troubled times.

Be Still and Know

SCRIPTURE READING: Psalm 46   KEY VERSE: Psalm 46:10

Be still, and know that I am God; I will be exalted among the nations, I will be exalted in the earth!

The writer of Psalm 46 knew what it meant to face turmoil and tragedy. Wars and violence were very much a part of Old Testament life. Entire nations were wiped out without warning. Imagine the fear and dismay of such perilous times.

You may know personally how it feels to abide in the instability of pain and suffering. At times you find yourself longing for something or someone to anchor and steady your hurting heart. Jesus is your anchor. He is your sure hope.

The psalmist told us that even though our world appears disjointed, turned upside down, and on the brink of desolation, God is with us. He never abandons His omnipotent station.

He is our hiding place when the storms of life lash out at us. He is our abode of trust, covering us with His divine veil of protection when powerful forces attack. Martin Luther captured this thought in the words: "A mighty fortress is our God." God is our refuge, and He cannot be shaken.

How do you tap into His sovereign watchcare? Verse 10 of Psalm 46 (NASB) holds the answer: "Cease striving [be still] and know that I am God." Lay aside your human effort, and call out to your Eternal Hope—Jesus Christ.

> *Dear heavenly Father, even though this world seems on the brink of desolation, You are my anchor. You are my sure hope. You are my hiding place in the storms of life. Thank You for the veil of Your divine protection.*

God Is in Control

SCRIPTURE READING: Psalm 121   KEY VERSE: Job 42:2

I know that You can do everything, and that no purpose of Yours can be withheld from You.

In his discussion on suffering and adversity in his best-seller *When Bad Things Happen to Good People*, Rabbi Harold S. Kushner states that Job had to conclude that God was not really all-powerful. Job is "forced to choose between a good God who is not totally powerful or a powerful God who is not totally good."

The thrust of his argument is that when bad things happen, God is apparently unable or uncaring. In other words, he claims that God is not the Sovereign Master of the universe.

When adversity strikes, we often are plagued with similar thoughts:

- Why doesn't God do something?
- Why did He let this happen?
- Doesn't He care?

The Scriptures reveal a God who is always in charge, regardless of the circumstances. We live in an abnormal world where evil is present; but God's providence is over all, and He uses His power for His purposes (Gen. 50:20).

God also cares. His Son met death on a cross because God's love transcended suffering. Whatever hardship you face today, know that God is in control of your life and He cares for you. Never doubt God's power or love.

Almighty God, how I rejoice that You are always in charge. Your providence reigns over all. You have the power to use every situation for Your purposes.

Reinforcing Your Faith

SCRIPTURE READING: Romans 5:1–5   KEY VERSE: Romans 5:3

*Not only that, but we also glory in tribulations, knowing that tribulation
produces perseverance.*

Y ou forgot a 9:00 A.M. meeting that you were supposed to attend. Your
computer lost a half day's work. You arrived home to discover a car wind-
shield smashed by a baseball. Have you had one of those days when everything
went askew? What about one of those weeks or months?

We like our days to be as cooperative as possible. We tolerate adversity but
certainly do not appreciate it. Often, however, God can accomplish more of His
purposes on these perplexing, aggravating occasions than on unclouded days.
God uses rough times to build character:

- When the boss says no, we develop perseverance.
- When a mate is ill for an extended time, long-suffering and kindness are
  cultivated.
- When a neighbor is harsh, goodness and love are surfaced by the Holy
  Spirit.

God also uses rough times to build trust.

Jerry Bridges writes in his book *Trusting God* that it is often "easier to obey
God than trust Him." Trusting God under a heavy cloud cover is the surest sign
of a growing faith. God wants us to lean on Him, even when we cannot always
see His presence. Let your hard days build sturdy character and reinforce your
faith. You may not enjoy them, but they will not be wasted.

*Dear God, nothing is wasted—not even the hard and difficult times. Use
them to build my character and reinforce my faith. Teach me the value of
adversity.*

Confronting Conflicts

SCRIPTURE READING: 2 Corinthians 4:7–18   KEY VERSE: 2 Corinthians 4:17

Our light affliction, which is but for a moment, is working for us a far more exceeding and eternal weight of glory.

C onflict affects people in different ways:

- Some internalize their difficulties, which can lead to sustained anger and frustration.
- Others fully vent their feelings and emotions, which may make them feel better momentarily but does not solve their problems.
- Still others try to ignore their problems, hoping they will disappear as time passes.

In God's plan, conflicts initiate the following scriptural scenario:

First, our conflicts should drive us to the Lord Jesus Christ. We look to God's Word to guide our conduct; we seek His face to steady our course. We lean on His strength, depend on His wisdom, and take refuge in His arms.

Second, we entrust our problems to the Lord's care. God is responsible for His children. Our conflicts concern Him, and He promises to sustain us if we cast our burdens on Him (1 Peter 5:6–7).

Third, we thank God for an outcome that glorifies Him. The Lord uses our conflicts to produce outstanding results that will benefit us on earth and in heaven.

By taking our problems to the Father, we have engaged our mighty God to work in our behalf. These problems can be solved as we allow Him to fight our battles for us (Ex. 14:14; Rev. 19:11).

O Lord, let every conflict drive me to You. Guide my conduct and steady my course. Use my problems to produce results that will benefit me on earth and in heaven. Thank You for an outcome that will glorify You.

JUNE 13

Through Troubled Waters

SCRIPTURE READING: Matthew 6:25–34   KEY VERSES: 1 Peter 5:6–7

Humble yourselves under the mighty hand of God, that He may exalt you in due time, casting all your care upon Him, for He cares for you.

Y ou lose your job. Your spouse files for divorce. You discover that one of your children is on drugs. A loved one is diagnosed with cancer and given only six months to live. Such times are extremely disorienting. They strike with such intensity that emotions can be buried beneath a tide of fear and anxiety.

Yet these pillars of truth can help You endure and triumph:

God knows your problems. Your woes have not taken God by surprise. He is aware of every detail of your troubles: "Your Father knows what you need, before you ask Him" (Matt. 6:8 NASB). God cares about your problems.

God loves you without limit. As the Good Shepherd, He will protect and defend you: "Do not fear or be dismayed because of this great multitude, for the battle is not yours but God's" (2 Chron. 20:15 NASB). God is able to deal with your problems.

God has the power to handle your problems. Because He knows and cares, He will act according to His wisdom and will: "Humble yourselves, therefore, under the mighty hand of God, that He may exalt you at the proper time, casting all your anxiety upon Him, because He cares for you" (1 Peter 5:6–7 NASB).

Precious heavenly Father, I am so grateful that You understand my problems. They have not taken You by surprise. You have the power to handle all of my difficulties.

Anger Toward God

SCRIPTURE READING: Jonah 3:4–4:11   KEY VERSE: Job 13:15

Though He slay me, yet will I trust Him. Even so, I will defend my own ways before Him.

Your daughter died of leukemia after years of painful treatment. You lost your job at the factory after twenty years of employment. These events—or even ones of lesser significance—may have resulted in a common emotion within you: anger.

The problem, however, is not just your anger but the object of your hostility: God. Is the Lord surprised by your outbursts? Is He angry with you? Will He punish you?

God is never threatened by your anger. He is never disappointed with you. He is never upset over your questions.

Yet while we are free to express our feelings toward our heavenly Father, we must be careful not to nurture them. Our anger toward God is never justified.

We may not understand why a daughter died or why we lost a job. We live in a sinful, abnormal world where God still allows evil.

But His love and justice are unquestioned, supremely demonstrated in the death, burial, and resurrection of the Lord Jesus Christ. He is for us, not against us. He is not unfair or undependable.

Holding on to our anger will only hurt us. Venting our feelings within the framework of trust in God is the only acceptable, profitable option.

Precious Lord, there are many things I do not understand, but I give them all to You. I know You are for me and not against me. Take my anger, and help me trust.

Working Through Problems

SCRIPTURE READING: Romans 8:31–34   KEY VERSE: Psalm 118:6

The LORD is on my side; I will not fear. What can man do to me?

C hristians face the same dilemmas that everyone else does. Christian soldiers in the Middle East must confront the same enemy as non-Christians. Believers in the business world must deal with the same volatile economic pressures as nonbelievers. Christians must encounter the same moral temptations as the unsaved.

Understanding that our faith does not eliminate our problems, we can, however, have a tremendous advantage in working through them.

Because we are Christians, God is "for us" (Rom. 8:31 NASB). We never face a circumstance without God's help and participating presence. God is intimately involved in our situations.

Because we are Christians, God will "freely give us all things" (Rom. 8:32 NASB). God does not withhold our needs in times of trouble. He will comfort, lead, and sustain us. We have His unlimited resources to draw upon in our difficulty.

Because we are Christians, we have Christ who "also intercedes for us" (Rom. 8:34 NASB). We may not know how or what to pray. But the Son of God is always praying on our behalf, presenting us before the heavenly Father on a constant basis.

What reassurance! Troubles? Yes. Hopelessness? Never!

Father God, how I rejoice that You are in me! I never face a circumstance without Your help and presence. Thank You for Your intimate involvement in every situation of my life.

Conquering in Christ

SCRIPTURE READING: Psalm 77   KEY VERSE: Isaiah 43:2

When you pass through the waters, I will be with you; and through the rivers, they shall not overflow you. When you walk through the fire, you shall not be burned, nor shall the flame scorch you.

The greatest truth the believer can cling to in time of need is that no problem, regardless of intensity or nature, can hinder the free, full flow of God's love toward himself.

The love of God is not just sentiment. It is not just a warm feeling or a sweet Christian saying. The love of God means that He is working to accomplish His purposes in your life in every stressful situation.

There is nothing random about your problem. It is not merely the result of fleeting earthly forces at work. Before you were born, before the universe was conceived, God knew about and figured your particular trouble into His master scheme.

You may not be able to understand what is happening or why this problem has arisen. But you do know the God who has the answers and the power to bring you through.

Each time of testing is an occasion to see God work and trust Him for the results. It is an opportunity to grow in dependence on Him and discover His greatness for yourself.

You are a conqueror in Christ in every situation because the Conqueror, Jesus Christ, is in control of you and your circumstances. Nothing or no one can outwit Him or overcome Him.

O Lord, You knew me before I was born. You figured all my problems into Your master scheme. I may not understand everything, but You do. You have the answers and the power to bring me through each difficulty. I am more than a conqueror through You.

He Will Revive You

SCRIPTURE READING: Job 42:1–6   KEY VERSE: Job 42:5

I have heard of You by the hearing of the ear, but now my eye sees You.

Faith works anywhere:

- At a bedside in the hospital
- At the dinner table on the family farm whose crop has been ruined by hail
- At work before the important staff meeting
- At the end of the month when the checkbook runs red
- At home when the neighbor will not let go of a personal grudge

Faith works at all times, in all places, because it trusts in God, who is always at work in heaven and earth to achieve His eternal, good purposes. Faith that conquers every obstacle triumphs when our chief concern is that God's will be done.

Each of us has an agenda to some degree. We want to see our sick loved one healed, our farm productive, our finances solvent, our relationships harmonious. While God does plan for our welfare, He sovereignly weaves our pain, disappointment, perplexity, and unanswered prayers to accomplish His ultimate purpose—to bring glory to Him in all things.

Once you are confident in God's supreme faithfulness to you, your faith in Him will carry you through any adversity. Your faith in God's promises, His character, and His unfailing love will sustain and strengthen you. Though you fall, He will upright you. Though you faint, He will revive you.

Dear Lord, when I fall, upright me. When I faint, revive me. Carry me through each adversity by a dynamic faith that conquers every challenge.

Praying in a Crisis

SCRIPTURE READING: James 5:13–18   KEY VERSE: James 5:13

Is anyone among you suffering? Let him pray. Is anyone cheerful? Let him sing psalms.

During the Persian Gulf War, prayer made a comeback in mainstream America. Commentators regularly mentioned prayer. The president prayed for our troops. But some of the most intense prayer arose from the hot sands of the Arabian desert.

"Praying makes me feel better, makes me a little more secure," said one army lieutenant who skipped a card game to attend a worship service. An army staff sergeant commented, "I have always prayed, but I need it now more than ever."

Adversity motivates people to prayer. Crises quickly filter the trivial and expose the essential. In the midst of crises, we must remember several crucial truths.

We must be rightly related to the God we petition. The nonbeliever may pray; but until he places his faith in Christ, his pleas are in vain. God desires to bring all men to saving faith, but He is not obligated to respond to the nonbeliever's prayers.

Another important principle is that while prayer moves God to act on man's behalf, it does not guarantee preferred answers. We cannot manipulate God. But crises turn us toward Him for His sovereign answers, the most critical being His provision for our sins through faith in Jesus Christ. We then ask in His name and trust Him for the outcome.

Heavenly Father, thank You for the privilege of prayer—that I can ask for Your provision and trust You for the outcome. In the face of every crisis, let me flee to You.

Encouragement for a Troubled Heart

SCRIPTURE READING: Psalm 138   KEY VERSE: Psalm 138:7

Though I walk in the midst of trouble, You will revive me; You will stretch out Your hand against the wrath of my enemies, and Your right hand will save me.

When Ruth Graham, wife of evangelist Billy Graham, was sent to a North Korean school as a young girl, she wrestled with loneliness and discouragement. Her missionary parents were hundreds of miles away—an especially frightening thought for an adolescent reared in a loving, Christian environment.

Alone and afraid, Ruth Graham learned a lesson that has befriended her for life: "In missionary school I learned to turn to the Bible for comfort and encouragement," she reflected. "Through the years I have continued that practice, and it has brought me more encouragement than any other source."

The words of Scripture are not only for instruction and correction but also for encouragement. If your heart is troubled, open your Bible. Read the God-breathed utterances given to uplift and sustain you.

Look at the lives of Old and New Testament characters, and trust in the unchanging God to work His wonder on your behalf. The Bible speaks peace. It is steeped in love. It is aglow with hope. Its words are living and vital, true bread and water for the weak and afflicted.

O God, Your Word never changes. It is forever settled in heaven. It is aglow with hope. It is living and vital. It is the bread that strengthens and the water that pours divine life into me.

Enduring Hope

SCRIPTURE READING: 2 Corinthians 1:3–7   KEY VERSE: 2 Corinthians 1:5

As the sufferings of Christ abound in us, so our consolation also abounds through Christ.

In only his second start since returning to the San Francisco Giants following cancer surgery on his left arm, Dave Dravecky crumpled to the mound in the early innings. The cancer-weakened bone in his arm had snapped. Further surgery was required, and baseball became his pastime.

His faith in Christ sustained him through the countless trips for treatment and the uncertainty of his future and health. He autographed each baseball picture featuring his long stride and cocked arm with Paul's statement of confidence to the Corinthians.

"My wife and I have committed these verses to memory," he said. "We realize that our life on earth is temporary and our circumstances and afflictions, however severe, are still light and fleeting when viewed from the perspective of eternity."

You need not lose heart in your heartaches. God is working through your trials in a mysterious but productive manner. As you place your focus on His eternal presence, you will have sure and sturdy hope.

Dave Dravecky has enduring hope. You, too, can be encouraged, knowing that God is in control of your life, both here and hereafter. His hand is loving, steady, and able.

Lord, give me an enduring hope that knows You are in control of my circumstances, now and in the future. You are loving, steady, and able to guide my life. I relinquish control to You.

Profiting from Suffering

SCRIPTURE READING: 1 Peter 4:12–16   KEY VERSE: 1 Peter 5:10

May the God of all grace, who called us to His eternal glory by Christ Jesus, after you have suffered a while, perfect, establish, strengthen, and settle you.

The best way to deal with suffering is to set your eyes on Jesus, not your circumstances. Most of us have little problem following Christ when things are going well, but at the first sign of a storm we instinctively run for cover.

After Jesus calmed the raging winds, He turned to His disciples and asked, "Why did you doubt?" No one knows the length and depth of suffering. However, we know from Scripture that God wants us to place our entire trust in Him during times of difficulty and heartache.

You may be struggling with a burden that has endured for years. You are tired, doubtful, and angry. Satan is tempting you to give up, but God has not given up on you.

Remember, His purpose for allowing suffering is to mold and shape you into the image of His Son. And nothing so sands and polishes a saint like the fiery trials of adversity.

Peter said, "After you have suffered for a little while, the God of all grace, who called you to His eternal glory in Christ, will Himself perfect, confirm, strengthen and establish you" (1 Peter 5:10 NASB).

Let nothing keep you from trusting Him, no matter how great the winds of affliction. Sink your roots deep into the grace and love of Christ.

Master, when I am tempted to give up, help me remember that You have not given up on me. Conform me to the image of Your Son. Sand and polish my life through the trials of adversity.

Brokenness: The Way to Blessing

SCRIPTURE READING: John 12:24–26   KEY VERSE: Psalm 119:75

I know, O LORD, that Your judgments are right, and that in faithfulness You have afflicted me.

R ub some seed corn between your fingers, and instantly you will be struck by its hardness. You can step on it, throw it, or try to crush it, and the seed will remain intact in most instances. An abundant source of life is stored within this rigid outer husk. The potential for thousands of kernels is bound up in one tiny seed corn.

As any farmer or gardener knows, prolific life is released only when the corn is buried several inches beneath the turned soil. There it lies in darkness and seeming oblivion for many days. The rains come, and the seed waits. The sun shines, and the seed waits.

Then one day the waiting is over. A small green shoot thrusts through the earth. In the months to come, the plant will grow, tassel, and produce ample food for man and beast. The joy of harvest would never be realized apart from the breaking of the seed's protective shell.

There is a corresponding spiritual process at work in Christians. It is brokenness—the principle by which God gloriously works to liberate us for abundant living. It is a hard way, but it is God's way to blessing, joy, and abundant life.

Precious Lord, thank You for the process of brokenness, which is at work in me. Let me realize that despite its pain, it is the road to blessing.

Broken for His Purposes

SCRIPTURE READING: Psalm 143   KEY VERSE: Psalm 143:11

Revive me, O LORD, for Your name's sake! For Your righteousness' sake bring my soul out of trouble.

B rokenness is not the exception in the Christian life—it is the norm. We like to recite the triumphs of stirring biblical characters: Moses and the Red Sea, David and Goliath, Paul and the spread of the gospel. Their moving exploits, however, are incomplete apart from the bleak contrast of their afflictions.

Moses wandering in the wasteland, David hiding in caves, Paul moving from one jail to another. Their times of idleness, misunderstanding, rejection, and isolation were thorny preparations for their triumphs. They were ushered into the work of the kingdom not amid applause and affirmation but on the wings of the storm.

The same principle is at work in Christians today. Following God is not like driving on a scenic highway with one majestic experience after another. The pathway of discipleship is often downward before it is upward, emptying before it is filling.

God uses men and women who have been broken by Him for His purposes. The breaking can be strenuous, but the result is a vessel fit for the Master's use. And isn't that what we should desire the most?

Dear God, break me for Your purposes. Make me a vessel that You can use. That is what I desire.

Merged into His Fullness

Scripture Reading: Exodus 3:1–10   Key Verse: Psalm 66:12

You have caused men to ride over our heads; we went through fire and through water; but You brought us out to rich fulfillment.

God uses the vexing route of brokenness to merge us into His fullness.

- Moses would have never seen the miracles of the Red Sea and the wilderness unless he had been weaned from the self-sufficiency of his youth.
- David would have never known the intimacy and care of God if he instantly stepped into the royal palace following his victory over Goliath.
- Joseph would have never grasped the magnificent sovereignty of God in feeding the nations if his brothers had not sold him into forced slavery.

God does not lack great and mighty things to show us. He waits on humble, hungry men and women who have admitted their inadequacy and have no other hope but Himself.

He achieves that transformation by striking at the root of self-sufficiency—pride. Pride gets in God's way. It expresses itself in some form of manipulation or overconfidence. It seeks to exalt self and cherishes the admiration of others.

The riches of God's storehouse are distributed to the meek of heart, the weak in spirit. The tightly clenched hand of pride cannot receive it. Only brokenness can release the grip.

Father God, help me release my grip on the things of this world so that I can receive the riches of Your storehouse. I have no other hope but You. You are my adequacy.

A Surrendered Heart

SCRIPTURE READING: Psalm 77   KEY VERSE: Psalm 77:6

I call to remembrance my song in the night; I meditate within my heart, and my spirit makes diligent search.

Failure to see God at work in the circumstances that accompany brokenness can result in several self-defeating responses:

- Many people become bitter. Emotionally they internalize their distress, leading to a critical and complaining spirit. Spiritually they are turned off to God, disinterested in His Word, the church, or His people.
- Others explode or simmer in anger. They are disturbed that God has allowed such difficulty. They grow hostile to any mention of His name.
- Some try to escape their situations. They either ignore the problem, hoping it will go away, or turn to escapist elements—drugs, immorality, fanaticism.
- Still others seek to manipulate their environment, hoping their cleverness can eventually solve the problem.

Unfortunately these avenues don't embrace the solution God offers—entrusting ourselves and our problems to Him, depending wholly on His help and grace.

Can you identify with any of these reactions to brokenness? If so, ask God to forgive you, and look anew and afresh to Him. A surrendered heart is the beginning of a new outlook based on God's encouraging perspective.

O God, I want to respond properly to brokenness. Don't let me be bitter or angry. Don't let me try to escape or manipulate situations. I surrender my heart and life to You.

The Broken Man

SCRIPTURE READING: Psalm 145   KEY VERSE: Psalm 145:14

The LORD upholds all who fall, and raises up all who are bowed down.

The minute seed corn that was buried in the ground burst forth into a cornucopia of grain. Likewise, the Christian, stripped of self-sufficiency and entered into a new dimension of life in Christ, is positioned for maximum fruitfulness in the kingdom of God.

The broken man enjoys a new measure of power in the Holy Spirit. He looks to the Spirit of God to work in and through him, putting no confidence in the flesh. He is charged with the life and energy of the Holy Spirit.

The submitted man is joyful in the Lord. He is no longer hostage to changing circumstances, riding the ups and downs of emotions or happenings. The joy of the Lord is his strength.

The yielded man is alert to the needs of others. God uses him to minister to other hurting people because he is not consumed with his own problems. He has wisdom and insight from the Lord to share, not his own futile reasoning.

He still must deal with the trials and ordeals of daily life; but there is a lift to his countenance, a surety about his ways. He relies wholly on Christ. He has freedom, liberty, and new devotion to Jesus and His work.

Lord, I submit. I yield my life to You. Make me joyful despite adversity and alert to the needs of others. Minister through me to hurting people. Give me new freedom, liberty, and devotion to Your work.

The Sweet Fruits of Brokenness

SCRIPTURE READING: Psalm 34   KEY VERSE: Psalm 34:4

I sought the LORD, and He heard me, and delivered me from all my fears.

The process of brokenness is not interminable. God knows your frame and will not overload you or bring unnecessary sorrow.

As the crushed seed erupts into bountiful life, the sweet fruits of brokenness are released during your turmoil and heartache.

Perhaps the most precious fruit is peace. You are no longer left to your own cleverness. You no longer have to rely on your strength. You are not vainly wrestling with God over who is in charge of your life.

The Holy Spirit fills the broken heart with the peace of Christ. It is the peace of submission, the peace of resting in Him, the peace of knowing your times are in His wonderful hands.

There is a new intimacy with Jesus. You trust Him. You rely on Him. You look to Him. You can do nothing apart from Him. He is all you need. He is sufficient. He undertakes all of your concerns and bears every burden.

The broken man or woman enters a new dimension in the relationship with Christ. It is the place of blessing, healing, and new beginnings. It is a time to rejoice in both the sovereignty and the goodness of God.

Almighty God, I claim Your peace! Bring me into a new level of relationship where nothing on earth can agitate my spirit. I want to walk in greater intimacy with You.

Healing the Pain of Brokenness

SCRIPTURE READING: 2 Corinthians 12:7–10   KEY VERSE: Psalm 51:17

The sacrifices of God are a broken spirit, a broken and a contrite heart—these, O God, You will not despise.

The promises of God are dear to the hearts of those who have experienced brokenness:

The sacrifices of God are a broken spirit; a broken and a contrite heart, O God, Thou wilt not despise. (Ps. 51:17 NASB)

The LORD is near to the brokenhearted, and saves those who are crushed in spirit. (Ps. 34:18 NASB)

He heals the brokenhearted, and binds up their wounds. (Ps. 147:3 NASB)

The Spirit of the Lord GOD is upon me, because the LORD has anointed me to bring good news to the afflicted; He has sent me to bind up the brokenhearted. (Isa. 61:1 NASB)

If you are in the midst of brokenness and bereft of hope, meditate on these Scriptures. They share the heart of our Father God who longs to embrace and heal the pain of your brokenness. He promises to be near you, sustain you, watch over you, and bring relief with His healing hand.

The end of brokenness is the healing touch of the Father, the touch of grace and mercy. It is the gift of His strength for Your weakness, His hope for your despair, His contentment for your anxiety.

Dear God, heal my heart. Bind up my wounds. Be near me in the midst of my brokenness, and let me sense Your presence. Exchange my despair for hope, my anxiety for contentment, my weakness for Your strength.

When God Is Silent

SCRIPTURE READING: Genesis 37   KEY VERSE: Psalm 54:7

He has delivered me out of all trouble; and my eye has seen its desire upon my enemies.

For more than ten years, things had gone from bad to worse for Joseph. Once a free man, he was sold into slavery by his own brothers to people who were his enemies. Through it all, he continued to obey God and work hard for his master. Then, he was falsely accused of assaulting his master's wife, and he was thrown into prison.

Where was God in the apparently negative events? Not once had Joseph received encouragement from family or friends. Even though Joseph knew God was guiding and blessing him, the times of waiting rigorously challenged his faith.

When God is silent, when He doesn't intervene, it may seem that He isn't involved in your life. But God is never still. He is always at work, especially in the "silent times." He uses every event, every situation, and every person in your life to prepare you for the future and fulfill His perfect purpose.

When finally released and ruling Egypt as second in command, with the power to save his family and people, Joseph at last understood God's special plan. Cling to Him in the tough times; trust Him with the details. You will rejoice as you see His faithfulness unfold.

> *Lord, even when You are silent, You are at work in my life. Help me trust in the silent times, knowing that You will use every event, situation, and person to prepare me for Your purposes.*

His Plans Are Unfolding

SCRIPTURE READING: Genesis 39   KEY VERSE: Genesis 45:8

It was not you who sent me here, but God; and He has made me a father to Pharaoh, and lord of all his house, and a ruler throughout all the land of Egypt.

Although brokenness is a process, we can unnecessarily extend the time frame. We prolong God's redemptive, constructive purposes when we fail to see God's hand in our adverse circumstances.

Joseph tasted the bitter fruits of unjust slavery and imprisonment for thirteen years before God elevated him to Pharaoh's administrator. Confronting his brothers who had mistreated him, Joseph said, "Do not be grieved or angry with yourselves, because you sold me here; for God sent me before you to preserve life . . . Now, therefore, it was not you who sent me here, but God" (Gen. 45:5, 8 NASB).

Do you see God in everything, understanding that He either sends or permits all circumstances, good and evil? If He is not Lord of all, then He cannot be Lord at all. He is the Sovereign of the universe. Joseph was able to see God's hand in his brokenness.

God is working all things for good in your shattered circumstances. He knows the heartache you face, and He will comfort your deepest pain.

His plans are unfolding, even in the darkness of your adversity. See God behind it, and you will have His light to see you through your troubles.

Precious heavenly Father, this road I travel is not always easy. Help me understand that Your plans are unfolding, even in the darkness of adversity. Let Your Word and Your love penetrate the shadows and light my way.

JULY

Journey to Freedom

REPRESENTING: Being delivered from the negative

KEY VERSE: Philippians 4:13

I can do all things through Christ who strengthens me.

It was a tragic sight. God's people were captives of enemy forces. Trudging down the dusty road in chains, they were herded from their promised land toward the wicked city of Babylon (1 Chron. 9:1; Jer. 39:1).

That is exactly how Satan wants you—chained by negative emotions, addictions, and habits. Held captive to past mistakes. Hopelessly entangled in emotional and spiritual bondage.

But you don't have to remain in captivity. Our spiritual expedition this month is a journey to freedom. In the following pages you will learn how to escape from unhappiness, pride, self-reliance, inadequacy, loneliness, and much more.

During this month, let God reverse your captivity, freeing you from negative emotions and attitudes. Put the past behind you. Let Him give you a new song and fill your life with joy and laughter. Then you will declare with the Israelites, "The LORD has done great things!" (Ps. 126:3).

The Great Escape

SCRIPTURE READING: Titus 3:3–7   KEY VERSES: Colossians 1:13–14

He has delivered us from the power of darkness and conveyed us into the kingdom of the Son of His love, in whom we have redemption through His blood, the forgiveness of sins.

Harry Houdini was a master escape artist. Tied by chains and ropes and placed in confining quarters, he could be counted on to free himself from his predicaments. One day Houdini did not escape—but died.

Although the nonbeliever may invent all kinds of escape devices to deal with his life on earth—drugs, vacations, riches, pleasures, good works—he never can escape eternal death. Born in sin and alienated from the Source of life, the Lord Jesus Christ, man is bound by the chains of death. All of his attempts to avoid the divine decree of eternal punishment are utterly futile.

There is only one path of escape from the judgment of everlasting separation from the God of the ages: personal faith in and reliance upon the Savior, Christ Jesus. The instant a person turns to Christ to forgive his sins, he has made the great escape from eternal death into eternal life.

What an escape! From darkness to light. From despair to hope. From futility to meaning. From the domain of Satan to the kingdom of God (Col. 1:13–14).

Have you looked to Christ as your only escape from sin's penalty of death? If not, run to the cross today—where Jesus shed His blood to pay for all of your sins—to receive your everlasting liberation.

Dear Lord, You released the chains of death that bound me and gave me eternal life. You brought me from darkness to light, from despair to hope, from futility to meaning. Thank You for making me part of Your kingdom.

The Message of Freedom

SCRIPTURE READING: Psalm 107:1–9   KEY VERSE: Psalm 119:25

My soul clings to the dust; revive me according to Your word.

We receive all kinds of messages in life. Messages tell us how to live, where to vacation, what to eat, how to cook it, and then how to exercise it all away.

God's first concern is always toward the spiritual part of a person's life, not the physical. Because of the relentless spotlight placed on the need to look and act a certain way, depression, eating disorders, and anxiety top the list of problems people are most likely to struggle with.

However, these are only symptoms of a more serious dilemma. When we seek to become something apart from Jesus Christ, we end up chasing a very elusive shadow. Even if we do achieve a certain status, there is always something else on the horizon demanding more from us. Someone is always ahead of us causing us to think we need something other than what we have in order to be happy.

The person who finds his identity in Jesus Christ has freedom and peace. If you are struggling with thoughts of inadequacy, ask God to make His love for you very clear. He will never place unhealthy expectations on you. Nor does He say you have to reach a certain status before He can love you.

The moment you accept His Son as your Savior, He comes into your heart with perfect love and acceptance. He created you and is bound in love to you forever.

Heavenly Father, I want to find my true identity in You. Free me from the bondage of my limiting inadequacies.

Freedom from Wrong Emotions

SCRIPTURE READING: John 10:7–15   KEY VERSE: John 10:10

The thief does not come except to steal, and to kill, and to destroy. I have come that they may have life, and that they may have it more abundantly.

You see a moving television program—tears flow.

A drunken man at the basketball game leans over and spills his drink on you—anger swells.

You drive up to your house surrounded by paramedics and ambulances—fear surges.

Each is an emotion, an intrinsic part of every individual's personal identity.

We talk of emotional moments. We say that some people are unemotional while others freely express their feelings.

Whether suppressed or inhibited, the emotional makeup of a person is an integral part of his behavior. As such, it can be a problematic area for many Christians.

The good news for the believer is that you are now inhabited by the person of the Holy Spirit. The Spirit searches the innermost parts of your being, seeking to touch every aspect of your personality. Progressively He can heal damaged emotions, control runaway passions, and harness selfish affections.

If your emotions are fragile or volatile, the Holy Spirit can act as the inner healer, providing an unseen source of comfort. Your emotional infirmities are His supernatural specialty.

O God, I yield my emotions to You. Holy Spirit, be my source of comfort. Help me realize that my emotional infirmities are Your supernatural specialty.

Unhappiness

SCRIPTURE READING: 1 Timothy 6:6–11   KEY VERSE: 1 Timothy 6:6

Godliness with contentment is great gain.

Written into our country's famous Declaration of Independence is the noble idea that each citizen possesses inalienable rights, among which are "Life, Liberty and the pursuit of Happiness." In the past few decades, that pursuit has become more frenzied than ever. We, a nation of millions who seek the good life, "grab all the gusto" we can.

The framers of our document of freedom did not explain that while we may have a right to happiness, finding it—and maintaining it—is another matter altogether. The more we look, the more elusive happiness seems.

Moses endured millions of Israelites who were anything but happy campers. Jeremiah and Noah preached for a lifetime under oppressive conditions with little effectiveness. Paul's home was the inside of jail cells for several years.

Yet we cannot say these and other Bible personalities were sad, disillusioned men. Anything but that. Despite their conditions, they radiated joy.

Perhaps they defined *happiness* differently. *Contentment* would best describe them.

Searching for happiness is a roller-coaster experience. However, you can consistently attain contentment.

Father, I want to consistently radiate Your joy, despite my circumstances. Instead of seeking the "good life," let me focus on You. Let me learn to be contented.

Self-Reliance

SCRIPTURE READING: Psalm 28   KEY VERSE: 2 Corinthians 12:9

He said to me, "My grace is sufficient for you, for My strength is made perfect in weakness." Therefore most gladly I will rather boast in my infirmities, that the power of Christ may rest upon me.

In *The Adventure of Prayer,* the late author Catherine Marshall revealed the power of helplessness:

Why is prayer so startlingly effective when we admit our helplessness? One obvious reason is because our human helplessness is bedrock fact. God is a realist and insists that we be realists too. So long as we are deluding ourselves that human resources can supply our hearts' desires, we are believing a lie.

This recognition and acknowledgment of our helplessness is also the quickest way to that right attitude which God recognizes as essential to prayer. It deals a mortal blow to the most serious sins of all—man's independence that ignores God.

Another reason is that we cannot learn firsthand about God—what He is like, His love, and His real power—so long as we are relying on ourselves and other people. And fellowship with Jesus is the true purpose of life and the only foundation for eternity. It is real, this daily fellowship He offers us.

So if your every human plan and calculation has miscarried; if, one by one, human props have been knocked out and doors have shut in your face, take heart. The message is: "Stop depending on inadequate human resources. Let Me handle the matter."

Lord, free me from self-reliance. Help me stop depending on inadequate human resources. Deliver me from the type of independence that ignores You.

Inadequacy

SCRIPTURE READING: Psalm 51   KEY VERSE: Psalm 60:12

Through God we will do valiantly, for it is He who shall tread down our enemies.

I n Psalm 51, David's psalm of contrition, he declared, "Behold, You desire truth in the inward parts, and in the hidden part You will make me to know wisdom" (Ps. 51:6).

God's truth, woven richly into our innermost beings, is the foundation for freedom. God wants His truth to sink deep to establish His perfect wisdom in our minds and hearts.

When we understand the truth of our position in Christ, we understand that we are sealed by the Holy Spirit—that we are secure in the family of God. No act or thought can ever alienate us from the love of God. We no longer have to depend on others or other things for our identity. We belong to Christ; we are His and He is ours.

When we understand the truth of our personhood in Christ, our feeling of inferiority can dissolve. We are of infinite worth to God, who died on our behalf. It is not our income level or social status that determines our value; it is God's estimation of our lives. We are so valuable to Him that He desires our company for all eternity.

When we understand the truth of our position in Christ, any incompetency or inadequacy we may feel is overcome. We have everything we need in the indwelling Christ. He makes us adequate for every demand.

> *Master, I often feel inadequate, but I know You are greater than my inadequacies. I am of infinite worth to You.*

Pride

SCRIPTURE READING: Daniel 4   KEY VERSES: Psalm 73:21–22

My heart was grieved, and I was vexed in my mind. I was so foolish and ignorant; I was like a beast before You.

Nebuchadnezzar thought he had it all. He didn't need God; he ruled all of Babylon, and all of its finery was at his absolute disposal.

The disturbing dream that Daniel interpreted for him had not come true; he certainly wasn't living as an animal yet. He stood on the roof of his palace, soaking in the scenery with pleasure. He said aloud with pride: "Is this not Babylon the great, which I myself have built?" (Dan. 4:30 NASB).

The moment the words left his mouth, Nebuchadnezzar knew he'd gone too far. He felt himself drop to his knees. He scrambled about on all fours and ate grass like a cow. No one would come near the wild man with shaggy hair and fingernails like sharp birds' claws.

Seven years later, at the end of the punishment period God prescribed, the king looked up at the heavens and began giving praise to God. For the once proud ruler, recognizing the truth of God's sovereignty brought him literal freedom from his beastly affliction.

When you do not acknowledge the Lord's right to use your life and possessions as He sees fit, God is grieved. Because He loves you, He wants you to honor Him and be submissive to His plans. The king who learned the hard way grasped a tough lesson: "His works are true and His ways just, and He is able to humble those who walk in pride" (Dan. 4:37 NASB).

Precious Lord, take it—this plague of pride. I want to be set free from it because it is one of the things You hate. Let me walk humbly before You.

Loneliness

SCRIPTURE READING: Psalm 139   KEY VERSE: Matthew 28:20

Teaching them to observe all things that I have commanded you; and lo, I am with you always, even to the end of the age.

The thought of loneliness usually stirs visions of being physically alone. Yet many feel lonely even in a crowd of people. Loneliness is an experience of the heart and cannot be simply chased away by material gain or the wealth of possessions. Only Jesus can truly satisfy a lonely heart.

Corrie Ten Boom wrote of her time spent in isolation in a concentration camp:

> A solitary cell awaited me. Everything was empty and gray . . . Here there was nothing, only an emptiness, a cold gray void. "O Savior, You are with me, help me; hold me fast and comfort me. Take away this anxiety, this desolation . . . Take me into Your arms and comfort me," I prayed. And peace stole into my heart. The weird noises still surrounded me, but I fell quietly asleep.
>
> I soon grew accustomed to the cell, and when worries threatened to overwhelm me I began to sing. What a change in my life! I talked with my Savior. Never before had fellowship with Him been so close. It was a joy I hoped would continue unchanged. I was a prisoner—and yet—how free!

No matter how dark your loneliness appears, God will bring light, hope, and a sense of total security if you will call out in faith to Him.

Dear heavenly Father, when I am overwhelmed with loneliness, let me realize that no matter how dark it may seem, Your light of hope and love still penetrates. I am not alone. You are with me.

Phobias

SCRIPTURE READING: Psalm 46   KEY VERSE: Isaiah 41:10

Fear not, for I am with you; be not dismayed, for I am your God. I will strengthen you, yes, I will help you, I will uphold you with My righteous right hand.

God's Word is alive with strength and courage to help us counter every phobia that plagues us. Isaiah 41:10 is a timeless prescription that has helped many Christians confront and conquer their fears because it is loaded with fear-busting truth.

"Fear not, for I am with you." You are not alone with your fears. God lives in you to help you. Knowing Christ is with you always brings great comfort and encouragement.

"Be not dismayed, for I am your God." God in all His power, wisdom, love, and mercy is on your side. He is personally acquainted with you. You are part of His family, and He looks after you in a fatherly manner.

"I will strengthen you, yes, I will help you." In your weakness, God promises to make you strong. He never tires or falters. His shoulders are eternally broad. How much can He help you? As much as you let Him.

"I will uphold you with My righteous right hand." God is your Advocate. He keeps and protects you. He is your Stronghold, your Refuge. Though you may be shaken, He never is. His everlasting arms are underneath to hold you in your most desperate moments.

Almighty God, I turn all my stressful fears and anxieties to You. I do not need to be anxious because You have promised strength and help. You will uphold me with Your righteous right hand.

Unworthiness

SCRIPTURE READING: Psalm 103   KEY VERSE: Isaiah 43:25

I, even I, am He who blots out your transgressions for My own sake; and I will not remember your sins.

God never ridicules us or makes us feel unworthy. Instead, we read these words of Jesus:

Just as the Father has loved Me, I have also loved you; abide in My love. (John 15:9 NASB)

If you abide in My word, then you are truly disciples of Mine; and you shall know the truth, and the truth shall make you free. (John 8:31–32 NASB)

I have called you friends, for all things that I have heard from My Father I have made known to you. (John 15:15 NASB)

Love and truth. God is love and the source of all truth. The love He has for you is the same love He has for His Son, the Lord Jesus Christ. He gives you this love through His grace and mercy. It is a pure love, not tainted by guilt or obligation.

Regardless of how deep your past transgression may be, God is near to free you with the truth of His Word. Nothing is stronger than His love. When He forgives, He forgets (Ps. 103:12; Isa. 43:25). Once you have confessed sin, there is no need to beg or plead for His forgiveness. It is a done deal!

You can walk freely in the light of His love because He calls you His child. Your life is inscribed within the palm of His hand.

You are the apple of His eye; all of heaven rejoices at the sight of your name written in the Lamb's blood.

> *Dear God, thank You that I am worthy! I walk freely in the light of Your love. I am Your child, the apple of Your eye. My name is written in the Lamb's blood. I belong.*

Selfish Desires

SCRIPTURE READING: Psalm 106   KEY VERSE: Psalm 106:15

He gave them their request, but sent leanness into their soul.

One noted evangelist put it this way: "You may get what you want, but you may not want what you get." It is sometimes easy to want something so much that we channel all of our efforts to attain it.

That is what the Israelites did in the wilderness. They grew so weary of their manna diet that they grumbled loudly for good, old-fashioned meat. God gave them their request, but it brought death along with it because of their rebellious hearts.

All of us can relate to that incident. After much toil, we finally receive our desire, only to discover that it brought a lot of heartache. How can you protect yourself from seeking the wrong object?

First, by delighting yourself in loving, worshiping, and serving God above all else: "Delight yourself in the LORD; and He will give you the desires of your heart" (Ps. 37:4 NASB). When you want to please and honor God more than you want anything or anyone else, your requests will be aligned with His will.

Second, by being willing to lay down your request before the Lord. Whatever you want, give it completely to the Lord for its fulfillment. Let Him judge whether He will grant your petitions. Leave it in His hands: "Commit your way to the LORD, trust also in Him, and He will do it" (Ps. 37:5 NASB).

> *O Lord, free me from selfish desires. Let me delight in You and worship and serve You above all else. I am laying all my requests before You, yielding each desire and leaving it in Your hands.*

Immorality

SCRIPTURE READING: Colossians 1:1–10   KEY VERSE: Colossians 2:10

You are complete in Him, who is the head of all principality and power.

Our usual defense against immoral thoughts or actions is a recommitment to personal discipline, chastity, or holiness. Gritty determination helps stem the tide of impure thinking or actions for a season; but for those who suffer its unrelenting temptation, immoral desires seriously erode any appearance of a joyful, content Christian life. God knows the severity of such passion, and He has provided a firm defense—although a radical departure from our ordinary tactics.

Our first line of defense against the onslaught of immorality in any form is to understand our new position in Christ. Consider this example: you are asked to put together a model airplane. The box cover portrays the plane, but the pieces inside have been switched. You can imagine the frustration of trying to get the model to match the picture.

If we don't understand our new identity in Christ, we will be flustered trying to match our behavior to this new Christlike image. Dr. Martyn Lloyd-Jones, a noted British preacher, explained, "You once were a child. Now you are a man. Therefore, quit acting like a baby."

Immorality can never match your new identity in Christ.

Precious heavenly Father, cleanse me from immoral thoughts, words, and deeds. I am a new creature in Christ. I want my behavior to match my new identity.

Neglect

SCRIPTURE READING: 2 Samuel 5:1–12   KEY VERSE: 2 Samuel 5:12

David knew that the LORD had established him as king over Israel, and that He had exalted His kingdom for the sake of His people Israel.

Have you ever been passed over at work for a promotion that you felt you deserved? Or have you ever not received due recognition for your work?

If so, you will be excited to know about a dynamic principle that runs through the life of David that kept him in line for God's blessing in similar circumstances. Though anointed as king, David spent many years on the run from his former boss, King Saul. On several occasions David had opportunity to kill Saul and seize the kingdom. In each instance he refused.

When Saul ended his life on a remote battlefield, David could have declared himself king over all of Israel. Instead he initially ruled over the single tribe of Judah. Seven and a half years later, the remaining tribes of Israel asked David to rule them.

The principle is this: David allowed God to promote him in His way and in His time. He refused to take the bull by the horns. David allowed God to give him credit.

Wherever neglect occurs in your life, remember that God will exalt you in due season. Then, like David, you can realize that "the LORD had established him as king over Israel" (2 Sam. 5:12).

Father God, cleanse me from selfish ambition. Establish and promote me in Your perfect timing. Give me the patience to wait.

Criticism

SCRIPTURE READING: Psalm 18:16–24   KEY VERSE: Proverbs 15:31

The ear that hears the rebukes of life will abide among the wise.

Your day started off great. Your devotional time was splendid, and you were on a roll at work—until a coworker walked up to your desk and took you to task over a memorandum you had written.

Suddenly God was distant, anger welled up within you like a flash flood, and resentment raced to the pole position. Your day was ruined.

Sound familiar? Is there anyone who has not undergone a similar negative transformation when on the receiving end of a reprimand? Our response, however, can determine whether criticism is constructive or destructive.

Criticism—just or unjust—is constructive when we listen. It is destructive when we immediately clamp down an emotional tourniquet, refusing its entrance.

Criticism is constructive when we sift it in a spirit of self-examination. It is destructive when we retain it as a reservoir of bitterness.

Criticism is constructive when it drives us to trust Christ as our defense and leave our reputation to Him. It is destructive when we seek to defend ourselves.

When you are criticized, learn and correct what you can with a humble spirit; that is wisdom. If it is without merit, lean on Christ as your Advocate; that is trust. Either way, you win.

Dear Lord, cleanse my critical spirit, then free me from the bondage of criticism by others. Let me heed constructive criticism and turn to You as my Advocate when it is without merit.

Fear

SCRIPTURE READING: Psalm 56:1–11   KEY VERSE: 2 Timothy 1:7

God has not given us a spirit of fear, but of power and of love and of a sound mind.

Paul Tournier, the eminent Swiss doctor, made a profound assessment of the Christian life: "Life is an adventure directed by God."

The seed of life-changing faith is contained in such a view. It can be the difference between a confident, rewarding life or a timid, fretful one. When you are confronted with perplexity, it can be the hinge upon which swings the response of either fear or faith.

Fear comes when you are overwhelmed by the magnitude or implications of a situation. It swells to paralyzing proportions when you think of the possibility of disastrous consequences. It can submerge you in waves of anxiety and insecurity.

But once you understand and embrace the truth that God is indeed in charge of your circumstances and has equipped you for every challenge, it is amazing how faith in Christ can change your outlook. Life isn't risk free. God has set a divine course for every believer that He oversees and directs with perfect wisdom and love.

Your faith is in His faithfulness to you, in His power that works on your behalf, in His grace that provides all your needs. God is in charge. Life is an exciting journey in trusting Him as your Guide and Companion.

Begin the adventure today, and drop your fears at His feet. He won't let you down.

Heavenly Father, here I am with all my fears—giving them to You. You have equipped me for every challenge. I know life isn't risk free, but whatever path I travel, You determine my destiny.

Inconsistency

SCRIPTURE READING: Ephesians 4:17–24   KEY VERSE: Psalm 57:2

I will cry out to God Most High, to God who performs all things for me.

An artesian well sits in a pasture along a picturesque rural road. Flowing from a small pipe, the water has provided cool refreshment for man and beast for decades. Its stream, issuing from deep within the earth, has never diminished or varied—even in times of severe drought.

Most believers long for such consistency since we are so often governed by our circumstances or emotions. A good day at home or work is spiritually fortifying. A flat tire or flat speech can be debilitating, leaving us spiritually deflated. That type of elevator Christianity takes its toll spiritually and leaves nonbelievers wondering about the reliability of our faith.

Like the artesian well, the source is the key. When the love and spirit of Christ control us through the indwelling Holy Spirit, we can live consistently. Christ is our life, flowing through our wills, emotions, and personalities with His purity and power, enabling, steadying us in turmoil and disappointment.

Christ never changes; He is always the same. We experience His unchanging life when we steadfastly count on His refreshing presence in every circumstance. Tough times come; but they can never separate us from the constant, steadfast love of God. He is our Source.

Father, I am often governed by circumstances and emotions. Free me from elevator Christianity. Make me consistent. Steady me in the face of turmoil and disappointment.

Conflict

SCRIPTURE READING: 2 Corinthians 4:7–18   KEY VERSE: 2 Corinthians 4:17

Our light affliction, which is but for a moment, is working for us a far more exceeding and eternal weight of glory.

Given the choice, most of us would choose membership in the status quo society: "Lord, things are going pretty well for me now. I'd rather not have trouble knock at my door just now."

That is a common sentiment. We want to maintain our comfort zone. We dislike change, especially the kind that is brought on by conflict.

The moment friction enters the picture—in our relationships or in our circumstances—the peaceful, easy feeling of the status quo disintegrates. But if we view conflict as an opportunity rather than an obstacle, we make amazing discoveries.

Conflict generates alertness to the presence of both God and Satan. When trouble strikes, we realize we are in spiritual warfare. We sense the adversary at work, but more important, we are sensitized to God's Word and His Spirit.

Conflict also generates action. No one has to tell us to open the Scriptures; no one must force us to pray. We are motivated and mobilized by the Lord to search the Scriptures and pray.

Conflict changes our attitudes. We become more grateful, more submissive, more dependent on God, more humble, and more understanding of others' needs.

O God, help me realize the positive benefits of conflict. Make me more alert to Your presence. Mobilize me to pray and study Your Word. Change my negative attitudes.

Alienation

SCRIPTURE READING: Psalm 25   KEY VERSE: Hebrews 13:5

Let your conduct be without covetousness; be content with such things as you have. For He Himself has said, "I will never leave you nor forsake you."

It seems the more populated our neighborhoods, cities, and planet become, the lonelier we feel. The mobility of our people, the high rate of divorce, the bent toward individualism, the time- and energy-consuming drives for success—all contribute to the increasing sense of alienation from one another. The consequences are serious: depression, superficial relationships, lethargy, stunted spiritual growth—even suicide.

If you are lonely and some of these characteristics describe you, there is hope. You can take active steps that will improve your situation since God has made you to enjoy Himself and influence others.

The beginning is a true understanding of your worth and value. Others may not notice you, but you are the apple of God's eye (Deut. 32:10). So much loneliness stems from feelings of insecurity and inferiority.

You are important (Isa. 43:4). You are made in the image of God (Gen. 1:26). You are His workmanship, unique and special (Eph. 2:10).

You can believe these truths from the Word of God because they are true. Allow the Lord Jesus Christ to change your self-image by viewing yourself as He does (Rom. 12:2).

Lord, others may not notice me, but I am not alienated from You. I am made in Your image. I am Your unique and special workmanship. Help me view myself as You see me.

Anger

SCRIPTURE READING: Psalm 37:5–8   KEY VERSE: Ephesians 4:26

"Be angry, and do not sin": do not let the sun go down on your wrath.

For most people, anger is not premeditated. We usually find our emotions erupting over unexpected incidents. The emotion of anger is not a sin; but left unchecked, it can mushroom quickly into sinful behavior. You can "be angry [and] not sin" (Eph. 4:26) when you follow these guidelines:

Do not be quick to become angry (James 1:19). If your anger triggers instantly, you have a sin problem. The Lord instructs us to be patient when wronged and long-suffering when abused (1 Cor. 13:4–5).

Do not hold on to your angry feelings. When you secretly nourish anger, you have sinned. Quickly put angry episodes behind you as you trust Christ to replace your anger with His love. Leave the results of your circumstances with sovereign God who can accomplish far more than your fury.

Do not justify your anger. Although there are occasions when anger is justified (a thug beating an elderly man on the sidewalk in front of your home), they do not occur often.

Are you handling your anger by biblical standards, or is anger handling you? If the latter is true, admit it as sin and trust the Lord Jesus Christ to remove your anger by loving through you.

> *Master, take control of my anger. Do not let me be quick to become angry. Help me release angry feelings and refuse to justify my anger. Let me learn to be angry and not sin.*

Peer Pressure

SCRIPTURE READING: Romans 12:1–3   KEY VERSE: 2 Corinthians 5:9

We make it our aim, whether present or absent, to be well pleasing to Him.

W e usually think of peer pressure affecting teens, but adults are just as influenced by the actions, dress, and customs of their associates. Fearful of rejection, we seldom venture beyond accepted norms. Seeking the approval of others is a tremendous motivating factor that influences even committed believers.

We should not think of this attitude as being strange. God tells us in the Bible not to be conformed to the world (Rom. 12:2).

Each day you must trust the Lord to keep you from being shaped by the world's financial, moral, and relational standards. The battle against such conformity can be won only when you truly seek to please God more than you seek to please others.

Pleasing the Lord should be the fervent ambition of every Christian. Pleasing Him means trusting the Holy Spirit to enable us to follow the Word of God as our authority and our guide in every part of living. Pleasing the Lord means obeying Him at any cost—even if it means experiencing the disapproval of others.

Make pleasing God your priority. When you do, you will find yourself conformed to His image, not conformed to the warped image of the world's empty and vain standards.

Precious Lord, I do not want my life to be shaped by the financial, moral, and relational standards of this world. I want to please You. I trust Your Holy Spirit to enable me to conform to Your Word in every area of my life.

Greed

SCRIPTURE READING: Proverbs 11:24–26   KEY VERSE: James 1:17

Every good gift and every perfect gift is from above, and comes down from the Father of lights, with whom there is no variation or shadow of turning.

What drove the two biggest business deals of the late eighties—the $25 billion takeover fight for RJR Nabisco and the $14 billion merger of Time Inc. and Warner Communications? Was it the conviction that bigger is better? Was it the search for corporate "synergies"? On paper, maybe. But three telling new accounts make it clear that the real moving forces were raw ego, greed, and ambition.

Such is the way *Time* magazine described the driving force of greed in our culture.

From corporate takeovers to individual ambitions, greed is a prime motivation for millions. We want more than we have; we want it *now*.

Clearly the Christian must move countercurrent to the prevailing tide of greed when it comes to a generous spirit. Generosity does not flow from educational, governmental, or financial systems. The polluted power of sin within each of us prevents generosity from naturally coming forth from us.

Generosity is a godly quality because God is the Author of cheerful giving (2 Cor. 9:7). Do you feel stingy? Are you slow to help others? Only a deliberate step of submission to the Lord Jesus Christ with a humble request for a giving heart can begin the blessings of a generous spirit.

Dear heavenly Father, deliver me from greed. Make me a cheerful giver. Bless me with a generous spirit.

Unforgiveness

SCRIPTURE READING: 2 Corinthians 5:14–19   KEY VERSE: 1 John 2:10

He who loves his brother abides in the light, and there is no cause for stumbling in him.

The path to freedom from an unforgiving spirit runs straight through the cross of Christ. When He died, forgiveness for man's sins—all of them—was provided.

When we receive Jesus through faith, we no longer should hold grudges or seethe over injustices. Christ Jesus has forgiven us. We are called to extend His forgiveness—even to our enemies. We did nothing to earn our forgiveness. Then we cannot make others earn our forgiveness, which may be the tool used by Jesus Christ to demonstrate His unconditional love to believer and non-believer alike.

Because of the Cross and Christ's presence in your life through the Holy Spirit, you have the supernatural capacity to extend His forgiveness. As a new creation in Christ, you are not a prisoner to your old habits of revenge and retaliation. Christ in you is your hope (Col. 1:27).

The love of God will not allow you to keep bitterness and resentment in your heart and still enjoy His fellowship. Now is the time to boldly forgive the one who has hurt you, not in your power but in the full forgiveness provided by the Lord Jesus Christ for every person at Calvary.

Lay your burden down. Let God's love flow through you, and then watch Him work.

> *Almighty God, thank You for forgiving me. Now give me the supernatural ability to extend forgiveness to those who hurt me. Let Your love flow through me to others.*

Poor Self-Image

SCRIPTURE READING: Ephesians 2:1–10   KEY VERSE: Ephesians 2:10

We are His workmanship, created in Christ Jesus for good works, which God prepared beforehand that we should walk in them.

C hristian psychologist Dr. James Dobson once took a poll of women who, by their own admission, were basically cheerful and secure individuals.

Dobson listed ten sources of depression. Included in the list were such topics as fatigue, boredom, in-law conflicts, and financial problems. The women were asked to identify which factor contributed most heavily to periods of depression.

The overwhelming reply was lack of self-esteem. Were the same poll taken by Christians at large, lack of self-worth would probably be ranked at the top.

Proper and healthy self-esteem is possible when we receive God's evaluation of ourselves, relying on His estimation of our worth, not the faulty opinion of others or our fluctuating personal performance.

God created us in His image. We are His workmanship. A Stradivarius is worthy because of its maker. We are worthy because God is our Maker.

The apostle Paul said, "I can do all things through Him who strengthens me" (Phil. 4:13 NASB). We have His adequacy, His power, His competency. Should we ever feel inferior again?

> *Dear God, thank You that my worth is not based on the faulty opinion of others or my own fluctuating performance. I am worthy because You are my Maker.*

Anxiety

SCRIPTURE READING: Matthew 6:25–34   KEY VERSE: Matthew 6:34

Do not worry about tomorrow, for tomorrow will worry about its own things. Sufficient for the day is its own trouble.

In her booklet *Overcome Your Worry*, Pamela Reeve shares how the character and sufficiency of God are the antidote for every form of worry:

The provision of our God covers the past, the present, and the future. Peace comes from the possession of adequate resources.

God can keep our minds at peace, even as He's promised, because we have adequate resources to take care of the sin and guilt of the past. We have the cross of Christ . . .

We have adequate resources for the present: That great Resource, the Holy Spirit, who will give us the wisdom we need, the enablement we need, the control we need—all that we need for the present.

. . . We have the adequate resources for the future if Christ is our Savior.

. . . All worry is basically distrust in the character and might of God. Exercising faith in God is the antidote to worry. Faith is believing that God is good.

. . . Are you worrying about something coming up ahead: Lack of finances, failing health, loss of a friendship? Keep filling your mind with the truth— God knows all about it. He has all the power to handle it for your good, and because He loves you so, He will.

O Lord, Your provision covers my past, present, and future. I rejoice that I can leave all my anxieties and worries with You.

Guilt

SCRIPTURE READING: Romans 8   KEY VERSE: Romans 8:1

*There is therefore now no condemnation to those who are in Christ Jesus,
who do not walk according to the flesh, but according to the Spirit.*

A W. Tozer, the noted Christian author and pastor, once talked about individuals who live in the "perpetual penance of regret."

Are you one of those persons? Do you constantly feel guilty? Are you
plagued with unrelenting remorse?

Has your faith in Christ placed you on the staircase to delight and joy, or
plummeted you into the cellar of perpetual regret?

The way out of your misery is receiving and extending the magnificent
grace of God. Believe this once and for all—your faith in Christ has cleared
your account with God. You are forgiven, for past, present, and future behavior.
Your debt is paid. Your penance cannot add one merit point to your already
perfect standing with your heavenly Father.

But take one more step. As you have received His forgiveness, pass it along
to people who have offended you. They owe you nothing. You cannot collect
anything from them—not acceptance, security, or affirmation.

Embracing God's grace to you and extending His grace to others will
destroy guilt's destructive cycle, replacing it with an unceasing celebration of
God's amazing, unconditional love.

*Precious heavenly Father, I must admit—guilt over my past often creeps in
to haunt me. Free me from guilt's destructive cycle. Replace my regrets with
an unceasing celebration of Your unconditional love.*

Jealousy

SCRIPTURE READING: 1 Samuel 18:1–12   KEY VERSE: James 3:16

Where envy and self-seeking exist, confusion and every evil thing are there.

Both Paul and James almost invariably used the same companion adjective or noun when describing jealousy. Wherever there is jealousy, there is also strife. Jealousy breeds conflict. It incites anger and bitterness. It promotes emotional and physical hostility.

Are you envious over another's success? Do you covet the looks or possessions of another? Do you feel as if you have been given a raw deal—while others seem to have a china closet full of silver spoons?

The emotional tangle of jealousy can be prevented when we understand God's principle of contentment. Biblical contentment means we thank God that He has given us everything we need. Others may be promoted while we languish. Others may have great physical talents or appearance while we are plain and mediocre.

But God, our Creator and Provider, will give us all good things as we trust in Him. Our lives can be fully satisfying when we know our Father is not impartial or unjust, but gives to each the full measure of grace needed for a productive, joyful life.

Father God, free me from the grasping tentacles of jealousy. Help me realize that I have all I need to live a productive and joyful life.

Depression

SCRIPTURE READING: 1 Kings 19:1–18   KEY VERSE: Psalm 42:11

Why are you cast down, O my soul? And why are you disquieted within me?
Hope in God; for I shall yet praise Him, the help of my countenance and my God.

Martin Luther, the great leader of the Reformation, often dealt with severe periods of depression. Depression is still a problem that knows no educational, cultural, or financial boundaries.

In his book *Healing for Damaged Emotions,* Dr. David Seamands prescribes some practical helps:

Avoid being alone. When you are depressed, you do not want to be around people . . . force yourself to be with people.

Seek help from others. You can no more pull yourself out of depression than you can get yourself out of quicksand by pulling at your own hair. Seek out people and situations which generate joy.

Praise and give thanks. All the saints agree on this one. It was [Samuel] Brengle's [the founder of the Salvation Army] way out. When he couldn't feel God's presence or really pray, he would thank God for the leaf on the tree or the beautiful wing of a bird.

Lean heavily on the power of God's Word. Throughout the centuries, His people have found the Psalms to be the most beneficial.

Depression is not a dead end. There is a way out. Trust Him to lead you and to help you apply these liberating truths.

Dear Lord, when clouds of depression surround me, help me remember to praise You. Let me realize it is not a dead end. There is a way out and Your light illumines the way.

Rejection

SCRIPTURE READING: Colossians 1:19–23   KEY VERSE: Psalm 117:2

His merciful kindness is great toward us, and the truth of the LORD endures forever. Praise the LORD!

In the Vietnam War, special bullets were sometimes used that caused far more physical destruction than ordinary bullets.

The experience and fear of rejection can likewise cause far more inner trauma than most other emotional afflictions.

Rejection strikes brutally at our most vulnerable spot—our sense of self-worth. If you have been rejected by another, the pain can be alleviated and the wounds healed by deliberately embracing God's unfailing love.

While selfish, ego-centered man sets up unattainable standards, the good news of the gospel is that Christians are now fully accepted by the perfect One Himself—God the Father. God never rejects us because of our performance or appearance. He loves us so completely that once we are reconciled through faith in Jesus Christ, we are forever secure in His love.

You meet God's standards through Christ's imputed righteousness. When others spurn you, turn immediately to Christ's waiting arms. His loving-kindness endures forever and will help you rise above the rejection of others.

O God, help me rise above the rejection of those around me. You accept me. I meet all Your standards through Jesus Christ. That is all that matters.

Spiritual Compromise

SCRIPTURE READING: 1 Corinthians 3:1–17   KEY VERSE: Matthew 6:24

No one can serve two masters; for either he will hate the one and love the other, or else he will be loyal to the one and despise the other. You cannot serve God and mammon.

Although compromise is acceptable in some realms, such as business or political negotiations, it is always a prelude to defeat in the spiritual arena.

Although we may barter with other individuals, there is no give-and-take with God. Spiritual compromise is attempted when we seek to dilute sin. We term it *shortcoming, fault,* or *bad habit.* But in God's eyes our disobedience is nothing less than black sin, which He hates and views as blatant rebellion.

Spiritual compromise is also enacted when we fail to take God's Word as anything less than divine inspiration, inerrant in every detail and authoritative over all of life. In each instance, we seek to lower God's standards by inserting our own viewpoint.

Premarital sex is not okay. It is sin. Gossip and slander are not permissible. Both are contemptible to God. Every act of compromise dulls your devotion to Christ and denies His lordship in your life.

Is there an area in which you are trying to rationalize your behavior, compromising God's unchanging standards? If so, admit your sin and live with full conviction that God's way is always the right way.

Almighty God, deliver me from spiritual compromise. My sin is not a shortcoming, a fault, or a bad habit—it is sin. Help me confront it for what it is, then forgive me.

Distraction

SCRIPTURE READING: 2 Corinthians 2:14–16   KEY VERSE: Philippians 3:8

Yet indeed I also count all things loss for the excellence of the knowledge of Christ Jesus my Lord, for whom I have suffered the loss of all things, and count them as rubbish, that I may gain Christ.

After winning a gold medal in the 1988 Olympics, the muscular wrestler was asked if he had any secrets of preparation. "My only secret is that I didn't let anything hinder my goal of winning," he related. "I refused to be distracted by any other competition."

That same zealous pursuit of our relationship with Christ is the highest goal for the believer. Paul termed it "undistracted devotion to the Lord" (1 Cor. 7:35 NASB).

That is true for every Christian—married or unmarried, rich or poor, small or great. God will not tolerate competition (Matt. 6:24).

The relevant question then is, Is there anything or anyone in your life who is in competition with Christ's claim on your life? Does money, marriage, your job, recreation, or your hobby vie for your allegiance to Christ? Do you seek Him first by daily acknowledging His lordship and obeying His will?

When other objects or people distract us from this primary focus to serve and worship the Lord, our spiritual growth is short-circuited. Having undistracted devotion to Christ means putting Christ first in all of our activities, submitting them to His will and guidance. When we do, we always win (2 Cor. 2:14).

Precious Lord, I am easily distracted from the paths of my spiritual journey. Free me from all that competes with Your claims in my life. I want to put You first in all things.

Spiritual Blindness

SCRIPTURE READING: 2 Corinthians 4:3–6   KEY VERSES: Matthew 13:15–16

"For the hearts of this people have grown dull. Their ears are hard of hearing, and their eyes they have closed, lest they should see with their eyes and hear with their ears, lest they should understand with their hearts and turn, so that I should heal them." But blessed are your eyes for they see, and your ears for they hear.

When telling of his conversion experience, the apostle Paul always included the footnote that he was a "Hebrew of Hebrews."

The people of Paul's day understood exactly what he was trying to convey. His terminology gave evidence that he was a well-educated Jewish purebred.

From the time of his birth, Paul was taught to think within the confines of the Law of Moses. As a young man, he spent his days in the synagogue where he studied under Gamaliel, one of history's greatest Jewish scholars.

His debates among Stoic philosophers underscored his vast knowledge. But in reality, Paul was quite blind. Mentally he might have been on the borderline of brilliance, but spiritually he lived in darkness. Only Jesus Christ could provide Paul with an education that would change not only his own life, but the lives of all who followed his teaching.

God's true wisdom and knowledge cannot be found in a human textbook. You may have a "degree of degrees"; but until you sit in God's classroom, you are living in spiritual blindness. Ask God to remove the scales from your eyes that may keep you in spiritual blindness. Open your heart to study His Word, and you will find the key to true understanding.

Dear heavenly Father, I can't make this journey if I cannot see the way. Let the light of Your Word clear up my spiritual blindness. Remove the scales from my eyes.

AUGUST

Journey to Jabbok

REPRESENTING: Experiencing renewal

KEY VERSES: Romans 12:1–2

I beseech you therefore, brethren, by the mercies of God, that you present your bodies a living sacrifice, holy, acceptable to God, which is your reasonable service. And do not be conformed to this world, but be transformed by the renewing of your mind, that you may prove what is that good and acceptable and perfect will of God.

The name Jabbok may not mean much to you, but it could become one of the most important words in your vocabulary. Jabbok means "a place of passing over," a place of change. It was at the Brook Jabbok that Jacob's life was forever changed. At Jabbock he was told, "Your name shall no longer be called Jacob, but Israel; for you have struggled with God and with men, and have prevailed" (Gen. 32:28).

Before Jabbok, Jacob was a master manipulator. He lied, deceived, and stole. After Jabbok, he was a changed man. His name, his personality—everything was different.

The Jabbok experience speaks of spiritual renewal, consecration, and change. Our journey during August is to spiritual Jabbok—*growth, surrender, consistency, intimacy, transformation, abiding, commitment*—these are all terms that describe our destination.

Butterfly Living

SCRIPTURE READING: 2 Corinthians 5:17–21   KEY VERSE: 2 Corinthians 5:17

If anyone is in Christ, he is a new creation; old things have passed away; behold, all things have become new.

To get a grasp of this verse, imagine the old you as a caterpillar and the new you in Christ as a matured butterfly. What you may find in your life experience, however, is that even though you are a butterfly, you are still drawn to the caterpillar way of life. How can you end this tension?

In his letter to the Romans, Paul wrote to exhort them to consistent "butterfly living." The temptations in their society to relapse into "caterpillar living" were strong, much as they are today. He wrote, "Do not be conformed to this world, but be transformed by the renewing of your mind, that you may prove what the will of God is, that which is good and acceptable and perfect" (Rom. 12:2 NASB).

This principle is so dynamic, you cannot afford to miss it. "Transformed" is a translation of the Greek *metamorphosis*, the process by which a caterpillar becomes a butterfly.

Renewing your mind is in essence taking on the mind of Christ; it means changing your thinking in accordance with the truth of God's Word. What you believe about God defines the quality of that relationship. Remember, you are not a caterpillar with wings glued on—you are truly a butterfly.

Dear Lord, thank You for changing my "caterpillar" mentality, so I can experience butterfly living. This month, as I reflect on the wonders of spiritual change, continue Your divine miracle of transformation.

Spiritual Excellence

SCRIPTURE READING: Galatians 5:13–15   KEY VERSE: Galatians 6:2

Bear one another's burdens, and so fulfill the law of Christ.

If you think that the way to become a better servant, live life for the Lord, is to try a little harder, think again. In his book *Walking with Christ in the Details of Life,* Patrick Morley explains,

> The common sense way to make a bigger contribution focuses on strengthening skills. The Christ way focuses on the enabling Holy Spirit . . .
>
> Spiritual excellence is not about ascending the ladder of leadership to greatness. It is about descending the ladder of humility to servanthood. Let's face it. It is a difficult thing to be a leader and a servant at the same time, impossible without the Spirit . . .
>
> The leader/servant is a man like John the Baptist. Though strong in personality and character, he understood his role. "He [Christ] must become greater; I must become less."
>
> Since learning that only the Holy Spirit can make one excellent, I have also discovered another secret. It is not that the Holy Spirit empowers a person to become more dynamic, eloquent, and persuasive—though all these might possibly come. Rather, it is that the Holy Spirit helps you to become nothing to yourself, you "become less." Not servile, but a servant.
>
> Don't ask the Holy Spirit to increase your skill; ask Him to increase Christ. As Jesus becomes greater, your impact will enlarge, but because Christ is growing larger, not you.

Heavenly Father, help me understand the true meaning of spiritual excellence. Let Christ increase. Let me decrease. Make me a servant.

Removing the Lock

SCRIPTURE READING: 2 Corinthians 3:1–6   KEY VERSE: 1 Corinthians 3:16

Do you not know that you are the temple of God and that the Spirit of God dwells in you?

If you have a bad habit that you cannot seem to get rid of no matter how much effort you exert, then that habit or problem has mastery over you. In a very real sense, you are its slave. Whether it's food or too much television or sports, whatever dictates your priorities has authority over you. It may feel as though sin has unlimited power, but that is not true. It is your feeling as you continue to allow yourself to be victimized by a false master.

The first step in recovery, besides the obvious one of recognizing the problem, is identifying and understanding your true position in Christ as a redeemed one. With His blood, you were literally redeemed, or paid for, and the ownership of your life was transferred from sin and self to almighty God.

Take hold of this powerful liberation statement: "For the love of Christ controls us . . . and He died for all, that they who live should no longer live for themselves, but for Him who died and rose again on their behalf" (2 Cor. 5:14–15 NASB). If the love of Christ controls you, there is no room for subownership by other passions or desires or people. Living in bondage is an unnecessary condition. It is like staying in prison when the lock is removed.

Are you a slave to anything besides Christ? You can declare your own independence day under His authority.

O God, I want to change! Remove the lock to any area of my life where I have refused You access. I declare my independence day!

An Inseparable Relationship

SCRIPTURE READING: John 21   KEY VERSE: John 21:6

He said to them, "Cast the net on the right side of the boat, and you will find some." So they cast, and now they were not able to draw it in because of the multitude of fish.

All the disciples knew to do was to go on about their business. Now that Jesus wasn't with them physically, they had to make many adjustments. What would life be like now that they were not traveling around the region with Him every day? What did it mean to be fishers of men? Was it all over?

The mood was probably quiet that night on the boat as they fished. Peter must have mused silently as he tugged at the nets, hoping for a catch. The light seemed to have gone out of his life. His heart was sore, for the last thing his Lord had heard him do was betray Him and deny he ever knew Him. Discouragement weighed him down with doubts and fears about the future.

Dawn came. As the light grew stronger, they could make out a figure on the beach. The man called to them, "Cast the net on the right-hand side of the boat and you will find a catch." When John said, "It is the Lord," Peter dived into the water to swim to shore.

Peter would never forget the conversation they had that day by the breakfast fire. He knew Jesus still loved him, and he had the chance to tell Jesus the same. Jesus knew exactly how to comfort Peter, reassure him of His eternal love, give him hope, and reignite his vision for the future. Jesus can do the same for you.

If you've shut Him out for any reason, He is still waiting for you on the shore.

Father, forgive me for the times I have shut You out of my life. Reassure me of Your love, give me renewed hope, rekindle my vision for the future.

Sin Does Not Fit

SCRIPTURE READING: Matthew 4:1–11   KEY VERSE: Matthew 4:11

Then the devil left Him, and behold, angels came and ministered to Him.

Have you ever watched a movie or television program and suddenly felt dirty because of the contents? Maybe you have been with friends and were caught off guard by something one of them said.

Deep inside you were embarrassed, but you tried not to look shocked. Later you thought through the situation and remembered a time when lewd language or actions would not have mattered much.

What has changed? You have. Paul wrote, "Therefore if any man is in Christ, he is a new creature; the old things passed away; behold, new things have come" (2 Cor. 5:17 NASB). At the point of salvation, you became a new creature. God through the presence of His Spirit regenerated your life. He has taken the old sinful you and infused new life into your being. You have been given a new life spiritually.

Sin and darkness no longer fit who you are in Christ. It's like wearing clothes several sizes too big. Sin doesn't fit, and it never will again. Because Jesus lives in you, His hope and His purity are yours, and you can say no to temptation and sin.

Study how Christ successfully faced and defeated the enemy in Matthew 4:1–11, and then read Paul's words in Ephesians 2:1–10 as he described your glorious transformation from spiritual death to eternal life.

> *Lord, sin doesn't fit me very well anymore, and it never will again. Thank You! Only Your love could make such a change.*

Be Still and Listen

SCRIPTURE READING: Galatians 5:16–23   KEY VERSE: Galatians 5:16

I say then: Walk in the Spirit, and you shall not fulfill the lust of the flesh.

Paul told us that if we walk by the Spirit, we will not carry out the deeds of the flesh (Gal. 5:16). Many times this is not an easy task. The only way you can walk in the Spirit is to be conscious of God's indwelling presence and your lack of ability.

The moment you try to live like Christ is usually the time you face difficulty. This happens because you set your focus on becoming something instead of allowing Christ to live His life through you. There will be times of failure in your life. These times are the very moments God uses to instruct you in great ways.

However, this can happen only if you are open to listening to the Spirit's voice. There can be no distraction inside you—no desire to get it right or work things out on your own. Let Jesus show you the way.

Submitting yourself to God's will opens the way for spiritual discernment. So many people try this or that in an effort to grow spiritually when all they really need to do is to learn how to sit before the Lord and be still in their spirits. Today when irritating thoughts come or something goes awry, allow the new you—the part of you that is controlled by God's Spirit—to take control of the situation.

Be still, if only for a moment, and listen for His voice. He will provide the needed wisdom, patience, guidance, and love you need to carry on in this life.

Master, because You live inside me, I have new and glorious freedom. Remove the distractions. Still my restless heart. Let the new me emerge.

Solitude with God

SCRIPTURE READING: Colossians 3:1–5   KEY VERSE: Colossians 3:3

You died, and your life is hidden with Christ in God.

Oswald Chambers wrote,

> A servant of God must stand so very much alone that he never realizes he is alone. In the early stages of the Christian life, disappointments will come—people who used to be lights will flicker out, and those who used to stand with us will turn away. We have to get so used to it that we will not even realize we are standing alone.
>
> Paul said, ". . . No one stood with me, but all forsook me . . . But the Lord stood with me and strengthened me . . ." (2 Timothy 4:16–17). We must build our faith not on fading lights but on the Light that never fails. When important individuals go away we are sad, until we see that they are meant to go; so that only one thing is left for us to do—to look into the face of God for ourselves.

A characteristic of life lived in the Spirit is the ability to enjoy solitude with God. This does not mean a life void of relationships. Instead it means that you have learned to look to Jesus for His companionship and approval before you look for the nod of others.

When trouble comes, walk swiftly in your mind to a place where only you and God reside. Our human minds have a tendency to replay frantic images that do not mirror the faithfulness of God. When you enjoy the company of the Savior, you experience a peace that goes beyond anything this world has to offer.

Lord, when others forsake me, help me remember that You are with me in my solitude. Let me hear Your voice calling me to that place where only You and I reside.

The Worth of Weakness

SCRIPTURE READING: 2 Corinthians 12:1–10   KEY VERSES: 2 Corinthians 12:9–10

He said to me, "My grace is sufficient for you, for My strength is made perfect in weakness." Therefore most gladly I will rather boast in my infirmities, that the power of Christ may rest upon me. Therefore I take pleasure in infirmities, in reproaches, in needs, in persecutions, in distresses, for Christ's sake. For when I am weak, then I am strong.

I n our society, physical strength is a hallmark of success and power. It doesn't take long to figure out the messages behind countless advertisements for fitness centers, health clubs, and exercise equipment.

Of course, staying in shape and taking good care of your body are worthy, healthful goals with the right perspective (1 Tim. 4:8). But the underlying assumption of people who value physical training as an ideal in itself is that weakness is shameful. For them, physical weakness represents who you are as a person, pathetic and helpless and unattractive.

In spiritual terms, weakness carries a far different message. It says, "I have a problem, and I need a Savior who can fix it." Weakness becomes an opportunity for God to demonstrate His power on your behalf: "'My [God's] grace is sufficient for you, for power is perfected in weakness.' Most gladly, therefore, I [Paul] will rather boast about my weaknesses, that the power of Christ may dwell in me. Therefore I am well content with weaknesses, with insults, with distresses, with persecutions, with difficulties, for Christ's sake; for when I am weak, then I am strong" (2 Cor. 12:9–10 NASB).

Do weaknesses prompt you to hide or attempt to make the changes by yourself? They should be your signal to ask the Lord for the help that only He can give.

Precious Lord, there is intrinsic value in weakness. Help me embrace it, realizing that therein lie dormant strength and unlimited potential for greatness.

Walking Away from God

SCRIPTURE READING: Psalm 73   KEY VERSE: Psalm 73:25

Whom have I in heaven but You? And there is none upon earth that I desire besides You.

H is family could have been in upheaval. Maybe he had just witnessed the promotion of a man he knew to be a fraud and a thief. Whatever the causes were, Asaph was discouraged to the point of questioning his faith or, rather, the point of his faith.

If trusting God was such a good thing, why were evil men getting away with murder? Why were the arrogant only getting richer and more powerful by the day, while humble and good people were suffering? These questions could just as easily be asked today. And maybe you have asked them.

What finally turned Asaph's heart around and put fresh wind in his spiritual sails? He realized once more these powerful truths: "Yet I am always with you [God]; you hold me by my right hand. You guide me with your counsel, and afterward you will take me into glory. Whom have I in heaven but you? And earth has nothing I desire besides you. My flesh and my heart may fail, but God is the strength of my heart and my portion forever" (Ps. 73:23–26 NIV).

The glory of the wicked, when viewed from an eternal perspective, was shown to be fleeting, shallow, and temporary. Asaph had to take a journey through doubt and anger and questioning before he could feel secure in God again. Never be afraid to take this journey.

> *Dear heavenly Father, when I look at others and question why, help me remember to view things from an eternal perspective. Let my journey through doubt and anger be swift so that I can feel secure in You again.*

Unconditional Surrender

SCRIPTURE READING: Judges 6   KEY VERSE: Judges 6:14

The LORD turned to him and said, "Go in this might of yours, and you shall save Israel from the hand of the Midianites. Have I not sent you?"

What would you say if you were going about your daily business and a stranger walked up and said to you, "The LORD is with you, O valiant warrior" (Judg. 6:12 NASB)?

Chances are, you would be surprised, confused, and maybe a little mistrustful of the stranger. Gideon certainly did not feel that he was a valiant warrior. Like the rest of the Israelites, he was in hiding, desperately trying to conceal his meager portion of grain from the oppressive Midianites.

But Gideon knew it was an angel of the Lord speaking to him, and his stumbling block to obedience was focusing on his personal inadequacy. He could think of many reasons why God should choose someone else: "O Lord, how shall I deliver Israel? Behold, my family is the least in Manasseh, and I am the youngest in my father's house" (Judg. 6:15 NASB).

In other words, his family was virtually unknown, and he was the least important member of a group of nobodies. Gideon soon learned that God did not want excuses; He wanted submission, obedience, and a yielded and trusting heart. God promised to be his sufficiency: "Surely I will be with you, and you shall defeat Midian as one man" (Judg. 6:16 NASB).

The Lord wanted Gideon to say yes without reservations, having faith that God would do the job. Only when he surrendered fully did God begin to use him in His plan to save Israel.

Almighty God, You don't want excuses; rather, You desire obedience. I submit my heart and life to You. You are my sufficiency. I say yes—without reservation.

Surrender Looks Like Victory

SCRIPTURE READING: John 15:1–18   KEY VERSE: John 15:16

You did not choose Me, but I chose you and appointed you that you should go and bear fruit, and that your fruit should remain, that whatever you ask the Father in My name He may give you.

To find out whether you are living the Spirit-filled life, take time to examine the motivation of your heart and not just the fruit of your labors. Anyone can put on a good outward appearance—volunteering to serve on various committees at church and holding positions of leadership are just two activities used to gain praise and accolades from others. Even a syrupy sweet smile and a polished greeting can add paint to a spiritually rough interior.

As believers, we need to know that we are capable of fooling ourselves. Putting on a spiritual front reveals a deeper problem—a lack of true humility and desire to know God on an intimate basis.

The Spirit-filled life is a life bathed in surrender to God. It is also a life of transformation in which we gradually take on the likeness of Christ. The emphasis is simple; whether in failure or in victory, disappointment or joy, Jesus is the focus of the entire being.

Many have gone out before us and left a well-worn pathway for us to follow. Men and women such as A. W. Tozer, Charles Spurgeon, Corrie Ten Boom, Amy Carmichael, and Oswald Chambers, to name a few. They point the way to a selfless life that overflows with the fullness of Christ.

Until you give God total control of your life, a battle will always be raging within your heart. Doesn't surrender look like victory in Him today?

O Lord, in Your plan, surrender is not defeat—it is victory. Take control of my life. Still the battle raging in my heart. I surrender to You.

Yes, Lord

SCRIPTURE READING: Romans 12:1–2   KEY VERSE: 1 John 1:9

If we confess our sins, He is faithful and just to forgive us our sins and to cleanse us from all unrighteousness.

For many, the phrase "surrendering to God" has negative overtones. They feel that surrendering somehow means giving up all individuality and freedom for life under a dictator. Of course, with the Lord Jesus Christ such a scenario couldn't be farther from the truth.

Yes, surrendering does mean saying yes absolutely to His will in complete obedience, but God created you to be you, in all your uniqueness. As you obey, you do so within the framework of your personality and makeup. He has a specific plan for you, one that would fit no one else. Obedience is the means by which you allow Him to achieve His purposes.

Have you ever sensed His gentle tug to do or say something in a particular situation, yet you didn't respond? How did you feel? The Lord has forgiven you, and He wants you to confess your sin and get rid of all feelings of guilt (1 John 1:9). But under the guilt, you probably also had a sense of missed opportunity.

God is good, He wants only good things for you, and He asks you to do good things. By obeying Him, you only stand to gain more blessing; by disobeying, you lose out on an experience of His power and love.

Ask God to reveal to you any disobedience, however subtle it may be, and keep your spiritual eyes wide open for the next opportunity to say, "Yes, Lord."

Dear God, thank You for the divine plan You have for me. You desire only good for me, and You ask me only to do good. It is easy to say yes!

Your Christian Growth

SCRIPTURE READING: Ephesians 2:1–10   KEY VERSE: Ephesians 2:10

We are His workmanship, created in Christ Jesus for good works, which God prepared beforehand that we should walk in them.

O ne aspect of the Christian life is maintaining a proper perspective concerning where we have come from and where we are going spiritually. It's not unusual for pride to slip in and cause an entire group of people to think more highly of themselves than they should. We need to remember that apart from Jesus Christ, we are totally unworthy of the kingdom of God.

Paul admonished the Ephesian believers to keep their spiritual pride in check. Just because they had gained new knowledge in Christ did not mean they were better off than anyone else. Jesus always pointed us to humility and service. Paul reminded the believers of the price God paid for their salvation that "even when [they] were dead in [their] transgressions," He made them "alive together with Christ" (Eph. 2:5 NASB).

This truth is foundational to our spiritual growth. The moment we turn from it, we bypass the true nature of God, which is one of eternal love and sacrifice. We are called to be witnesses of Christ's work and glory on earth.

Be careful how you view yourself. Remember the apostle Paul's words: "All of us also lived among them at one time, gratifying the cravings of our sinful nature" (Eph. 2:3 NIV). God's loving desire for you is written in Daniel 12:3 (NIV): "Those who lead many to righteousness" will shine "like the stars forever and ever."

Keep me growing, Lord! I've learned a lot, but there is so much more I need to know. Help me to never stop learning and changing.

The Growth Process

SCRIPTURE READING: Philippians 3:7–16   KEY VERSES: Philippians 3:13–14

Brethren, I do not count myself to have apprehended; but one thing I do, forgetting those things which are behind and reaching forward to those things which are ahead, I press toward the goal for the prize of the upward call of God in Christ Jesus.

Penelope Stokes acknowledges in *Grace Under Pressure:*

Just as physical growth takes many years and much struggle, spiritual maturity comes hard as well. It takes time to grow—time to learn and mature—and the process isn't as simple in reality as it looks on paper.

When we strive against the time necessary for our development, we live in frustration. But when we can relax in God's timetable for our growth, depending upon His grace for the work His Spirit wants to do in our lives, we can experience the joy and wonder of growth, change, and fruitfulness.

Do you remember as a child being anxious to grow up? It seemed forever until that certain birthday when you would be able to do more things and be treated like a grown-up. Of course, by the time you got there, that age did not seem so old.

Such longings are typical in the Christian life as well, especially when you look at the example of a mature believer whom you admire. It's okay to look forward to where God is taking your life, as long as you understand that there are no shortcuts.

Paul expressed his balanced desire for maturity this way: "Brethren, I do not regard myself as having laid hold of it yet; but one thing I do: forgetting what lies behind and reaching forward to what lies ahead, I press on toward the goal" (Phil. 3:13–14 NASB).

Lord Jesus, the growth process often seems long. Spiritual maturity isn't simple. Help me forget the past and press toward the goal You have set for me.

Checking Your Progress

SCRIPTURE READING: Ephesians 4:17–24   KEY VERSE: Psalm 37:37

Mark the blameless man, and observe the upright; for the future of that man is peace.

Like physical growth, spiritual growth is not necessarily something you feel yourself doing. You detect growth by seeing where you are now and looking back at where you've been. You can check your progress along the way as well if you know what to look for.

Increasing awareness of sin. You will develop a keener sense of sin in your life, a sharper awareness of your private motivations. As you expose your innermost thoughts to the truth of God's Word, reality comes into clear focus, and it is much more difficult to justify wrongdoing.

Increase in spiritual battles. The heat is turned up when you begin to wrestle with issues of obedience in everyday life. Attacks may come from all sides, even from those you thought supported you. You will learn to rejoice as you "get dressed" in spiritual armor (Eph. 6).

Increased desire to serve. When you possess love overflowing, you want to give it away. That's the nature of God's grace—it's a gift to be shared. Whether it's a deed people can see or a commitment to praying for someone, you will develop a heart for others.

Decreased desire to be critical. The more you are aware of God's grace for you, the less inclined you are to be harsh with others. Mercy breeds mercy, and you become a bearer of love.

Father God, increase my awareness of sin. Give me new desire to serve. Keep me strong for the spiritual battles I encounter as I continue to grow in You. Make me a bearer of love.

The Great All

SCRIPTURE READING: John 14:21–23   KEY VERSE: Hebrews 11:6

Without faith it is impossible to please Him, for he who comes to God must believe that He is, and that He is a rewarder of those who diligently seek Him.

A. W. Tozer underscored the vital necessity of reckoning with the unseen reality of God and His power:

The spiritual is real . . . We must shift our interest from the seen to the unseen. For the great unseen reality is God. "He that cometh to God must believe that he is, and that he is a rewarder of them that diligently seek him" (Hebrews 11:6). This is basic in the life of faith.

Every man must choose his world . . . As we begin to focus on God, the things of the Spirit will take shape before our inner eyes.

Obedience to the Word of Christ will bring an inward revelation of the Godhead (John 14:21–23).

A new God-consciousness will seize upon us, and we shall begin to taste and hear and inwardly feel the God Who is our life and our all.

More and more, as our faculties grow sharper and more sure, God will become to us the great All and His Presence the glory and wonder of our lives.

Tozer concluded with this prayer. Lift it as your own today:

Dear Lord, open my eyes that I may see; give me acute spiritual perception; enable me to taste Thee and know that Thou art good. Make heaven more real to me than any earthly thing has ever been.

AUGUST 17

Molded by the Master

SCRIPTURE READING: Jeremiah 18:1–6   KEY VERSE: Jeremiah 18:4

The vessel that he made of clay was marred in the hand of the potter; so he made it again into another vessel, as it seemed good to the potter to make.

Young Christians often complain that the Christian growth process is slow and tedious. They become discouraged and stop growing because they want instant knowledge without exerting any effort. Seasoned Christians have some of the same difficulties only in a different way. They perceive themselves as having all the knowledge necessary to live the Christian life, so they stop growing and risk becoming hardened to the intimate love of God.

The Lord has a solution for both of these spiritual abnormalities. It is called being molded into the likeness of Christ, and it's much more than a one- or two-year process. It is a process through which we grow abundantly as children of God. There is no time for boredom or pride because we are too much in love with Christ.

Elisabeth Elliot wrote: "God will never disappoint us. He loves us and has only one purpose for us: holiness, which in His kingdom equals joy." Holiness is a priority with God. When we seek to be like Christ, we seek holiness.

But to become holy, we must submit ourselves to the shaping and molding of God's loving hands. Clay cries out to be molded into something of beauty. The Potter longs to mold and shape your life. Allow Him to take whatever time He needs to create in you joy and devotion of immeasurable worth.

Heavenly Father, mold me into the likeness of Your Son. The clay of my spiritual being cries out to be made into something of beauty.

Life at Its Best

SCRIPTURE READING: 2 Samuel 7   KEY VERSE: 2 Samuel 7:18

King David went in and sat before the LORD; and he said: "Who am I, O Lord GOD? And what is my house, that You have brought me this far?"

D avid was stunned by Nathan's announcement. God was crafting a divine covenant with the former shepherd that exceeded David's fondest hopes. His household and the people of Israel would reap of God's extraordinary beneficence.

The king and warrior was overcome with gratitude: "Who am I, O Lord GOD, and what is my house, that Thou hast brought me this far?" (2 Sam. 7:18 NASB).

In a different sense but of far grander import, God has formed a covenant with each believer in Christ. It is the new covenant of forgiveness of sin and the gift of God's righteousness. The incredible blessings of life in Christ, eternal and abundant, are inextricably bound up in this profound new relationship with deity.

This new life in Christ—a new beginning, a new perspective, a new destiny, a new power—is the only context to define life at its best. It does not get any better than intimate fellowship with our Guide and Sustainer, Jesus Christ.

Our response, when we ponder the immense weight of "every spiritual blessing in the heavenly places in Christ" (Eph. 1:3 NASB), should mimic the awe and wonder of David. Who are we that God has chosen us to know and enjoy Him?

Don't gauge your level of success or satisfaction by materialistic criteria. You live in a covenant relationship with the Savior and King.

Father, who am I that You have chosen me to know and enjoy fellowship with You? I am overwhelmed by the privilege of my covenant relationship with You.

Living a Consistent Life

SCRIPTURE READING: Ephesians 3:14–21   KEY VERSE: Ephesians 3:16

He would grant you, according to the riches of His glory, to be strengthened with might through His Spirit in the inner man.

Whether it has been several years or only a few days since you accepted Christ as your Savior, you can probably remember the dramatic changes that the Lord began to work in your life. It may even be difficult to comprehend all that you said and did before because your heart is so different now.

Paul described this as a literal night-and-day change in your very being, personhood, and identity: "This I say therefore, and affirm together with the Lord, that you walk no longer just as the Gentiles also walk, in the futility of their mind, being darkened in their understanding, excluded from the life of God" (Eph. 4:17–18 NASB).

You now live in the light and are Christ's new creation (2 Cor. 5:17). From darkness to light, you moved in a new direction full of hope and the promise of being made over in Christ's image day by day.

What all believers face on occasion, however, is the roller-coaster feeling of spiritual inconsistency. One day you feel so close to the Lord, you could tell everyone about learning to abide in Him. The next day you struggle so much with basic sins, you wonder how the Lord will ever use you. Are you still a new creation? Absolutely.

You will continue to grow in Him for the rest of your life, and as you mature, the Lord smoothes out the rough places with His love.

O God, I want to get off the roller coaster of spiritual inconsistency. Let the reality that I am a new creation, growing and maturing in You, smooth out the rough places in my life.

Intimacy with God

SCRIPTURE READING: Psalm 139   KEY VERSE: Psalm 139:7

Where can I go from Your Spirit? Or where can I flee from Your presence?

Even though intimacy with God involves a journey that takes place over a lifetime, the Bible teaches that there is never a time when God is unaware of you. He knows all about you—all the good and all the bad—and His love for you remains infinitely the same.

Salvation is just the beginning of a much closer relationship that builds and deepens over time. God is already there, intimately waiting for you to love and respond to Him. The more you grow in your knowledge of Him, the more you will come to understand that God gave everything He had to offer when He gave His Son for you as an atonement for your sins.

The cross where Jesus died is an eternal symbol of His personal care and love toward you. But the work of the Cross does not end at Calvary. It continues in every aspect of life, calling you to leave your old ways—your sin—behind and follow Him with an intimate, loving desire.

Only through intimacy can He teach you to view life with hope and compassion. This is especially needed today when there is so much discouragement. Never be discouraged. Jesus Christ is your strength and your sure hope. He overcame the jeers and insults of man so that He might prove His love to you. All that you could ever need or long for is within Him. Will you trust Him for that today?

> *Lord, my heart cries out for intimacy with You. All that I need or long for is in You. I want to know You in the power of Your resurrection and the fellowship of Your suffering.*

The Abiding Life

SCRIPTURE READING: Romans 8:1–11   KEY VERSES: Romans 8:5–6

Those who live according to the flesh set their minds on the things of the flesh, but those who live according to the Spirit, the things of the Spirit. For to be carnally minded is death, but to be spiritually minded is life and peace.

A favorite childhood Bible song has lines such as these: "Oh, be careful little eyes what you see," and "Oh, be careful little feet where you walk." Children can do body motions along with the music to help them remember the words.

The message may seem childishly simple, but it's equally valid for adults. You need to be careful what you see and where you go. Why?

According to Romans 8:5–6 (NASB), "Those who are according to the flesh set their minds on the things of the flesh, but those who are according to the Spirit, the things of the Spirit. For the mind set on the flesh is death, but the mind set on the Spirit is life and peace."

In John Bunyan's *The Pilgrim's Progress,* Christian decides not to heed the warning to stay on the path. The beautiful green grass beside the path is so soft and inviting, so much better on the feet. Little does he know that when he steps into its lushness, he has set foot in the deceptive By-path Meadow. It isn't long until he ends up a prisoner of the Giant Despair in Doubting Castle.

Letting your focus wander can have the same negative consequences. Setting your mind is a process of deliberate thought. Many times when you get up in the morning, your mental direction is not steered toward the Lord. That is why you must make the conscious decision to center your daily mental activity on spiritual concerns.

Master, I often detour through By-path Meadow and end up in despair and doubting. Establish my thoughts on You. Give me a spiritual mind, focused on the things of Your Holy Spirit.

Fruit Producing

SCRIPTURE READING: John 15:1–8   KEY VERSE: John 15:5

I am the vine, you are the branches. He who abides in Me, and I in him,
bears much fruit; for without Me you can do nothing.

What kinds of sounds do you hear in a grape arbor or other fruit orchard? You can probably hear birds chirping, the wind rustling through leaves, and many other usual outdoor sounds.

You do not hear the sounds of the vines or trees groaning and straining. The plants are not laboring to produce their fruit; the fruit just comes out of the branches naturally as a part of the growing process. The vine does not have to concentrate on producing grapes. When the vine is healthy and has all the water and nutrients it needs, the grapes come forth.

Jesus compared your life to the branches on a grapevine. He said, "I am the vine, you are the branches; he who abides in Me, and I in him, he bears much fruit; for apart from Me you can do nothing" (John 15:5 NASB).

The secret to fruit producing is as basic for you as it is for a real grapevine: stay attached to the Vine and focus all of your energy and attention to simply being there, or abiding, in Christ. Worship Him, praise Him, meditate on His words, seek solitude in Him, and let yourself be absorbed into His purposes.

Through the power of the Holy Spirit, who bears testimony that you are attached to the Vine, your "grapes" will grow. Your fruit is a direct reflection of the quality of your relationship with Christ.

Precious Lord, help me give up groaning and straining and simply learn to
abide. I'm tired of trying to do it in myself. Produce Your fruit in me.

Good: An Enemy of the Best

SCRIPTURE READING: Proverbs 3:5–12   KEY VERSE: Proverbs 3:6

In all your ways acknowledge Him, and He shall direct your paths.

During the fifties, a television program aired called *The Life of Riley*. You may remember watching it. The idea was to portray a life that anyone would want to live. During the opening credits, the star of the series was shown lying back in a hammock with his arms folded behind his head, while others hurriedly cut grass and cleaned the yard behind him. However as the story unfolded, viewers quickly saw how unpredictable life can be.

The tragedy is that many people spend a lifetime trying to live the life of Riley. They opt for what appears fun and pleasurable rather than God's best. Oswald Chambers emphasized,

> The greatest enemy of the life of faith in God is not sin, but good choices which are not quite good enough. The good is always the enemy of the best.
>
> Many of us do not continue to grow spiritually because we prefer to choose on the basis of our rights, instead of relying on God to make the choice for us. We have to learn to walk according to the standard which has its eyes focused on God. And God says to us, as He did to Abram, "walk before Me" (Gen. 17:1).

Life at its best is not a lifetime void of trouble and pain, but a lifetime of joy and peace. The experiences we encounter along the way lead to deep wisdom and personal knowledge of divine hope and grace.

Dear heavenly Father, good is good, but best is better. I don't want to settle for anything less than the best. You choose what is right for me.

Free to Live God's Way

SCRIPTURE READING: Galatians 5:1–15   KEY VERSE: Galatians 5:1

Stand fast therefore in the liberty by which Christ has made us free, and do not be entangled again with a yoke of bondage.

When approving an inmate for parole, prison officials are supposed to consider the likelihood of recidivism, or repetition of the offense. People who have committed certain crimes, especially the more violent ones, have a higher rate of recidivism than others. The sad fact is that some prisoners are never able to escape their pattern of criminal behavior.

Why? Until their thinking changes, the resulting actions stay the same, no matter how good rehabilitation efforts might be. The same is true for a sinful habit in your life. Before you can shake off its negative influence, you must alter your mind-set.

Romans 12:2 (NASB) explains the bondage-breaking process: "Do not be conformed to this world, but be transformed by the renewing of your mind, that you may prove what the will of God is, that which is good and acceptable and perfect."

As you read God's Word and study His principles carefully, they gradually become a natural part of your thought process. When the new comes in, the old is tossed out. The Lord is then able to work His truth into your innermost being, establishing new, Christlike habits.

You don't have to be confined by the restrictions of an old sin problem. Whether you are in a jail that is real or one of your own making, Jesus wants to set you free to live in His ways.

Almighty God, set me free to live Your way. Remove the restrictions of sin. Toss out the old. Make room for the new.

The Power Within

SCRIPTURE READING: 1 Corinthians 1:26–29   KEY VERSE: 1 Corinthians 1:27

God has chosen the foolish things of the world to put to shame the wise, and God has chosen the weak things of the world to put to shame the things which are mighty.

In his book *The Person and Work of the Holy Spirit*, R. A. Torrey wrote,

The Holy Spirit dwells in every child of God. In some, however, He dwells way back of consciousness in the hidden sanctuary of their spirit. He is not allowed to take possession as He desires of the whole man, spirit, soul, and body. Some therefore are not distinctly conscious of His indwelling, but He is there nonetheless.

What a solemn, and yet what a glorious thought, that in me dwells this August person, the Holy Spirit. If we are children of God, we are not so much to pray that the Spirit may come and dwell in us, for He does that already. We are rather to recognize His presence, His gracious and glorious indwelling, and give to Him complete control of the house He already inhabits, and strive so to live as not to grieve this holy one, this divine guest.

How considerately we ought to treat these bodies and how sensitively we ought to shun everything that will defile them. How carefully we ought to walk in all things so as not to grieve Him who dwells within us.

When we grieve God's Spirit through sin or wrongful attitudes, we miss the full benefits of His presence. The power that indwells us is the same power that indwelled Christ while He was on earth. Pray and ask Him to reveal Himself to you today in a fresh new way.

O Lord, thank You for the power of the Holy Spirit that is at work in me. Reveal Yourself to me today in a fresh new way.

Total Commitment

SCRIPTURE READING: Jude 1   KEY VERSE: Jude 3

Beloved, while I was very diligent to write to you concerning our common salvation, I found it necessary to write to you exhorting you to contend earnestly for the faith which was once for all delivered to the saints.

Constantine was the first Roman emperor to take a serious interest in Christianity. During his rule, much was done to ease persecution against the church and to advance the gospel message.

J. D. Douglas noted, "In a dream . . . Constantine saw a vision of a monogram composed of the first two Greek letters of the name of 'Christ.' The next day he had his soldiers inscribe that monogram on their shields and marched into battle." The victory they gained was a political and military victory as well as a victory for Christianity over heathenism.

Constantine's religious sentiments resulted in laws favoring Christianity. In A.D. 325, he organized the first ecumenical council, the Council of Nicaea, which was devoted to settling doctrinal disputes and unifying the church. One of the most important decisions reached was a ban against Arianism, a heresy that denied Christ is coeternal with the Father.

But even though Constantine took a bold step toward Christianity, compromise diluted most of his efforts. Pagan worship continued. Constantine maintained his pagan title "Pontifex Maximus." He contended for the faith but invited compromise into his heart.

What banner waves above your heart? One of total commitment or one of compromise?

Dear God, I pull down the banners of self-will, self-sufficiency, and compromise that reign in my life. I lift the banner of total commitment to You.

Abiding in Christ

SCRIPTURE READING: John 15:9–17   KEY VERSE: John 15:17

These things I command you, that you love one another.

In John 15, Jesus instructed us to abide in Him. The visual picture is one of a branch abiding in a vine. Christ taught that God is the Vinedresser, pruning and shaping the branches so that they will bear much fruit. *Abiding* means "remaining and continuing." It is an active word, even though from a worldly perspective we often view it as a word of passivity. However, nothing is farther from the truth. When we abide in Christ, we are in a process of growth unlike anything we have known before.

Notice how the young tender shoots of the grapevine appear in the spring and begin running along the arbor. God tenderly watches over His branches and with the greatest of care and skill cultivates the vine so that it produces a maximum harvest.

The sole purpose of the branches is to bear fruit. They are not destined to live on their own apart from the vine, nor are they allowed to grow wild. They maintain, they continue, and they rest in the vine.

We live under the grace of God and are given full access to His infinite peace as we abide in Him. When turmoil comes, we can go to a place of refuge. It is a place of abiding contentment in the inner chamber of our hearts. You need never fear when you are abiding in Christ. His peace and rest are yours.

Precious heavenly Father, thank You that I have a place of refuge in times of turmoil. Peace and rest are mine when I abide in You.

A Personal Invitation from God

SCRIPTURE READING: Isaiah 1:18–21   KEY VERSE: Isaiah 1:18

"Come now, and let us reason together," says the LORD, "though your sins are like scarlet, they shall be as white as snow; though they are red like crimson, they shall be as wool."

The Bible typically portrays sin as black or dark, but in Isaiah 1:18 (NASB), the imagery changes: "Though your sins are as scarlet, they will be as white as snow; though they are red like crimson, they will be like wool."

In Bible times, these colors were some of the brightest colors that could be produced, and they were absolutely colorfast. You didn't just wash out a scarlet stain from a piece of cloth. If the material was dyed with scarlet, it stayed red. The idea of something dark red becoming as white as snow or wool was certainly out of the question.

Yet that is what Christ's red blood does to your sins. It wipes them away completely, and all God sees when He looks at you is purity—no spots or smudges of unrighteousness soiling the fabric of your life.

You can find a good example of this spiritual principle in science. If you take a white card with a big red dot on it and look at it through a special red photographic light filter, you cannot see the spot at all. The entire card appears white. Through the filter of Christ's blood, you are "eternally white" in the eyes of God.

Does God see you through the covering of Jesus' blood, or are you still trying to scrub out the flaws in your heart and life by your own effort? You were not designed to be self-cleaning. Let Him do the job.

Lord Jesus, thank You for the invitation to be washed white as snow. I accept. Wash away the crimson stains of my sin. Remove all the spots and smudges.

Strength to Say Yes

SCRIPTURE READING: Hebrews 12   KEY VERSE: Hebrews 12:1

We also, since we are surrounded by so great a cloud of witnesses, let us lay aside every weight, and the sin which so easily ensnares us, and let us run with endurance the race that is set before us.

I magine trying to go about the day with your legs tied together, with the rope just loose enough to allow minimal mobility. You would eventually get things done, but even the simplest task would be slow work. Between falling and tripping over your feet, you might avoid injury long enough to reach your destination.

That is a picture evoked by the word *ensnares* in Hebrews 12:1. This term was used to refer to snaring an animal with a trap or a net, leaving it alive but rendering it incapable of getting away. Habits of sin work in a similar fashion; ones that are allowed to remain a part of consistent behavior become a snare in your life.

You may be able to function in certain basic areas, and your appearance or career may not be affected immediately, but sin eventually trips you up and prevents the full and unencumbered life God wants you to experience. The "little" problem of fudging on an expense report may later turn into full-scale embezzlement as sin's hold wraps tighter around your life.

If something bad has a hold on you right now, turn it over to the Lord before it gains a firmer grip. Jesus wants you to feel the exhilaration that comes from making choices that please Him, and He always provides the strength to say yes to His principles.

Father God, give me the ability to say no to things that ensnare. Clear my pathway of all that would trip and entrap. Give me divine strength to say yes to Your principles.

The Focus of Your Faith

SCRIPTURE READING: Psalm 100   KEY VERSE: Psalm 100:5

The LORD is good; His mercy is everlasting, and His truth endures to all generations.

An imperfection in a piece of cloth or silverware may be unattractive but has few functional implications. However, a flaw in the construction of your home or engineering of your car can have serious consequences.

When it comes to the matter of faith, it is wise to periodically examine the spiritual integrity of your trust in Christ. A defect in this area can impair the quality of your relationship with the Lord and your response to His leadership.

Ask yourself these questions:

- Does God or my personal concerns occupy the center stage of my faith?
- Am I more interested in knowing what the will of the Father is, or just what the will of the Father is for me?

If you are not careful, your own neediness can crowd out the centrality of who God is in your walk of faith. Perhaps unintentionally, you allow pressing problems to supersede your chief duty to know God and enjoy Him forever.

Certainly God understands your desire to have your needs met (and He is more than willing to do so). However, He wants you to be supremely occupied with Him, to delight yourself in His personhood.

When the focus of your faith lies in the greatness and grandeur of God, you have little trouble believing He is faithfully and lovingly at work for your well-being.

Dear Lord, You are the focus of my faith. Keep me supremely occupied with You. Don't let my problems and needs crowd out the centrality of who You are.

Keep Building and Growing

SCRIPTURE READING: 1 Corinthians 3:10–15   KEY VERSE: 1 Corinthians 1:9

God is faithful, by whom you were called into the fellowship of His Son, Jesus Christ our Lord.

Developers and builders work hard to make sure that structures meet the required building codes. From electrical wiring to masonry and framing, all materials must be of a specified quality and assembled in a safe manner. If they are not, then the security and physical well-being of the future occupants are at risk.

As a believer, you are involved in the long-term building of your spiritual "house." Christ is the strong foundation, and He guides the ultimate construction of your faith and character. Along the way, as you choose to submit to His carpentry, you select the building materials that go into your spiritual house.

Being obedient, using your tongue for the edification of others, acting as a peacemaker, refusing to give in to selfishness, and doing anything that reflects the fruit of the Spirit—all are solid building blocks of a life being conformed to the image of Christ. One day Jesus will judge the quality of the house of your life: "Now if any man builds upon the foundation with gold, silver, precious stones, wood, hay, straw, each man's work will become evident; for the day will show it, because it is to be revealed with fire; and the fire itself will test the quality of each man's work" (1 Cor. 3:12–13 NASB).

Remember, though, that this evaluation has nothing to do with salvation. Jesus will inspect your structure only for the purpose of giving good gifts in the measure of the work you did here.

Dear heavenly Father, I've started this journey of commitment and change. Please help me continue. Someday You will review the quality of my spiritual house. I want to pass inspection.

SEPTEMBER

Journey to Receive a Spiritual Mantle

REPRESENTING: Ministering to others

KEY VERSE: 1 Peter 4:10

As each one has received a gift, minister it to one another, as good stewards of the manifold grace of God.

Before we begin our spiritual journey this month, take a few minutes and read 2 Kings 2:1–15. It is the story of Elisha's journey with the prophet Elijah to receive the double-portion anointing for ministry and to take up Elijah's mantle.

There is a spiritual mantle—a legacy of divine power—that God wants to place on you to equip you for His work. God is looking for men and women with the spirit and power of Elisha.

Following Elisha's example, we travel together this month to receive the double-portion anointing for ministry. During our journey, we will discover the importance of walking worthy of our calling with wise use of time and talents. We will learn how to serve, minister to, and encourage others.

Get ready—the mantle of God's anointing is about to fall.

Walking Worthy of Your Calling

SCRIPTURE READING: Ephesians 4:1–2   KEY VERSE: Ephesians 4:1

I, therefore, the prisoner of the Lord, beseech you to walk worthy of the calling with which you were called.

In coming to the United States shortly after her release from a Nazi concentration camp, Corrie Ten Boom, author of *The Hiding Place,* was answering the call of God for her life.

However, that calling did not go unchallenged. Time after time Corrie's presence in the United States was questioned. The little support she had in the beginning dwindled. She was tempted to become discouraged but refused. Beneath any thoughts of rejection were a peace and a hope that God would honor her obedience.

When others rejected her, Corrie held fast to the promises of God. Finally her commitment paid off. A door of opportunity opened through a well-known Christian evangelist. Soon Corrie Ten Boom became one of the most recognized Christian speakers of our time. She weathered life's most severe storms and was found worthy of God's call.

God has called you to be a light of His love and forgiveness to a world locked away in utter darkness. Therefore, walk worthy of His call. When discouragement comes, stand firm in your faith, and God will mold you into an instrument of His love to others.

Dear Lord, You have called me to be a light as I travel through this world. Use me to minister to others I encounter on my journey.

The Servant Spirit

SCRIPTURE READING: John 13:1–20   KEY VERSE: Matthew 20:27

Whoever desires to be first among you, let him be your slave.

Why was Peter so stunned and overcome with shame when Jesus knelt to clean his feet? Foot washing was servant's work, a menial and dirty task, certainly not a job for an esteemed and beloved Leader. In one humble and brilliant gesture, Jesus demonstrated what their attitude and actions should be: "If I then, the Lord and the Teacher, washed your feet, you also ought to wash one another's feet. For I gave you an example that you also should do as I did to you" (John 13:14–15 NASB).

This servant's spirit should characterize everything you do. Of course, it's easy to think of a hypothetical situation and say, "Yes, I would do anything to help out." But the real test of your willingness to serve comes when you are confronted with the actual need.

You see trash all around a picnic site. Do you pick up the litter, or do you eat and walk away, hoping that someone who is paid to do it will clean up?

Your elderly neighbor needs a driver to take her to the store and the doctor. Would you volunteer?

The key to overcoming hesitation to serve is keeping the right attitude. When you see others as Jesus sees them, you want to meet their needs with enthusiasm. You discover the joy of serving when you follow the Savior's lead.

Heavenly Father, I want to serve others with joy, touching their lives with Your love, extending my hands to a hurting world. Make me a servant.

Motivation for Commitment

SCRIPTURE READING: Daniel 6   KEY VERSE: Matthew 5:16

Let your light so shine before men, that they may see your good works and glorify your Father in heaven.

Even though the Persian decree demanded that worship be given only to King Darius, Daniel continued to worship God. He knew that violation of the decree would lead to the lions' den, yet he refused to compromise his convictions.

We all have moments when we feel like Daniel—times when we stand for what we know is right, but we end up feeling as if we have been cast into a den of lions. It happens in our jobs, community ties, families, and even our churches.

The thing that separated Daniel was his devotion to God. He was not concerned about what others thought of him. Above everything else, Daniel wanted to live only for God. Nothing could change the upward direction of his worship.

When people see your life, do they see Jesus? Daniel's witness was so strong that it made a lasting impression on the king. From the top of the lions' den, King Darius shouted down, "Your God whom you constantly serve will Himself deliver you" (Dan. 6:16 NASB).

May the words of our Savior motivate us to an even stronger commitment: "Let your light shine before men, that they may see your good deeds and praise your Father in heaven" (Matt. 5:16 NIV).

O God, often I feel as if I am in a den of lions, surrounded by hostile people and circumstances. In these times, help me remain faithful in devotion and duty so that You will be glorified.

Living a Consistent Life

SCRIPTURE READING: Ephesians 4:17–24   KEY VERSE: Ephesians 4:24

You put on the new man which was created according to God, in true righteousness and holiness.

A Christian college professor urged her students to make sure their lives were consistent with the message of God's Word: "Never let an air of inconsistency blow through your lives. If this happens, the world will notice it, and your testimony for Jesus will be damaged."

Consistency is difficult. The Lord knows this and is ever present to keep us pointed in the right direction. However, the matter of consistency also is a matter of self-will. We must want to be like Jesus in order for there to be a sweetness to our lives that others notice and see as being essential to the Christian lifestyle.

In Ephesians 4, Paul explained how the believer is to approach life. He admonished the young church in Ephesus to leave their old ways and thought patterns, especially the ones that reminded them of their lives before they were saved.

A radical change takes place on the inside when our souls are transferred from eternal death to eternal life. The evidence of this transformation is that now that we have given our lives to Jesus, we no longer desire to live in sin's habitat.

Washed in the saving blood of Jesus Christ, we are new creatures. The old is gone. Once we lived as those who do not know Jesus as Savior and Lord; praise be to God, though, as believers, we have a new consistency to our lives that brings eternal peace and hope.

Father, I want to be like You. Let my life exude a sweet aroma that others will notice. Help me be consistent in my Christian walk.

Sifted for Service

SCRIPTURE READING: Luke 22:31–34   KEY VERSE: Luke 22:32

I have prayed for you, that your faith should not fail; and when you have returned to Me, strengthen your brethren.

I f you want to be greatly used of God, you must be willing to be sifted for His service. This principle is much like the process of winnowing wheat. In New Testament times that was done by threshing the grain on high ground. The chaff was blown away by the wind while what was useful remained.

Peter was no exception to the winnowing process. Jesus told the future apostle: "Satan has demanded permission to sift you like wheat; but I have prayed for you, that your faith may not fail; and you, when once you have turned again, strengthen your brothers" (Luke 22:31–32 NASB).

It was the night of our Lord's arrest. If ever there was a time Peter wanted to stand firm, that was it. Yet he ended up denying Jesus three times. What emotional pain and sorrow must have gripped his mind. But think back to Jesus' words: "When once you have turned again, strengthen your brothers." This is the hope we have in Christ; that even when we fail Him, even when He has to winnow us like wheat, He never gives up on us.

By sifting your life through trials and frustrations, God brings to the surface the things that are impure. Had Peter refused to be sifted, he never would have been fit for service. If you sense God's sifting hand in your life, submit your will to Him and allow Him to prepare you for His service.

> *Lord, help me realize that my trials and frustrations are not without purpose. You are separating the good from the bad, the spiritual grain from the chaff. You are sifting me for service.*

The Sifting Process

SCRIPTURE READING: Matthew 20:25–28   KEY VERSE: Matthew 20:16

The last will be first, and the first last. For many are called, but few chosen.

God has a plan for your life. However, it doesn't snap into place overnight. It takes a lifetime to achieve all He has planned for you. He prepares you for service by giving you spiritual gifts and natural talents, and by allowing you to face many difficulties. He uses the difficulties to sift away the impurities in your life. The difficulties also sand and polish the rough edges of your life until they are removed. In the end, you become a reflection of His glory.

When God begins His process of sifting in your life, you may feel as though your entire life is being shaken. Don't worry. He is positioning you for a great blessing. Another indication of the sifting process of God comes when you sense His silence. He is testing to see whether you will trust Him even though He is not making Himself known to you through material blessings.

One of the hardest forms of sifting comes through suffering, whether physical, mental, or emotional. Amy Carmichael, a devoted servant of God, spent the last years of her life confined to her bed. God allowed her to be tested beyond what seemed bearable, especially for one who loved being in contact with others. Most of us will never face that kind of trial. However, the life of Christ burned brilliantly within her. Today her books, written during her time of suffering, are testimonies to God's faithfulness and glory.

Master, help me realize that You work in silence, suffering, and times of shaking to accomplish Your purposes in my life. Use these difficult circumstances to prepare me for the future You have planned.

The Fragrance God Loves to Smell

SCRIPTURE READING: 1 Peter 5:6–10   KEY VERSE: 1 Peter 5:10

May the God of all grace, who called us to His eternal glory by Christ Jesus,
after you have suffered a while, perfect, establish, strengthen, and settle you.

God is always in charge of the sifting process. There is never a time when the trials and tribulations of life are beyond His control. Even when you feel frustrated and confused, God is in the driver's seat. Satan never has the upper hand. And though the enemy may seek to discredit you, God has justified you through your acceptance of His Son.

God uses sifting not only to remove the impurities in our lives, but also to surface the qualities He desires to use greatly. Most of us have heard about how fire refines gold. It is in the heating up of the material that the dross is made visible and removed. The hotter the fire, the purer the gold.

God doesn't sift and refine us in relaxed and beautiful settings. Often the purging comes in times of tempest and trial. In her devotional classic *Streams in the Desert*, Mrs. Charles Cowman wrote,

> Sometimes God sends severe blasts of trial upon His children to develop their graces. Just as torches burn most brightly when swung to and fro; just as the juniper plant smells sweetest when flung into the flames; so the richest qualities of a Christian often come out under the north wind of suffering and adversity. Bruised hearts often emit the fragrance that God loveth to smell.

Dear Lord, when my heart is bruised, let it emit the fragrance You love. Bring forth Christlike qualities in my tough times.

Vision Without Boundaries

SCRIPTURE READING: Matthew 28:16–20   KEY VERSE: Matthew 28:19

Go therefore and make disciples of all the nations, baptizing them in the
name of the Father and of the Son and of the Holy Spirit.

Four stirring, motivational forces were behind the disciples' desire to proclaim the gospel message: (1) their personal experience with the Lord; (2)
the promise of Christ's presence with them; (3) the promise and the coming of
the Holy Spirit; and (4) the memory of the way Jesus dealt with those who were
hurting. Theirs was a vision without boundaries.

However, their ministry certainly did not begin that way. There was a time
on the Sea of Galilee when doubt and confusion ruled their minds. That was
until Jesus stood up in the boat and commanded the waves and the winds to be
still.

There was a night when all but one deserted our Savior, and that one was
frightened and overcome with sorrow. The disciples wanted to believe Christ
was the One promised by God, but their vision was shortsighted—much like
ours at times.

Jesus knew the Father's plan reached to eternity. It was His destiny to
become the Lamb of God who would take away the sins of the world. No
boundaries erected by man or Satan could stop the plan of God.

The same God who raised Christ from the grave is alive in every believer.
Never place boundaries on the vision God brings: "He who began a good work
in you will perfect it until the day of Christ Jesus" (Phil. 1:6 NASB).

What a wonderful, glorious Friend, Master, and Savior we have in Jesus.

Dear heavenly Father, remove every boundary that limits Your work in my
life. Expand my spiritual borders. Give me vision without boundaries.

Unlimited Vision

SCRIPTURE READING: Isaiah 6:1–8   KEY VERSE: Jeremiah 29:11

*I know the thoughts that I think toward you, says the LORD, thoughts of peace
and not of evil, to give you a future and a hope.*

Illness destroyed Helen Keller's sight and hearing when she was not yet two
years old, leaving her cut off from the world," writes William Bennett in *The
Book of Virtues*.

For nearly five years she grew up, as she later described it, wild and unruly . . .

Anne Sullivan's arrival at the Kellers' Alabama home from the Perkins
Institution for the Blind in Boston changed Helen's life . . . Through the sense
of touch she was able to make contact with the young girl's mind, and within
three years she had taught Helen to read and write Braille. By sixteen, Helen
could speak well enough to go to preparatory school and college. She graduated
cum laude from Radcliffe in 1904, and devoted the rest of her life to helping
the blind and deaf-blind, as her teacher had done.

In recalling the first day she spent with Anne Sullivan, Helen wrote, "It
would have been difficult to find a happier child than I was as I lay in my crib
at the close of that eventful day and lived over the joys it brought me, and for
the first time longed for a new day to come."

Anne Sullivan had a vision without boundaries, and she shared it with
American author and speaker Helen Keller.

Are your goals limited by fear or doubt? God has a plan for your life that
is broad and full of hope. Even now He waits to reveal it to you.

*Almighty God, I repent of the fear and doubt that limit my vision. Your
plan for me is greater than I can imagine. Even now, You wait to reveal it to
me. Lord, I am ready to receive it.*

The Power Within

SCRIPTURE READING: 1 Corinthians 1:26–31   KEY VERSE: 1 Corinthians 1:27

God has chosen the foolish things of the world to put to shame the wise, and God has chosen the weak things of the world to put to shame the things which are mighty.

God has equipped you for every good work. The presence of the Holy Spirit is His guarantee that no matter what you face, He is committed to providing the power and strength you need to accomplish the task, get through the hurt, and end up victorious in Him.

D. L. Moody had only a fifth grade education, but he became one of the greatest evangelists of our time. He was never ordained to the ministry, yet God used him to lead thousands to the saving knowledge of Jesus Christ. The book *More Than Conquerors* tells us that "during the nineteenth century when mass media consisted of only printing presses and public oratory, more than 100 million people heard or read the gospel message of D. L. Moody. The evangelist spoke to at least 1.5 million in London during four months in 1875, long before radio and television." God chooses the weak things to shame those who think they are strong (1 Cor. 1:27–29).

There is only one way God can be glorified in your life, and that is through your willingness to lay aside your ability, talent, and personal desires in order to follow Him in obedience. Sacrifice and submission lead to a life of tremendous hope, freedom, and eternal joy. D. L. Moody could do nothing apart from the Savior, and what he did through the power of the Holy Spirit can never be duplicated.

O Lord, thank You for equipping me for every good work. Your presence is my guarantee of success. Help me accomplish the task, get through the hurt, and end up victorious in You.

Encouraging Sagging Saints

SCRIPTURE READING: 1 Corinthians 16:10–21   KEY VERSE: Hebrews 6:10

God is not unjust to forget your work and labor of love which you have shown toward His name, in that you have ministered to the saints, and do minister.

Stephanas. Fortunatus. Achaicus. Aquila. Priscilla. Although names not on the tip of your tongue, these people were instrumental in the formation of the early New Testament church. Paul mentioned their indispensable labor in his parting instructions to the church at Corinth. Without defining their specific contributions, he remarked that their ministries refreshed and revitalized believers, including himself.

The local church today frequently errs in the notion that its pastor and staff members are the sole nucleus for the work of the gospel. They have vital functions, but the saints themselves share and participate in the growth of Christ's body.

Your name may not be on the bulletin. You may not be a deacon or elder. But you have been equipped with spiritual gifts to strengthen the saints. A note with a brief word of encouragement, a phone call to someone in your Sunday school class, lunch with a discouraged parent, a small gift to someone in need—these are discreet but practical and encouraging ways to lift the spirits of sagging saints.

Ask God to show you how you might refresh fellow workers. Let Him lead you in appropriate ways to demonstrate His gentle love: "God is not unjust so as to forget your work and the love which you have shown toward His name, in having ministered and in still ministering to the saints" (Heb. 6:10 NASB).

Dear God, teach me to be an encourager and a source of hope to others. Show me how to refresh my fellow workers, demonstrating Your love in appropriate and practical ways.

A Spokesman of God's Truth

SCRIPTURE READING: Hebrews 13:20–21   KEY VERSE: Mark 2:17

When Jesus heard it, He said to them, "Those who are well have no need of a physician, but those who are sick. I did not come to call the righteous, but sinners, to repentance."

George Whitefield, an English evangelist who lived from 1714 to 1770, delivered more than eighteen thousand sermons in his lifetime of being a traveling preacher. In England and America, his strong voice carried through fields to the crowds of thousands that gathered wherever he went. He was so passionate to spread the gospel that he continued preaching even in poor health.

The people around him recognized that the Lord gave him almost super-human energy and drive. In their book *The Light and the Glory*, Peter Marshall and David Manuel described the scene in New Hampshire at his last sermon:

> When the time came to speak, he could barely breathe, and one of them said to him, "Sir, you are more fit to go to bed, than to preach."
>
> "True, sir," gasped Whitefield. Then, glancing heavenward he added, "Lord Jesus, I am weary in Thy work, but not of it. If I have not finished my course, let me go and speak for Thee once more in the fields, and seal Thy truth, and come home and die!"

God answered his prayer. After delivering a more than two-hour sermon, the exhausted Whitefield went to a pastor friend's home; he died the next morning as he gazed out the window at the sunrise. Because one man was will-ing to be a spokesman of God's truth, two nations were touched with His love.

O Lord, make me a spokesman of Your truth. I have not finished my journey. Don't let me grow weary along the way. Keep me faithful to the end.

Following Jesus

SCRIPTURE READING: Matthew 4:12–25   KEY VERSE: Matthew 4:19

He said to them, "Follow Me, and I will make you fishers of men."

When Jesus called Peter and Andrew to be His disciples, all He said to them was, "Follow Me." Peter and Andrew had heard Him teach before; that was not the first moment they had laid eyes on Jesus or heard what work He was about. Yet at the moment of calling, Jesus said only a few words.

The hearts of Peter and Andrew were already prepared to answer His call; they immediately left their nets and livelihood and went with Jesus. The two disciples had an extreme sensitivity to the Spirit of God. They were able to recognize the difference between God's prompting and the urging of their hearts.

Peter and Andrew also possessed a mind-set of service. The New Testament had not yet been written, but their lives exemplified these verses about their Savior: "Have this attitude in yourselves which was also in Christ Jesus, who, although He existed in the form of God, did not regard equality with God a thing to be grasped, but emptied Himself, taking the form of a bond-servant, and being made in the likeness of men" (Phil. 2:5–7 NASB). They were ready to sacrifice anything for the cause of Christ, even the security of a known future as fishermen.

Jesus Christ gives you the same call: "Follow Me." It does not matter where you are in life. All that matters is that you adapt your own plans to His.

Precious heavenly Father, two words have changed my life—Follow Me. I have heard the call. I am ready to respond. I will follow You.

Acting Out Your Commitment

SCRIPTURE READING: Luke 9:23–26   KEY VERSE: Luke 9:23

He said to them all, "If anyone desires to come after Me, let him deny himself, and take up his cross daily, and follow Me."

In the back of your mind, when you hear the words *deny* and *cross*, you usually think of suffering. You might even get the vague idea that yielding to God's will for your life is going to mean always walking a hard road or giving up everything you ever hoped for in favor of a foreign plan.

Denying yourself doesn't mean eating only bread and water or not letting yourself have good things. Jesus was talking about submission, the one-time act of saying to the Lord that He is in charge, that Christ is your Master and Savior and is free to use your life any way He pleases.

"Taking up your cross daily" is the step-by-step process of acting out that commitment and affirming it each day as you make decisions. If you want to take a certain action, but you know that God has a specific command against it, then you must make a choice—your way or God's way. And because He is absolutely loving and absolutely holy, you know that His direction is in your best interest and for your ultimate good.

Self-denial is Christ-acceptance. Saying yes to Him means opening up your life to adventure that leads only to blessing. Begin to act out your commitment today!

Lord Jesus, my answer is yes—I will follow You! Help me act out my commitment today as I walk Your way.

The Cost of True Discipleship

SCRIPTURE READING: Luke 14:25–35   KEY VERSE: Luke 14:27

Whoever does not bear his cross and come after Me cannot be My disciple.

Jesus certainly knew how to drive away a crowd. When He spoke of whole-hearted commitment and absolute surrender to His mission, the multitudes melted away. The only ones left were those who recognized that He spoke the words of life, uncompromising yet loving truth about what it means to really know Him.

Oswald Chambers wrote in *My Utmost for His Highest* about the kind of total absorption Christ wants us to have:

> There is no such thing as a private life, or a place to hide in this world, for a man or woman who is intimately aware of and shares in the sufferings of Jesus Christ.
>
> God divides the private life of His saints and makes it a highway for the world on one hand and for Himself on the other. No human being can stand that unless he is identified with Jesus Christ. We are not sanctified for ourselves. We are called into intimacy with the gospel, and things happen that appear to have nothing to do with us.
>
> But God is getting us into fellowship with Himself. Let Him have His way. If you refuse, you will be of no value to God in His redemptive work in the world, but will be a hindrance and a stumbling block.

Jesus wants all of your devotion, not just a portion. You cannot have other priorities plus Jesus. He is the priority.

Precious Lord, adjust my priorities. Call me into greater intimacy with the gospel. Deepen my relationship and fellowship with You.

Do Not Grow Weary

SCRIPTURE READING: 2 Thessalonians 3:6–15   KEY VERSE: 2 Thessalonians 3:13

As for you, brethren, do not grow weary in doing good.

At various points throughout history, some Christians have been accused of being too teleological in focus. That is, they emphasized the life to come and their ultimate destination of heaven to the exclusion of concern for this present world. You have probably heard this comment: "He is so heavenly minded, he is no earthly good."

In Paul's day in the church at Thessalonica, many believers took this warped emphasis to the extreme. They were convinced that Jesus was returning at any moment, so they ceased working and waited for Him. You can imagine what chaos the imbalance caused within the early church, with some believers working harder and carrying the load for the others.

Second Thessalonians 3:12–13 (NASB) contains this reproof: "Now such persons we command and exhort in the Lord Jesus Christ to work in quiet fashion and eat their own bread. But as for you, brethren, do not grow weary of doing good."

It is all right to look forward to spending eternity with Jesus after we die and leave this earth; He wants us to eagerly anticipate His generous blessings to come. Yet the here and now matters to Jesus too. He wants you to grow in His fellowship, maturing and strengthening and becoming a better-equipped representative of His grace to a lost world.

Heavenly Father, keep my focus on this lost and dying world. Help me grow in fellowship with You, maturing and strengthening to become a better representative of Your grace.

Your Time

SCRIPTURE READING: Ephesians 5:15–17   KEY VERSE: Psalm 90:12

Teach us to number our days, that we may gain a heart of wisdom.

Time is life and how you spend it. It is the sum of your accomplishments and memories. Are you satisfied with your time management, or do you feel as if your schedule for the day, the week, the month is already filled with obligations of a career or commitments to others?

You can change. You can manage time without its managing you. Like Moses, you can ask God to teach you to number your days, that you may present to Him a heart of wisdom (Ps. 90:12).

Begin with setting goals and priorities. What are your gifts and talents? What has God called you to do with them? How can you take small steps to reach them? This winnows out the insignificant and forms a mental picture of the essentials.

If necessary, find a space of a day or so to think soberly about where you have been and where you want to go. Pray, read, ponder, and write down what God impresses on your heart. Commit yourself to spend time daily with God. Doing that in itself may seem burdensome at first if your schedule is harried. However, you will find the time as God grants insight and prudence for your varied agenda.

Getting the big picture helps connect the daily dots of appointments, meetings, interruptions, and assorted duties. Time will become your ally, not your enemy.

O God, teach me to number my days. Help me manage time wisely. Let it become my ally instead of my enemy.

Your Talents

SCRIPTURE READING: Luke 19:12–27　　　　KEY VERSE: Luke 19:17

He said to him, "Well done, good servant; because you were faithful in a very little, have authority over ten cities."

An essential ingredient for success in the personal or corporate realm is productivity. Businesses must be profitable if they expect to survive. Employees must work hard and wisely if they are to progress.

Although the believer's identity and security in Christ should never be confused with his performance (the Father unconditionally loves and accepts him), God expects him to be productive in the use of his natural talents and spiritual gifts. This is clear in the parable of the talents where the industrious servant is rewarded and the indolent worker is reprimanded for his lack of initiative and effort.

The fear of failure is perhaps the greatest obstacle for many Christians. We flunk a course, flub an assignment, disappoint a boss, and decide we must not be made of the right stuff. What heresy! Failure is never final in God's eyes. Look at David, Moses, Mark, and others who blew it but still found great favor with God. All God desires is that you learn from your mistakes and trust Him to help you.

A productive, satisfying life can be your experience. There will be unexpected lapses and momentary pauses as you seek to maximize your talents, but in the end, you will hear God say, "Well done, my good servant" (Luke 19:17 NIV). This is reward enough.

> *Father, I praise You that failure is never final in Your eyes. Remove my fear of failure, and replace it with divine confidence. Help me learn from my mistakes.*

Molded by the Master

SCRIPTURE READING: Jeremiah 18:1–6   KEY VERSE: Jeremiah 18:4

The vessel that he made of clay was marred in the hand of the potter; so he made it again into another vessel, as it seemed good to the potter to make.

Jeremiah is often called the weeping prophet, for very little within his writings evokes ease and comfort. Israel was in a dark period. The people had turned from God and were beginning to reap the consequences of their sin.

In chapter 18, the prophet used the example of a master potter working a lump of clay into a beautiful vessel to portray God's desire for His people. Israel's rebellion, however, had spoiled God's handiwork.

Jeremiah knew the course of destruction Israel had chosen. "Behold, like the clay in the potter's hand, so are you in My hand, O house of Israel," declared the Lord. The people answered God by saying, "It's hopeless! For we are going to follow our own plans, and each of us will act according to the stubbornness of his evil heart."

Jeremiah's age-old cry of alarm could be directed to us today. God, the Master Potter, still seeks to mold us into vessels of purity and holiness. However, many have been drawn aside by the temptations of the world.

Don't repeat Israel's mistake. Dedicate yourself to God, for His purpose and glory alone. You will then reap the blessings God freely bestows on those who love and honor Him.

Lord, I dedicate myself to You, Your purpose, and Your glory. Take this lump of clay I call my life and mold it into a beautiful vessel.

Stewards of His Grace

SCRIPTURE READING: 1 Peter 4:7–10   KEY VERSE: Romans 12:13

Distributing to the needs of the saints, given to hospitality.

H is Sunday school class began a supper club designed to help members get to know one another and to be a ministry to people outside the church.

Hosting one of the dinners was an ideal opportunity for involvement, but he was afraid to offer. *I'm living alone now,* he thought. *I don't cook that well, I don't know much about being a host, and it's been a while since I've had people over.* With great hesitation, he finally put his name on the list.

As the day approached, he was amazed when several class members called and volunteered to help him get ready. Some made food, some brought chairs, and others even donated festive decorations. The dinner was a success, and everyone felt welcomed and loved.

Hospitality isn't just for certain homemakers with large homes or a special knack for party throwing. The same command is given to all believers: "Be hospitable to one another without complaint. As each one has received a special gift, employ it in serving one another, as good stewards of the manifold grace of God" (1 Peter 4:9–10 NASB).

It doesn't matter how experienced or equipped you are. What counts is offering what the Lord has given you. God uses everything for His glory. Your home and belongings become a blessing many times over when you open them up to someone else.

> *Father God, use everything I have for Your glory—my home, my finances, my talents and abilities. Whatever I have, it's Yours.*

You Are a Missionary

SCRIPTURE READING: Romans 10:1–15   KEY VERSE: Romans 10:14

How then shall they call on Him in whom they have not believed? And how shall they believe in Him of whom they have not heard? And how shall they hear without a preacher?

Glancing over the bulletin as you settle into the pew on Sunday, you notice the sermon topic is missions. Privately you relax a little, anticipating stories of people in faraway places instead of a message of challenge and conviction.

As the pastor begins to speak, you tune out mentally. After all, you are not a missionary. You don't even know any missionaries personally. Why should you listen?

For a very good reason—Jesus gave the Great Commission to all His children (Matt. 28:18–20). God is the One who convicts and saves and sanctifies, but He calls you to be a part of that process on earth by being a witness for Christ.

Are you being disobedient if you do not leave home to tell others about Jesus? No. God does not call all believers to be traveling missionaries. He wants most of His children to stay at home and be testimonies to those around them.

But if you are a home missionary, you also have the privilege and responsibility of supporting those God has called. As brothers and sisters in the Lord and fellow laborers, they need your daily prayer and encouragement.

The next time someone talks about missions, listen closely. You're a missionary too.

Master, You have called me to be a witness. I am a missionary. Help me understand and fulfill this divine mandate.

People in Process

SCRIPTURE READING: Matthew 13:3–9, 18–23   KEY VERSE: Matthew 13:23

He who received seed on the good ground is he who hears the word and understands it, who indeed bears fruit and produces: some a hundredfold, some sixty, some thirty.

The seed and the soil are inseparably linked in nature's cycle of growth. Good seed must lodge in good soil if there is to be a harvest.

Jesus' parable of the soil and seed is familiar to most of us. His message is clear; it is the condition of the soil, not the content of the seed or the actions of the sower, that governs a person's response to the gospel of Christ.

This should bring a sigh of relief to many fervent evangelicals who wonder why people don't instantly and enthusiastically embrace Christ as Savior when the gospel is presented. There is no need to burden yourself with thoughts such as, *If only I had remembered that fourth point.* Nor should you run out and enlist in yet another study course in evangelism.

The seed, God's Word, is always good. It is the soil—the person's heart, personality, will, and emotions—that must be prepared to receive Christ.

God works by His Spirit through people and circumstances to attract men and women to faith in Christ. Evangelism is a process, and sharing your faith is part of the equation. But don't despair when the feedback is negative. When the conditions are right, faith will blossom.

Precious Lord, work by Your Spirit to attract those around me to Christ. When the timing is right, help me share the gospel in a way that faith will blossom.

God's Plan for Your Life

SCRIPTURE READING: Romans 1:14–16   KEY VERSE: Romans 1:16

I am not ashamed of the gospel of Christ, for it is the power of God to salvation for everyone who believes, for the Jew first and also for the Greek.

In his book on world missions, *In the Gap*, David Bryant shares a letter from a young student whose spiritual eyes had been opened to the importance of a missionary spirit:

> What really hit home to me the most was the fact that God wants us to live beyond the getting of things in life. Even as a Christian, I could see myself becoming an average college graduate, concerned only about getting through, getting out, and getting a job. I was feeling boxed in by my career in special education because preparing for it was taking too much of my time and energy.
>
> But as God spoke to me about being part of the great adventure of life by being a World Christian I started to see my career through God's eyes. I can see now that a career in special education is significant only as it relates to God's total plan for life as a World Christian.

Perhaps you, too, have felt "boxed in" by career or family. These are not liabilities at all, since work and family are integral parts of God's plan. Seek out information from your local church about the need for prayer and financial support for missions. Order a mission-centered magazine such as *The Short Term Mission Handbook*.

God's plan for your life is bigger than you can ever imagine.

Dear heavenly Father, give me a missionary spirit. Make me a World Christian. Open my spiritual eyes to new opportunities to become involved in Your divine plan.

You Are a Minister

SCRIPTURE READING: Zechariah 4:5–7   KEY VERSE: Colossians 1:27

To them God willed to make known what are the riches of the glory of this mystery among the Gentiles: which is Christ in you, the hope of glory.

He had been a Christian for ten years and often prayed for God to allow him to work for a Christian organization. However, as the years went by, God provided no change in his line of work. Eventually he began to wonder, *How can God use me in a place like this?*

Too often we look at those who work for churches and ministries and think what they are doing is the most important work for the kingdom of God. It is important, but so is what you are doing right where you are. Only you can accomplish what God has given you to do. Working in a Christian organization is no more sacred than working in a factory or department store as long as your motive is to honor God.

You may work with someone who is trapped in sin. You don't know it, but he feels helpless and longs for a way out. Because you know the Way, you also know the person who can break through his darkness with the light of eternal hope.

You are a minister of the gospel right where God has planted you. Praise Him for giving you this opportunity, and make every effort to take advantage of it. You are His only hope to a lost and dying world (Col. 1:27).

Almighty God, thank You for the opportunity to be a minister. Show me how to take advantage of it. Use me today—right where I am!

So Send I You

SCRIPTURE READING: John 20:19–23   KEY VERSE: John 20:21

Jesus said to them again, "Peace to you! As the Father has sent Me, I also send you."

George Grenfell (1849–1906), missionary and explorer of the Congo, made the following entry into his diary:

> Thank God we are safely back! It might have been otherwise, for we have encountered perils not a few. But the winds, which sometimes were simply terrific, and the rocks, which knocked three holes in the river steamer as we were running away at night from cannibals, have not wrecked us. We have been attacked by natives about twenty different times, we have been stoned and shot at with arrows, and have been the marks for more spears than we can count.

For thirty-two years, Grenfell labored in Africa planting churches. His memoirs read more like a war novel than a mission's report and detail wild hardships, dangers, and disappointments. Tenacious in his efforts to spread the gospel, he launched six voyages up the Congo River. The result was the establishment of several mission stations in an area that until his coming had remained unreachable.

This is not a time for fainthearted Christians. Grenfell sailed up the Congo for the gospel's glory. When you are faced with trials, remember these words: "So send I you," as well as the One who said them (John 20:21 KJV).

> *Dear God, this is no time for fainthearted Christians. Increase my dedication and commitment to fulfill Your call. You have sent me. I will go.*

Staying on Course

SCRIPTURE READING: Philippians 3:7–10   KEY VERSE: Philippians 3:8

Yet indeed I also count all things loss for the excellence of the knowledge of Christ Jesus my Lord, for whom I have suffered the loss of all things, and count them as rubbish, that I may gain Christ.

Jesus was very clear when He gave parting instructions to His followers: "Go therefore and make disciples of all the nations, baptizing them in the name of the Father and the Son and the Holy Spirit" (Matt. 28:19 NASB).

This is the mission of the church today—or should be. Some churches, large and small, drift away theologically and doctrinally from the absolute truth of Scripture. Others suffer from a lack of Christ-centered leadership, with much friction between the pastor and the staff. And some leaders forfeit the trust of the congregation by willfully pursuing sin. If not addressed, these problems bog down the church and cause it to lose sight of the ultimate purpose.

Take a serious look at the vitality and activity of your church:

• Is Bible teaching a priority?
• Is evangelism emphasized?
• Are people involved in service to the community?
• Is the worship service meeting the needs in your life?
• Are there real opportunities for fellowship and support?

If you find the answers to these questions less than satisfying, ask God to show you how to pray for its leaders. Be willing to obey Him, and make it your goal to worship with people who are committed to Christ above all else.

O Lord, let my church be a place where Your Word, worship, and evangelism are emphasized. Draw us to serve our community. Make our fellowship one of mutual support. Bless our leaders. Help us stay on course to accomplish our mission.

Wait on the Lord

SCRIPTURE READING: Psalm 27   KEY VERSE: Psalm 27:14

Wait on the LORD; be of good courage, and He shall strengthen your heart; wait, I say, on the LORD!

Most of us have heard the adage: "Timing is everything." The truth is, much of life does depend on correct timing. Runners pace their stride according to it. Olympic swimmers train by it. If a car's timing is off, it won't run well. Even the seasons change according to the earth's timing.

Timing is especially crucial for the Christian. David learned proper timing while hiding out from King Saul. Had he jumped ahead of God's plan and killed the envious king, he would have been out of sync with the Lord's will.

We can probably name at least once when, instead of waiting on the Lord, we moved on in our own strength. Whether we realized it or not, we missed a tremendous blessing.

Pushing to achieve what you want may result in a reached goal, but the victory is always bittersweet without God's anointing. Abraham learned this when he jumped ahead of God's plan for his life. Hagar was a human choice (Gen. 16). Sarah was God's divine choice.

When you wait on the Lord, you exercise faith. Ask Him to make the path He has chosen for your life very clear. It's better to wait and be sure than to move ahead, only to receive His second best.

> *Precious heavenly Father, I know it is better to be sure than to move ahead and receive only second best. Give me patience to wait instead of moving in my own strength. Make the path You have chosen for me clear.*

The Making of an Encourager

SCRIPTURE READING: 2 Corinthians 5:18–20   KEY VERSE: 2 Corinthians 5:20

We are ambassadors for Christ, as though God were pleading through us: we implore you on Christ's behalf, be reconciled to God.

In 2 Corinthians, Paul outlined several responsibilities we have as believers living by the grace of God. First, we are to comfort others with the same comfort we received from God. Second, we are to be reconcilers between sinful man and holy God. In the original Greek the word *reconcile* denotes a change from enmity to friendship. A person exchanges his sinfulness for a life of forgiveness and grace through Jesus Christ.

How many people do you know who are lost in sin and still feel worthy of God's love? Not many. Most have an overwhelming sense of guilt. They think there is no way for God to love them. But God loves each of us unconditionally. His forgiveness is based not on what we do right but on what Jesus did for us at Calvary.

Once saved, we become representatives of His love to people who desperately seek freedom from sin. To other believers, we are to be encouragers, committed to holding one another up in prayer and love.

Ask the Lord to guide you as you go through the day. Lay aside your judgmental attitude, and always remember you were once lost in sin until Jesus came to you through someone who was willing to share His love. Be committed to being trustworthy. When a person tells you an intimate detail, guard it with your life and refuse to betray his trust.

Father God, I want to be an encourager. Show me how to comfort others and direct them to reconcile with You.

Your Place in the Marketplace

SCRIPTURE READING: Ephesians 6:5–9   KEY VERSE: Colossians 3:23

Whatever you do, do it heartily, as to the Lord and not to men.

The slogan of a major automobile manufacturer is this: "Quality is job one." The company tells customers that its priority is sending top-notch cars off the assembly line. Manufacturers know that consumers look for quality in everything they buy. You don't want to purchase items you know are below par and don't represent someone's best effort.

The way you do your job every day reflects your personal quality standard. With each assignment or phone call or meeting, you tell others how you value your job and your employer. Do you work just enough to get by, or do you work at maximum capacity?

You can discover real and lasting motivation when you understand that your accountability is to Jesus Christ (Col. 3:24).

Perhaps your boss is unreasonable or your job doesn't meet your expectations. Maybe you aren't paid what you feel the position is worth. Remember, Jesus is the One who understands your needs and gives you the strength for every task, no matter how difficult or how trivial it may seem.

In every job, your goal is the same—to point those around you to your Savior and Master by working with a passion for excellence.

> *Dear Lord, help me work with a passion for excellence in all I do. Help me remember I am accountable to You. Let my personal standards point those around me to You.*

The Risk of Obeying God

SCRIPTURE READING: Luke 5:1–11   KEY VERSE: Luke 5:4

When He had stopped speaking, He said to Simon, "Launch out into the deep and let down your nets for a catch."

Once Jesus finished speaking to the crowd from the bow of Peter's boat, He turned to the brawny fisherman and said, "Put out into the deep water and let down your nets for the catch of a lifetime."

The idea seemed intriguing to Peter, but was it plausible? He was a leader, a man others turned to for wisdom concerning the sea. Jesus' request appeared preposterous, if not crazy. No one fished in the Sea of Galilee during the daytime. Fishing was done at night and in shallow water.

Yet Peter obediently responded, "Master . . . at Your bidding I will let down the nets" (Luke 5:5 NASB). Disregarding the questionable looks of his peers, Peter raised the ship's sails and headed out into deep water. The result of his obedience was a great abundance of fish, so many that the nets began to break and the boat began to sink.

What has God placed His finger on in your life that requires you to launch out into the deep? Is it a new job, a relationship that needs healing, an unmet goal?

Peter wasn't alone in the boat, and neither are you. Jesus sailed out there with him. So raise the sails of your life, put out into the deep, and prepare for a huge catch!

> *Dear heavenly Father, I know there are risks, but I am ready. I am willing to leave my comfort zone. I am raising the sails of my life, launching out into the deep, and preparing for a huge catch.*

OCTOBER

Journey to Revival

REPRESENTING: Refocusing on the Word and praising God

KEY VERSES: 2 Timothy 3:16–17

All Scripture is given by inspiration of God, and is profitable for doctrine, for reproof, for correction, for instruction in righteousness, that the man of God may be complete, thoroughly equipped for every good work.

The captives were returning! After years in Babylonian bondage, God's people were making their way across the rocky hills back to their promised land. Among the throngs of travelers was a man named Ezra, who had "prepared his heart to seek the Law of the LORD, and to do it, and to teach statutes and ordinances in Israel" (Ezra 7:10).

The book of Ezra and Nehemiah 8 record the tremendous revival that occurred when Ezra led God's people to renewed emphasis on the Word of God, prayer, and meditation.

Following Ezra's example, our spiritual journey this month leads to renewed emphasis on the Word of God, prayer, and meditation. We will learn the power of praise, how to pray, and how to lift the level of our praying. We will also discover the tremendous benefits of meditation—of sitting and waiting in God's presence.

Are you ready to go? Grab your Bible and a cup of coffee. Find a quiet corner. Take the phone off the hook. Put up the DO NOT DISTURB sign and let's begin.

Meeting with God

SCRIPTURE READING: Psalm 63   KEY VERSE: Colossians 4:2

Continue earnestly in prayer, being vigilant in it with thanksgiving.

A re you devoted to praise, prayer, and the Word? This kind of commitment to communing with God—sharing the deepest desires of your heart and praising Him for His goodness—is not a mystery. It's not a spiritual secret known only to a chosen few. By following some basic steps for preparation, you can develop the habit of meeting with God regularly:

Set a definite time. With hectic schedules and daily pressures, it's easy to let the day slip by unless you've made an "appointment" with God. Treat this worship as a meeting you can't break, and push other items on your list to a later time.

Set a definite place. It's best to find a quiet nook or secluded area where you won't be disturbed.

Establish a definite purpose. Prepare your heart with Bible study, and come to Him with a desire to build a relationship. If you ask Him, God will give you a growing passion to know Him more. Then time with God will be time you won't want to miss.

> *Dear Lord, deepen my relationship with You as I renew emphasis on prayer, meditation, and the Word. Help me make it a priority to meet with You regularly.*

Walking with God

SCRIPTURE READING: Psalm 23   KEY VERSE: Psalm 23:3

He restores my soul; He leads me in the paths of righteousness for His name's sake.

Think of the times when you and a friend walked down a country road, strolled along a stretch of beach, or took a long walk in the neighborhood. Perhaps you shared some concerns. Maybe you just talked pleasantly. Or you didn't say much at all. You simply enjoyed the company of a good friend.

This is the encouraging tenor that can describe your relationship with Jesus Christ. In several instances, the Bible talks about men walking with God (Gen. 5:22; 6:9). In the New Testament, believers are urged to walk in the Spirit, to keep in step with the Spirit's leadership. The grand, sweeping idea in all instances is that you can enjoy the sweet friendship of the personal Christ.

Sure, God wants obedience and holiness. But when we walk with Him— talking, listening, sharing, confessing—such spiritual traits naturally mark us. God is your Friend. He made you for glad-hearted fellowship with Him. He delights in your good company, spending time revealing His character, love, and wisdom to you.

You can be completely honest with the Father. You can talk about anything with Him. He isn't embarrassed, and you won't ever be condemned.

Your life in Christ is a relationship, and it is with the best Friend you could ever want. Enjoy His company and come into His presence with a joyful heart.

Lord, You are my best Friend. I come into Your presence to talk, listen, confess, and share. Thank You for Your friendship.

Made for Praise

SCRIPTURE READING: Psalm 19   KEY VERSES: Psalm 19:1–4

The heavens declare the glory of God; and the firmament shows His handiwork. Day unto day utters speech, and night unto night reveals knowledge. There is no speech nor language where their voice is not heard. Their line has gone out through all the earth, and their words to the end of the world. In them He has set a tabernacle for the sun.

Our Maker designed all creation to be to the praise of His glory. The tiniest pebble and the tallest mountain bear testimony to God's power and love. Warbling birds, chirping crickets, and croaking frogs all lend their special voices to the chorus.

Those who appreciate nature and the wonders of the environment from a godless perspective cannot fathom their real message. God intended the majesty of creation, even though its manifestations are now flawed by sin, to point us to Him (Rom. 1).

Have you ever been outdoors on a clear night in an open space, where there are no artificial lights to get in the way? You cannot count the thousands of stars in the sky. In that moment outside, your feelings of awe may well up so strongly inside, you are unable to speak.

Psalm 8:1 (NASB) is a wonderful prayer: "O Lord, our Lord, how majestic is Thy name in all the earth, who hast displayed Thy splendor above the heavens!"

O Lord, my Lord, how majestic is Thy name in all the earth, who hast displayed Thy splendor above the heavens!

Preparation for Praise

SCRIPTURE READING: 1 Chronicles 16:1–36   KEY VERSE: 1 Chronicles 16:24

Declare His glory among the nations, His wonders among all peoples.

S ome churches hold special services just for praise. The usual order of worship is set aside so that the entire time can be spent in the act of adoration of the Lord. Singing, prayer, and personal testimonies of God's goodness are often key ingredients in such gatherings.

The idea of a praise service isn't a new one, though. In the days of King David, the ark of the covenant was about to be returned to Jerusalem after months in the house of Obed-Edom (1 Chron. 14–16). However, David had earlier made a grievous mistake and angered the Lord. He decided to bring the ark to Jerusalem by transporting it in a manner directly opposing what God commanded.

David learned his lesson well, and his heart was filled with rejoicing at the blessing that would soon come to his people as a result of their obedience. At his directive, the priests made burnt sacrifices to God. A loaf of bread and some meat were given to every man and woman in the land, and spirits were bursting with anticipation.

Then came the final and most important part of the worship preparation: "He [David] appointed some of the Levites as ministers before the ark of the LORD, even to celebrate and to thank and praise the LORD God" (1 Chron. 16:4 NASB). David consecrated a time of praise, and that is what God wants you to do in response to His work.

Father, prepare my heart for praise. Let me learn its value and practice it regularly in response to Your wonderful works.

The Cure for a Heavy Heart

SCRIPTURE READING: 1 Peter 2:1–10   KEY VERSE: 1 Peter 2:9

You are a chosen generation, a royal priesthood, a holy nation, His own special people, that you may proclaim the praises of Him who called you out of darkness into His marvelous light.

Praise seems to be a natural part of what we want to do when things are going our way. But on the days when the dishwasher breaks or the children are sick or the mechanic gives you bad news about the car, it is much more difficult to be effusive with thanksgiving.

God understands how your emotions are built; He made them. He also knows the cure for a heart weighed down by concerns and irritations—praise.

Praise focuses your attention upon God. When you take a long and deliberate look at the character and ways of the Lord who loved you enough to die for you, your eyes are naturally shifted away from the difficulty and onto His ability to care for you.

Praise increases your faith. Telling God what you love about Him always involves reciting His past actions of might and power on your behalf. You can look back at the times He sent special provision at just the right moment and thank Him for them. This process results in a heart that expands with joy and security in Him.

Praise gives you a sense of identity. When you praise God, you act as one who belongs to Him. According to 1 Peter 2:9 (NASB), you are a member of "a people for God's own possession, that you may proclaim the excellencies of Him who has called you out of darkness into His marvelous light." That is reason enough to praise Him forever.

Lord, on difficult days—when I don't feel like it—I still want to praise You. Thank You for delivering me from darkness into light. That is reason enough to praise You forever.

A Heart of True Praise

SCRIPTURE READING: John 12:1–8   KEY VERSES: Psalm 73:25–26

Whom have I in heaven but You? And there is none upon earth that I desire besides You. My flesh and my heart fail; but God is the strength of my heart and my portion forever.

The scene was familiar. Jesus was at Lazarus's house in Bethany, reclining at the table with His friends. How He loved spending time there. However, the dynamics of their relationship had changed dramatically. Only six days ago, Jesus raised Lazarus from the dead in a miracle that drew many to faith.

Mary's relationship with the Lord had changed as well. She knew His death was at hand. Warren Wiersbe comments, "She anointed both His head and His feet. It was an act of pure love on her part, for she knew her Lord was about to endure suffering and death . . . In a sense, Mary was showing her devotion to Jesus before it was too late . . . Her act of love and worship was public, spontaneous, sacrificial, lavish, personal, and unembarrassed."

Quietly she knelt down next to Jesus at the table, and without a word, she delicately poured out every ounce of perfume onto His feet. Then she wiped the costly rivulets away with her hair until the entire house was filled with the aroma of the nard and with the even sweeter fragrance of her sacrifice.

Praise doesn't have a single, narrow definition. Praise can be Mary's gentle, silent gift that expressed the longing of her heart to worship. Praising is singing songs and saying private prayers. As you grow in the Lord, your praise will assume many forms; and all are worthy when given out of love for God.

Master, give me a heart of true praise. Spontaneous. Lavish. Personal. Unembarrassed. I praise You!

Your Umbilical Cord to God

SCRIPTURE READING: Jeremiah 33:1–3   KEY VERSE: Psalm 17:6

I have called upon You, for You will hear me, O God; incline Your ear to me, and hear my speech.

How often do you find yourself dropping into bed at night without having told God you love Him? God is not controlled by emotions, but He does have them. Think of Jesus crying at Lazarus's tomb, compassionately looking into the face of Mary as she anointed His feet with oil, or rearranging His daily plans to meet with the woman at the well. His love, His deep sense of caring, motivated Him to reach out to others.

We reach out to Him through prayer. This is your umbilical cord to God. If it becomes damaged through sin or complacency, your fellowship with Him is the first thing that suffers. The enemy's intent is to draw you away from spending time with Christ in prayer. He will do anything to distract, discourage, and cause you to doubt God's good will for your life.

How do you combat this type of covert activity? For one, be creative in your prayer time. God knows your daily schedule. Ask Him to help you organize your day so that you may spend time with Him at some point. Rising earlier or staying up later are simple options.

The heart is the key. God sees your intentions—good or bad. If you are sincere in your desire to pray to Him, He will open the door to intimacy between you and His Son.

Precious Lord, strengthen the cords of prayer that bind my spirit to Yours. Help me organize my day so that I can spend more time with You. Open the door to intimacy between us.

Teach Us to Pray

SCRIPTURE READING: Luke 11:1–4   KEY VERSE: Mark 1:35

In the morning, having risen a long while before daylight, He went out and departed to a solitary place; and there He prayed.

In the first chapter of the book of Mark, we are given a rare glimpse into the early days of Jesus' ministry. The twelve disciples had not been chosen, but Andrew, James, John, and Peter were already emerging as followers of Christ.

In Mark 1:35–37 (NASB), we read for the first time of Jesus' prayer life: "In the early morning, while it was still dark, He arose and went out and departed to a lonely place, and was praying there. And Simon and his companions hunted for Him; and they found Him, and said to Him, 'Everyone is looking for You.'"

Jesus' behavior was not the norm. He didn't always go to the temple to pray as everyone else did. Instead, He arose early to be alone with God. But His goal in prayer wasn't to complete a ritual; it was to communicate with His heavenly Father and to gain refreshment for His soul.

Later, Luke recorded a different scenario as Jesus interacted with His disciples. The same men were the ones thirsty for what Jesus was experiencing with the Father. They, too, wanted to know that type of holy communion and pleaded, "Lord, teach us to pray" (Luke 11:1).

God loves us and He wants to make His love apparent. Would you, too, yearn along with the disciples, "Lord, teach me to pray"?

Teach me to pray, Lord. I want to experience the same intimate communion that You had with the Father. Help me set aside time to learn.

Prayer Protection

SCRIPTURE READING: Ephesians 6:11–18   KEY VERSE: Ephesians 6:11

Put on the whole armor of God, that you may be able to stand against the wiles of the devil.

It's late in the evening. You sit down to enjoy God's Word and pray. But soon after you bow your head, your mind wanders. An evil thought creeps in and won't go away. *Where did that come from?* you wonder. You try once more to put your focus on the Lord. As the minutes go by, however, you feel sleepier and sleepier. Before you know it, you're waking up the next morning.

This scenario is a familiar one, and for good reason. Satan is pleased when your attention is diverted, and you feel like a failure in your prayer life. He knows God can use you most effectively when you pray, and harming your prayer life is the fastest way to short-circuit your ability to serve Him.

That's why God has given you special prayer protection. The spiritual armor that guards your faith is also designed to keep you firm and strong as you talk to God. The breastplate of righteousness will keep your mind pure; the shield of faith will help you put out "the flaming missiles of the evil one" (Eph. 6:16 NASB).

Ask God to fit you with His armor when you pray. Trust the Lord to guard your time with Him. If you fail, don't be depressed. God still waits for you. The victory in the battle of prayer is yours.

> *Almighty God, I claim Your prayer protection—the breastplate of righteousness, the shield of faith, the helmet of salvation, the girdle of truth. Victory in the battle of prayer is mine!*

Praying in a Crisis

SCRIPTURE READING: James 5:13–18   KEY VERSE: Philippians 4:6

Be anxious for nothing, but in everything by prayer and supplication, with thanksgiving, let your requests be made known to God.

Have you ever noticed how squirrels react to oncoming cars? Many times they run to one side of the road only to return to the middle. They teeter back and forth in indecision and often come out on the losing end of the contest.

How do you respond to crises? Are you cool and surefooted, or do you race around, frantically searching for a solution?

God promises to meet your needs regardless of the circumstance. But in doing so, He wants you to come to Him in faith during crises. Through prayer, He brings encouragement, hope, and guidance.

When we pray, God turns His attention toward us. Even though there is never a moment when we are outside His thoughts, prayer brings us into an even closer relationship with Him. He sees our faith and responds in faithfulness.

God knows when you face a crisis, and He goes before you to bring about a solution on your behalf.

The apostle Paul told us, "Be anxious for nothing, but in everything by prayer and supplication with thanksgiving let your requests be made known to God. And the peace of God, which surpasses all comprehension, shall guard your hearts and your minds in Christ Jesus" (Phil. 4:6–7 NASB).

> *O Lord, I often panic in crises and frantically search for my own solutions, not realizing You have gone before me to make a way. Calm my anxieties, and teach me to trust in You.*

Thy Kingdom Come

SCRIPTURE READING: Matthew 6:5–15   KEY VERSE: Matthew 26:39

He went a little farther and fell on His face, and prayed, saying, "O My Father, if it is possible, let this cup pass from Me; nevertheless, not as I will, but as You will."

C S. Lewis wrote, "Prayer is request. The essence of request, as distinct from compulsion, is that it may or may not be granted. And if an infinitely wise Being listens to the requests of finite and foolish creatures, of course He will sometimes grant and sometimes refuse them." Lewis was clearly writing from personal experience because he said later, "If God had granted all the silly prayers I've made in my life, where should I be now?"

Have you ever looked back at past circumstances and been grateful God did not give you what you wanted? It is a common experience. As human beings, we cannot see life from God's infinite and all-wise perspective.

That is why Jesus taught us how to pray with these words: "Our Father who art in heaven, hallowed be Thy name. Thy kingdom come. Thy will be done, on earth as it is in heaven" (Matt. 6:9–10 NASB). He told us to begin with the humble acknowledgment that we do not know best, but God does.

Jesus in the Garden of Gethsemane, shortly before His arrest and crucifixion, prayed, "My Father, if it is possible, let this cup pass from Me; yet not as I will, but as Thou wilt" (Matt. 26:39 NASB). Setting all theological debates aside, it is important to recognize Jesus' submission to the Father.

If you have not ever thanked God for being a wise Father to you, begin today.

Dear God, thank You for the times You have denied my requests. You know best. Thank You for being a wise Father.

The Priority of Prayer

SCRIPTURE READING: Daniel 6   KEY VERSE: Psalm 84:2

My soul longs, yes, even faints for the courts of the LORD; my heart and my flesh cry out for the living God.

The story of Daniel in the lions' den is one of high drama. The action is so captivating that it is easy to overlook the reason why King Darius had Daniel thrown into the pit of hungry beasts.

The cause of Darius's anger was not nearly as dramatic as the outcome. It was Daniel, quietly going about his daily business of prayer. Ordinarily his faithfulness would not have been a problem, but Daniel's enemies decided to use it against him by making it a crime to pray to anyone except Darius.

What was Daniel's response?

Now when Daniel knew that the document [the law to pray to Darius] was signed, he entered his house (now in his roof chamber he had windows open toward Jerusalem); and he continued kneeling on his knees three times a day, praying and giving thanks before his God, as he had been doing previously. Then these men came by agreement and found Daniel making petition and supplication before his God. (Dan. 6:10–11 NASB)

Daniel was not about to alter his commitment to prayer to protect himself. He could have prayed somewhere else besides his upper chamber with windows. But Daniel knew that to give in was to demonstrate a lack of faith.

Most important, prayer was more than an issue over which to make a statement. Daniel did not want to give up prayer because it was his means of fellowship with almighty God.

Precious heavenly Father, help me make prayer a priority. As I make this spiritual journey into Your presence each day, I know You will meet me there.

Devoted to Prayer

SCRIPTURE READING: Matthew 14:13–23   KEY VERSE: Luke 5:16

He Himself often withdrew into the wilderness and prayed.

E ven with all of the crowds pressing around Him, with continual requests and a desire just to be with Him, Jesus sought time alone with His Father. Jesus made clear what He believed is the most important part of fellowship with God. In spite of the demands on His energy, He made communing with God His priority.

Is prayer the first thing on your list for the day? The last? Somewhere in between? Read what the apostle Paul said to the believers in the church at Colosse: "Devote yourselves to prayer, keeping alert in it with an attitude of thanksgiving" (Col. 4:2 NASB).

The word *devote* here doesn't convey the complete meaning of the original Greek, which was "giving constant attention to" or "persevering." We are to make the conscious decision to set aside time to talk to the Father and to listen to Him as He works in our hearts by the Holy Spirit and His Word.

It is tremendously helpful to set a specific time to pray. Make an "appointment" with the Lord, and write it down on your list for the day. If you keep in mind that you are making arrangements for a special encounter with God, you will treat this meeting accordingly.

You can combat the clamor of the day to find victory and joy in prayer, and a vital part of doing so is finding freedom from avoidable distractions.

Ask God to show you how rich your relationship with Him can be.

Father God, I make a conscious decision today to set aside time to talk with You. Set me free from avoidable distractions. Show me how rich our relationship can be.

Starting a Prayer Journal

SCRIPTURE READING: 1 Thessalonians 5:16–18   KEY VERSE: Psalm 48:9

We have thought, O God, on Your lovingkindness, in the midst of Your temple.

Have you ever considered the value of keeping a prayer journal? It's a record of your prayer relationship with God so that you can remember what you talked about with Him.

It works in this way. After you pray, write in a small notebook what you have said, along with the date. As God answers a particular item, draw a single line through the request, so that you can still read it, and put the date of the answer at the end of the line. When you review the journal, you can rejoice at His provision. You will be able to say, "God loves me. He is interested in me. I am growing in my faith, and He is working in my life."

What a thrill it is to trace His involvement and see your spiritual growth unfold as you trust Him, releasing all of your worries and problems to Him. As you pour out your heart to Him, you feel His tender care.

In addition, prayer is a purification process. God changes more than just your outlook on external things; He opens your eyes to aspects of your behavior and attitude that were not obvious before. As you respond to His conviction and make the appropriate changes through His strength, your character is molded more and more into the likeness of Jesus.

A prayer journal will help you observe and chronicle this process for yourself and others.

> *Lord, I cherish the ways You've answered me in the past. Thank You for loving me and working in my life.*

Changing People Through Prayer

SCRIPTURE READING: Colossians 1:3–12   KEY VERSE: Colossians 1:3

We give thanks to the God and Father of our Lord Jesus Christ, praying always for you.

Paul had a tender longing for the churches he helped to establish because he was physically separated from them by time and sheer distance. Yet he could pray for them, lifting their needs and desires to the Lord for fulfillment. You can do the same thing for loved ones, and in the process of working on their behalf God also moves in your life.

Paul's effective prayer for the Colossian believers was characterized by three life-transforming qualities.

First, it was continuous. He said, "We have not ceased to pray for you" (Col. 1:9 NASB). As often as they came to his mind and he was stirred by love, he asked God to fill them with wisdom and a knowledge of His will.

Second, his prayer was God centered. He must have known of many particular needs, perhaps for food or clothing or protection from government interference. But Paul did not list them in detail; instead, he focused on who the Lord is and what He can do, which includes a very individual concern.

Third, in the area of God's ability, Paul was very specific. He asked God to help them walk in a manner worthy of Christ, to hold them in obedience, to give them discernment in decisions. Those spiritual benefits apply to any situation.

Heavenly Father, make me faithful in praying for others with whom You have entrusted me spiritually. Keep them walking worthy of You. Give them discernment in their decisions, and make them obedient in their response to Your commands.

Powerful Praying

SCRIPTURE READING: Colossians 1:9–14   KEY VERSE: Hebrews 10:19

Therefore, brethren, having boldness to enter the Holiest by the blood of Jesus.

A striking feature of Paul's prayers is their sheer power. He was a gifted evangelist with a mastery of language that God used to capture intense spiritual truth. His prayers serve as models of how you can approach God in prayer with the boldness and confidence that are yours because of Jesus' sacrifice.

Paul's prayers dealt with issues and ideas that would bring victory in any situation. In Colossians 1:9 (NASB), he asked for the believers of the Colossian church to "be filled with the knowledge of [God's] will in all spiritual wisdom and understanding."

You need the Lord's infinite and exacting wisdom every moment of your life, and asking God to fill your heart and mind with wisdom means consciously acknowledging that you need Him. This prayer is so rock-solid because it is based in part on a promise of wisdom in James 1:5, and praying from the basis of God's promises is an excellent way to be sure that you ask Him for something within His purposes.

Paul's whole motivation for requesting wisdom and power from God was the glorification of Jesus: "So that you may walk in a manner worthy of the Lord, to please Him in all respects, bearing fruit in every good work and increasing in the knowledge of God" (Col. 1:10 NASB).

You don't have to settle for timid requests. You can pray within the privilege of your eternal position as a beloved one in Christ.

Father, give me power in prayer. Give me boldness in place of timidity. Make me a warrior in the spiritual realm.

Lifting the Level of Your Praying

SCRIPTURE READING: Ephesians 1:15–23   KEY VERSE: James 4:2

*You lust and do not have. You murder and covet and cannot obtain. You fight
and war. Yet you do not have because you do not ask.*

Doctor R. A. Torrey caught the crowd before him off guard as he quoted
James 4:2: "You do not have because you do not ask." He went on to explain,

These words contain the secret of the poverty and powerlessness of the average
Christian, of the average minister, and of the average church . . .

Many wonder why do I have so little victory over sin? Why do I win so few
souls to Christ? Why do I grow so slowly into the likeness of my Lord and Savior
Jesus Christ? And God answers . . . "Neglect of prayer. You have not, because you
ask not." . . .

Prayer has as much power today, when men and women are themselves on
praying ground and meeting the conditions of prevailing prayer, as it ever has
had. God has not changed, and His ear is just as quick to hear the voice of real
prayer and His hand is just as long and strong to save as they ever were.

When you pray, ask God to reveal His will for your life and the situation
you are facing. Don't just get caught up in praying for material gain. God provides where there is a need. His greatest desire is for you to learn to trust Him
in prayer.

Torrey's admonishment is valid, and the only way to receive the blessings
of Christ is to get to know the God of all peace and comfort. Lift the level of
your praying, and you will see the evidence of His hand over your life.

*Lift the level of my praying, Lord. Reveal Your will for my life and circum-
stances, then help me obediently follow the pathway You have chosen for me.*

Praying for Others

SCRIPTURE READING: Romans 15:29–33   KEY VERSE: Acts 2:42

They continued steadfastly in the apostles' doctrine and fellowship, in the breaking of bread, and in prayers.

Often the phrase "pray for me" is used with a casual air, as a typical closing for talks with other believers when discussing problems or difficulties. There is nothing wrong with using this phrase frequently, of course, but the importance of the request can be lost in the shuffle when it becomes part of the conversational routine.

The apostle Paul never asked for prayer in an offhand manner. When he said, "Pray for me," he fully expected those who heard his appeal to bring his needs before the Lord in earnestness on a regular basis.

Paul wrote, "Now I urge you, brethren, by our Lord Jesus Christ and by the love of the Spirit, to strive together with me in your prayers to God for me" (Rom. 15:30 NASB). He knew how much he needed the Lord's direction and protection as he entered potentially hostile regions, rarely knowing what kind of reaction the gospel message would receive.

God does not require your prayers in order to function in others' lives; instead, He allows your times of communication with Him to be used as demonstrations of His intimate involvement in daily affairs. In Romans 15:32 (NASB), Paul expressed anticipation for the future and his desire to find "refreshing rest" in their company. Part of that mutual joy resulted from the vital connection of prayer, and that is the satisfaction you can receive from prayer for others.

O God, it is a solemn responsibility with which You have entrusted me. Make me faithful to pray for others on a regular basis.

A Temple for His Presence

SCRIPTURE READING: 2 Chronicles 7:12–18   KEY VERSE: 2 Chronicles 7:15

My eyes will be open and My ears attentive to prayer made in this place.

Solomon had just completed the construction of the temple. Sacrifices were made to God along with a commitment to follow the Lord all the days of his life. God was pleased, and in 2 Chronicles, He acknowledged Solomon's devotion: "My eyes shall be open and My ears attentive to the prayer offered in this place" (2 Chron. 7:15 NASB).

In her book *Adventures in Prayer,* Catherine Marshall declared,

> God insists that we pray, not because He needs to know our situation, but because we need the spiritual discipline of asking. Similarly, making our requests specific forces us to take a step forward in faith.
>
> The reason many of us retreat into vague generalities when we pray is not because we think too highly of God, but because we think too little. If we pray for something definite and our request is not granted, we fear to lose the little faith we had. So we fall back on the safe route of highly "spiritual" prayers— the kind that Jesus brushed aside as not true prayer at all, just self-deceptive "talking to ourselves."

As Solomon stepped back and viewed the glory of the temple of God, he was struck with the awesome reality of God's presence all about him. The shekinah glory of God literally filled the place.

When you pray, allow God to expose the true devotion of your heart. Ask Him to cleanse you and make you a temple fit for His presence.

Master, expose the true devotion of my heart. Cleanse me and make me a temple fit for Your presence.

Lord, Make Me!

SCRIPTURE READING: Ephesians 3:14–21   KEY VERSE: Ephesians 3:16

He would grant you, according to the riches of His glory, to be strengthened with might through His Spirit in the inner man.

I n his book *Walking with Christ in the Details of Life,* Patrick Morley explains the growth of the prayer life:

> We are needy people. When God found us, we were consumed with needs: relational, emotional, financial, moral, psychological, and spiritual needs ... It seems quite natural, then, that until our temporal lives begin to straighten out, temporal needs would preoccupy our early prayers. The distinctive of our prayers in this first phase of our spiritual life is that they are prayers of petition ...
>
> When once we see the faithfulness of God to care for us, we want to learn how to follow Him. We come to that point where we want to surrender the silliness of our own ideas to the way of the Lord. Instead of praying, "Lord, give me," we start praying, "Lord, make me." Surrendering to the will of God becomes pre-eminent in our thinking.

This maturity in attitude is implied in what the apostle Paul prayed for the Ephesian church. The day-to-day concerns of the believers were essentially no different from yours today, but notice what Paul requested for them: "That He would grant you, according to the riches of His glory, to be strengthened with power through His Spirit in the inner man" (Eph. 3:16 NASB).

The Lord wants you to come to Him for even the smallest detail. But He wants you to feel free to pray for deeper spiritual riches as well.

Precious Lord, make me! I surrender to Your will. Strengthen my inner man with power through Your Spirit according to the riches of Your glory.

Our Textbook

SCRIPTURE READING: 2 Timothy 3:10–17   KEY VERSE: Psalm 119:2

Blessed are those who keep His testimonies, who seek Him with the whole heart!

Noah Webster, the early nineteenth-century scholar most famous for his dictionary, wrote the following in the preface of his American edition of the Bible:

> The Bible is the chief moral cause of all that is good, and the best book for regulating the . . . concerns of men . . . The principles of genuine liberty, and of wise laws and administrations, are to be drawn from the Bible and sustained by its authority. The man, therefore, who weakens or destroys the divine authority of that Book may be accessory to all the public disorders which society is doomed to suffer . . . There are two powers only, sufficient to control men and secure the rights of individuals . . . the combined force of religion and law.

Over the centuries, countless men and women have dedicated and sometimes sacrificed their lives for the cause of bringing God's Word to people who need it desperately. From translators and linguistic experts to international missionaries, these individuals understood the importance of each person having access to a Bible and being able to read it in his own language.

The best way to cherish the Scriptures is to use them as 2 Timothy 3:16–17 describes, as a living guide for real life. Don't let it sit on a shelf or by your bed gathering dust. God's timeless truth has the power to transform your life when you give it the opportunity.

Dear heavenly Father, thank You for Your Word. It has strengthened me. It has kept me. It has changed my life.

Drifting from His Word

SCRIPTURE READING: Psalm 119:9–16   KEY VERSE: Psalm 119:105

Your word is a lamp to my feet and a light to my path.

The Bible is as relevant today as it was when it was first written. The pages of Scripture are timeless principles explaining God's nature and redemptive plan for mankind.

The Bible also gives us an account of the various ways God deals with His people. It even helps us understand ourselves better. Scripture is a constant source of encouragement, instructing us to have hope in hopeless situations and to seek God and His victory when defeat seems imminent.

If you truly want to know God, know His Word. Everything He has spoken through Scripture is for a purpose—not just so that we might have a list of rules and regulations, but so that we might know Him better.

When we fail to read and study the Bible, our communication line to God is weakened. Drifting from His Word leads to self-reliance and isolation from God. We begin to live separate from His will by trying to accomplish things in our own strength. Without this guidance, life is empty and disappointing.

It is never too late to build a fruitful relationship with the Lord. The moment you pick up His Word, He takes the initiative to reveal Himself to you: "Thy word is a lamp to my feet, and a light to my path" (Ps. 119:105 NASB).

Almighty God, I do not want to drift from Your Word. It is a lamp to my feet and a light to my path. Without it, I cannot make this spiritual journey.

Cherish the Word

SCRIPTURE READING: Deuteronomy 6:1–9   KEY VERSE: Deuteronomy 6:6

These words which I command you today shall be in your heart.

A re you a list maker? Most people at least jot down their grocery items on a piece of paper before heading to the store. It's so easy to forget the little details that we need to keep checklists to help us remember.

We're just as forgetful concerning God's Word many times. The Lord understands our natural weaknesses and our tendency to mentally push aside thoughts we don't deem urgent at the moment. That is why He commanded His people to keep His words ever before them:

> *These words, which I am commanding you today, shall be on your heart; and you shall teach them diligently to your sons and shall talk of them when you sit in your house and when you walk by the way and when you lie down and when you rise up. And you shall bind them as a sign on your hand and they shall be as frontals on your forehead. And you shall write them on the doorposts of your house and on your gates. (Deut. 6:6–9 NASB)*

In other words, they were to put God's Word in the paths of their daily lives, everywhere they went and as a part of all they did. How can you do the same today? Find some verses that pertain to your personal circumstances, and write them out on cards. Keep the cards with you or in a prominent place in your home. You'll be surprised how quickly they become a part of your everyday thinking and you will learn to cherish His Word.

> **Dear God, write Your Word on my heart. O Lord, teach me to cherish it and make it a vital part of my everyday life.**

Sharpen Your Shovel

SCRIPTURE READING: Proverbs 1   KEY VERSE: Psalm 19:10

More to be desired are they than gold, yea, than much fine gold; sweeter also than honey and the honeycomb.

If you were an explorer, and you had a guaranteed, accurate map directing you to buried treasure, you would be committed to uncovering it, wouldn't you? Nothing would deter you from the expedition. You would have a shovel in hand and a single-minded purpose that was not deterred by any difficulty.

Did you know that God's Word is a treasure? It's true, and not just in an obscure or abstract way. The Bible is truth, God's unerring, unfailing, and eternal revelation to mankind. Every principle is rock-solid; you can bank your very life on what it says.

King David, who possessed much wealth, expressed the worth of Scripture in these poetic terms: "The law of the LORD is perfect, restoring the soul; the testimony of the LORD is sure, making wise the simple. The precepts of the LORD are right, rejoicing the heart . . . They are more desirable than gold, yes, than much fine gold; sweeter also than honey and the drippings of the honeycomb" (Ps. 19:7–10 NASB).

These are the words of a rich man, yet he found the Word of the Lord richer still. If you have read the Bible for years, you can certainly testify to its growing sweetness. If you are just beginning to "mine" in Scripture, you need to sharpen your shovel and get ready to dig—you'll never reach the bottom.

O Lord, sharpen my spiritual shovel. I want to mine the wealth of Your Word. I am ready to dig into Your limitless resources.

Your Fertility Factor

SCRIPTURE READING: Matthew 13:1–9 KEY VERSE: Matthew 13:9

He who has ears to hear, let him hear!

The parable of the sower and the seeds is a story about how we listen to God's Word. Some people are unreceptive, some are so-so, and some are fertile and ready to burst forth with growth. Here are some key ways to enhance your "fertility factor":

Commit yourself to listening carefully. When you are involved in Bible study, wherever you are, make the conscious decision to keep your ears open and your concentration focused.

Resist all outside clutter. Part of concentration means getting rid of distractions. If you're at home, don't position yourself next to the phone or the TV or the refrigerator. Even with all the willpower in the world, you set yourself up for a wandering mind.

Evaluate your spiritual needs right away. When the study session is over, take some time to look back over your notes and determine which points are personally applicable. If the message was especially long or intense and you need to back away for a while, write down a specific time for later to review what you learned.

These tips may seem obvious at first glance, but developing a disciplined routine in Bible study pays off tomorrow as you form good habits. With proper management, good soil becomes productive over the years as nutrients seep in and penetrate each layer.

Precious heavenly Father, make the soil of my life more productive as the nutrients of Your Word penetrate each layer. Enhance my fertility factor.

Are You a Good Listener?

SCRIPTURE READING: James 1:21–25   KEY VERSE: James 1:22

Be doers of the word, and not hearers only, deceiving yourselves.

A re you a good listener? One young man became so perplexed over his inability to remember, he decided to tape much of what was told to him. He even went so far as to keep a tape recorder in the car to record his thoughts and prayers to God. In our fast-paced world, many of us may find ourselves desiring to follow his example.

However, the mind's ability to remember, process, and code information is amazing. Yet researchers tell us we use very little of the brain's capacity to think, reason, and recall past events. Even if you feel that you are a poor listener, God can change that.

Your brain is like a muscle; the more you use it, the stronger it becomes. Memorizing Scripture increases your ability to think and reason. Doctors agree that when you force the brain to activity, even if it has been injured, it will seek a way to get the task done. Truly we are fearfully and wonderfully made.

An important part of being a good listener is making sure you have a teachable spirit. If you have a closed mind to God's Word, or if you are passive in your spiritual outlook, chances are, you will retain very little of what God is saying.

Ask the Lord to make you sensitive to His voice. Plan your spiritual activity to include times spent in prayer and seeking His will for your life. If your greatest desire is to know Him, He will give you the desires of your heart.

> *Father God, make me a good listener. Give me a teachable spirit that is open to Your Word. Make me sensitive to Your voice. Deliver me from spiritual passivity.*

Life's Most Important Activity

SCRIPTURE READING: Exodus 3:1–6   KEY VERSE: Exodus 3:4

When the LORD saw that he turned aside to look, God called to him from the midst of the bush and said, "Moses, Moses!" And he said, "Here I am."

God got Moses' attention in a spectacular way. Moses was going about his daily business when he saw the bush consumed in flame, yet not being consumed: "When the LORD saw that he turned aside to look, God called to him from the midst of the bush, and said, 'Moses, Moses!' And he said, 'Here I am'" (Ex. 3:4 NASB).

You've heard this story many times before, but have you ever noticed that Moses "turned aside to look"? In other words, he stopped what he was doing and moved his focus in a different direction—the direction of God. When he did, he was rewarded with a special, life-changing encounter.

You can have a time of meeting with God, too, by entering His presence in prayer and by reading His Word. Remember, Jesus lives in you through the power of the Holy Spirit, so His presence is always with you. However, you have active fellowship with Him as you meditate on His words to you.

Meditation quiets your spirit. God told Moses to be mindful that he was standing on holy ground. Moses was so awed and reverent that he followed God's command to remove his shoes.

Meditation enlarges your view of God. Moses walked away with a new mission and a sense of God's huge purposes for His people. You will discover more about God's purposes for you when you turn aside to worship Him.

Dear Lord, quiet my spirit. Enlarge my view of Your omnipotence. Give me a new mission and sense of purpose as I wait before You.

Sitting Before the Lord

SCRIPTURE READING: 2 Samuel 7:18–28 KEY VERSE: 2 Samuel 7:18

King David went in and sat before the LORD; and he said: "Who am I, O Lord GOD? And what is my house, that You have brought me this far?"

A re you confused? Unsure of what the next step might be? Anxious about the future? Perplexed over the problems that still beset you?

Perhaps the time is right to meditate on God's Word. God's Word is wisdom for your uncertainty, peace for your anxiety, comfort in times of trouble and turmoil. Meditating on the Scriptures is much like enjoying a good meal. How much would you savor the flavor and nourishment of your favorite food if you placed it on your fork, put it in your mouth, and then immediately took it out again?

When we meditate on God's Word, we taste its rich goodness and receive its energizing life. God's truths are absorbed into the inner man. They are no longer hollow or superficial. There is nothing complex about biblical meditation. Get out your Bible, and locate some Scriptures that are relevant to your need. Then ask God two questions: "Lord, what are You saying here?" and "Lord, what are You saying to *me* through this passage of Scripture?"

The answer may come quickly. You may need to wait, but know that God hears you and will answer you. Apply what you know to be true, and lean on God's sufficiency. He will sustain you and see you through your problem.

Father, I am confused, anxious, and perplexed. I wait in Your presence.
What do You have to say to me today?

The Benefits of Meditation

SCRIPTURE READING: Psalm 145   KEY VERSE: Psalm 145:5

I will meditate on the glorious splendor of Your majesty, and on Your wondrous works.

Meditation on God's Word brings countless benefits to your relationship with the Lord. Do you long for deeper intimacy? Do you want the source of strength that comes from acknowledging God as Provider? Coming before the Lord with a genuine desire to know Him more is the foundation of your faith.

Meditation quiets your spirit. You cannot humble yourself before God and open up your thoughts and feelings to Him without experiencing His gentle touch. Your spirit calms down from the stress of living as you realize how much He cares for you.

Meditation purifies your heart. Have you ever been reading your Bible and felt God tugging at your heart about something you said or did? That is the work of the Holy Spirit, who is making you more like Christ. In the process called sanctification, God brings your heart in tune with His.

Meditation increases your discernment. "All Scripture is inspired by God and profitable for teaching, for reproof, for correction, for training in righteousness" (2 Tim. 3:16 NASB). You'll know what is right by the standard of His Word.

Meditation confirms good counsel and exposes the bad. When you know what God says, you can evaluate the words of others. Compare all counsel to God's Word before you accept it. Meditation is the first step to knowing what He says.

O God, I wait before You. Please quiet my spirit, purify my heart, and increase my discernment. Confirm the good counsel I receive, and expose the bad. Strengthen the foundation of my faith.

A Fresh Encounter with God

SCRIPTURE READING: Isaiah 6:1–9   KEY VERSE: Psalm 139:3

You comprehend my path and my lying down, and are acquainted with all my ways.

Have you ever approached your devotional time with the idea of actually meeting with God? It is easy to reduce a quiet time to little more than a perfunctory Bible reading or study and a quick prayer if you forget the real purpose of setting aside that time.

God wants you to have a real and fresh encounter with Him each day. You don't generate this meeting through any formula or particular method; you simply come before Him with a humble, repentant heart and a genuine desire to know Him more.

You gain a sense of His presence. Isaiah knew immediately that he was in the presence of the living God. When the meeting ended, Isaiah walked away a changed man. You cannot experience God's presence and be the same; God's holiness is life changing, and through the Holy Spirit, He lives inside you forever.

You are never without His presence. You sense your unworthiness. As you come face-to-face with God's holiness, you realize your needy state. His awesome brightness eclipses even the angels in heaven.

The standard of His righteousness illuminates the sin in your life. You need to understand His forgiveness. The purpose of recognizing sin is not for condemnation and guilt, but for repentance. Christ forgives all your sins, but He wants you to confess them in order to experience His wondrous grace.

Precious Lord, I want to have a fresh encounter with You today. I want to know You better. Meet with me, and when our meeting ends, let me walk away changed.

The Moments That Sustain You

SCRIPTURE READING: Psalm 34   KEY VERSE: Psalm 34:5

They looked to Him and were radiant, and their faces were not ashamed.

You are made for fellowship with the Lord. Blaise Pascal said, "Happiness is neither within us only, or without us; it is the union of ourselves with God." Though you may try to fill that void with busyness or a flurry of activity, your deep-rooted need for intimacy with God remains.

Do you set aside a specific time each day to come into His presence, pray, and meditate on His Word? Every area of your life feels the impact of the loss if you do not. That meeting time with God is worth protecting.

In his book *Peaceful Living in a Stressful World*, Ron Hutchcraft explains,

> We're built to begin our day with our Creator. It started with Adam who met "the Lord God as He was walking in the garden in the cool of the day" (Genesis 3:8). Since then, men and women have been incomplete—whether they recognize it or not—without their morning walk with God.
>
> David told us while literally running for his life, "Seek peace and pursue it." With stress his constant pursuer, how could he be so preoccupied with peace? He explained: "I sought the Lord, and he answered me; he delivered me from all my fears. Those who look to him are radiant . . . Taste and see that the Lord is good" (Psalm 34:4–5, 8). David could then go on to "pursue peace" because he had found his quiet center. It came from his time with the Lord!

Dear heavenly Father, as I travel life's pathway, let me never forget what sustains me and gives me strength for the journey—prayer, meditation, and the Word.

NOVEMBER

THEME

Journey to Mount Horeb

REPRESENTING: Knowing God's voice

KEY VERSE: Isaiah 30:21

Your ears shall hear a word behind you, saying, "This is the way, walk in it," whenever you turn to the right hand or whenever you turn to the left.

The prophet Elijah was discouraged. He believed he was the only one left who truly loved and served God. He knew his life was in peril from his enemies. Elijah needed new direction. He desperately needed to hear from God. So he trudged up the rocky pathway to Mount Horeb to be alone. There he heard "a still small voice" (1 Kings 19:12).

The voice Elijah heard calmed his fears. It gave him strength and hope. It provided new direction. It was the voice of God.

God still speaks today. The only question is, Are we listening? This month we travel in the footsteps of Elijah to our own spiritual Mount Horeb. There, above the rush of this world, we wait to hear what God will speak to us. Our guide for this spiritual journey—the Holy Spirit—is experienced and trustworthy. If you listen closely, His direction will be clear.

Are You Ready to Listen?

SCRIPTURE READING: 1 Kings 19:1–18   KEY VERSE: 1 Kings 19:12

After the earthquake a fire, but the LORD was not in the fire; and after the fire a still small voice.

The prophet Elijah was exhausted physically, emotionally, and spiritually. *Is this what happens to a man who obeys God?* Elijah must have wondered.

He was depressed to the point of desiring death, on the run, and desperately wanted to hear from God. Where should he go? What hope was there for a future? Through an angel, God fed him to restore his physical strength, but Elijah still wasn't ready to hear what God had to say.

For forty days and nights, Elijah traveled to Mount Horeb (Sinai), moving slowly in his despair. He cried out to God once more: "I alone am left; and they seek my life, to take it away" (1 Kings 19:10 NASB).

How did God answer his plea? Not in the way that Elijah expected. Elijah stood on the mountain waiting. The sudden, violent wind did not bring God's answer. God was not in the rock-shattering earthquake either. The sudden inferno did not contain His answer. After the great commotion, Elijah heard a gentle blowing, and then God spoke to give him direction for his future.

God wanted Elijah to have the right heart attitude to receive His words. Elijah needed to be thoroughly emptied of himself, of self-reliance, of the need to control. When Elijah gained a proper perspective of God's tender sustenance and sovereign power, he was ready to really hear what God had to say. Is your heart ready to listen?

Dear Lord, I want to hear Your voice. Empty my reservoir of self-reliance, and give me a proper perspective of Your sovereign power. Make me ready to listen.

Your Eternal Guide

SCRIPTURE READING: John 16:7–15   KEY VERSE: John 16:13

When He, the Spirit of truth, has come, He will guide you into all truth; for He will not speak on His own authority, but whatever He hears He will speak; and He will tell you things to come.

When you are a tourist on the road, nothing is quite as valuable as a knowledgeable tour guide. This informed person can help you see the best sights and find your way around an unfamiliar place. The tour guide also knows what locations to avoid. Even though you could basically get around without one, you are wise to choose this person's insight and experience.

In the Christian life, the Holy Spirit is your Guide. This is how Jesus described the work of the Holy Spirit to His disciples: "When He, the Spirit of truth, comes, He will guide you into all the truth; for He will not speak on His own initiative, but whatever He hears, He will speak; and He will disclose to you what is to come" (John 16:13 NASB).

Jesus knew that He would be leaving this world soon, to be killed and then to rise again and ascend to heaven. For three years, He had walked side by side with His disciples. They always had the benefit of His physical presence and direction. The shock of Jesus' absence would confuse and depress their human hearts, and Jesus wanted to prepare them for the coming changes.

The Holy Spirit lives inside each believer through the grace of Jesus Christ. He takes the words of Scripture and makes them real and active in your life. His continual work is to disclose the truths of God one-on-one. He is your Comfort and eternal Guide.

Heavenly Father, I praise You for the gift of the Holy Spirit, who lives in me. Thank You for His comfort and guidance along my spiritual journey.

The God Who Speaks

SCRIPTURE READING: Matthew 3:13–17   KEY VERSE: Hebrews 1:4

Having become so much better than the angels, as He has by inheritance obtained a more excellent name than they.

The opening verses of the book of Hebrews are known for their power and majesty. The writer used a formal, written technique to impart truths that are foundational to the rest of the book and, more important, to faith in Christ:

> *God, after He spoke long ago to the fathers in the prophets in many portions and in many ways, in these last days has spoken to us in His Son, whom He appointed heir of all things, through whom also He made the world. And He is the radiance of His glory and the exact representation of His nature, and upholds all things by the word of His power . . . He sat down at the right hand of the Majesty on high; having become as much better than the angels, as He has inherited a more excellent name than they. (Heb. 1:1–4 NASB)*

It is vital to understand how the coming of Christ fits into God's grand scheme of history and of dealing with His people. Since He created the universe and mankind, God has demonstrated His deep desire to communicate. The wonders of creation and the Scriptures find their fulfillment in the person of Jesus Christ.

When you accept Christ, you embrace the living revelation and Word of God. God's eternal conversation sounded through the ages when He said, "This is My beloved Son, in whom I am well-pleased" (Matt. 3:17 NASB).

> *O God, I am so thankful that You spoke in ages past and You still speak today! I release the revelation power of Your Word to work in my life without reservation.*

"In the Beginning God"

SCRIPTURE READING: Hebrews 1:1–4   KEY VERSE: Psalm 135:1

Praise the LORD! Praise the name of the LORD; praise Him, O you servants of the LORD!

Our God is an awesome God who has seized the initiative in revealing Himself to mankind. Apart from God's revelation, man would be mired in ceaseless ignorance and frustration. John Stott painted this awe-inspiring portrait of God in his book *Basic Christianity:*

> "In the beginning God." The first four words of the Bible are more than an introduction to the creation story or to the book of Genesis. They supply the key which opens our understanding to the Bible as a whole. They tell us that the religion of the Bible is a religion of the initiative of God.
>
> Before man existed, God acted. Before man stirred himself to seek God, God has sought man. In the Bible we do not see man groping after God, we see God reaching after man.
>
> The Bible reveals a God who, long before it even occurs to man to turn to Him, while man is still lost in darkness and sunk in sin, takes the initiative, rises from His throne, lays aside His glory, and stoops to seek until He finds him.

Before the foundation of the universe, God loved you and prepared a way for you to know Him and hear His voice. Meditate on that for a moment, and spill out your gratitude in worship.

> *Father, before I sought You, You sought me. I do not have to grope after You because You are continually reaching out to me. You prepared a way for me to know You and hear Your voice. I praise You!*

God Is Speaking

SCRIPTURE READING: John 1   KEY VERSE: John 1:1

In the beginning was the Word, and the Word was with God, and the Word was God.

After reading John 1:1, A. W. Tozer commented,

An intelligent, plain man, untaught in the truths of Christianity, coming upon this text, would likely conclude that John meant to teach that it is the nature of God to speak, to communicate His thoughts to others.

And he would be right. A word is a medium by which thoughts are expressed, and the application of the term to the eternal Son leads us to believe that self-expression is inherent in the Godhead, that God is forever seeking to speak Himself out to His creation. The whole Bible supports this idea. God is speaking. Not God spoke, but God is speaking. He is, by His nature, continuously articulate. He fills the world with His speaking voice.

Although God communicates primarily through His Word, He is not limited in His expression. He often uses pastors, friends, and others to bear witness to His will for our lives. Be sure the voice you hear is God's by establishing a close, personal relationship with Him. Ask Him to reveal Himself to you through His Word. A person who focuses his thoughts on God will be led by God and will gain the mind of Christ.

Lord, reveal Yourself to me through Your Word. Help me focus my thoughts on Your will, be led by You, and gain the mind of Christ.

The Key to Listening

SCRIPTURE READING: 2 Samuel 7   KEY VERSE: Psalm 46:10

Be still, and know that I am God; I will be exalted among the nations, I will be exalted in the earth!

God had just made a covenant with David. Among many things, God promised to give him a son (Solomon), who would someday build the temple for God that David had dreamed of. The throne of rulership over Israel would never depart from David's house, though interrupted at times, and would one day find its ultimate fulfillment in Jesus Christ.

What an overwhelming set of promises, and what a mighty demonstration of complete grace! God made this covenant with David *before* he sinned with Bathsheba. God knew what David would soon do, but He in grace chose to love him and establish a never-ending relationship with him. David's response to God's words through the prophet Nathan is a prime example of why David is called "a man after [God's] own heart" (1 Sam. 13:14 NASB).

David's heart priority was on worshiping and loving his God. He said, "Now therefore, O LORD God, the word that Thou hast spoken concerning Thy servant and his house, confirm it forever, and do as Thou hast spoken" (2 Sam. 7:25 NASB).

God desires your humble worship, thanksgiving, and the complete giving over of your heart to Him. That is what David did, and that is why his fellowship with God was so sweet. If you seek intimacy with God, falling down before Him in worship is the place of beginning.

Master, I seek a greater intimacy with You. I know it will come through worship, so teach me how to worship in spirit and truth.

Recognizing God's Voice

SCRIPTURE READING: John 10:1–18   KEY VERSE: John 10:11

I am the good shepherd. The good shepherd gives His life for the sheep.

In today's busy, increasingly urban world, many people do not know basic facts about farm animals. If you know something about them, test your knowledge about sheep with these statements, answering true or false.

____ Sheep are able to seek out their own sources of food and water.

____ Sheep help one another when a sheep is wounded or stuck.

____ Sheep are strong and able to carry packs on their back.

____ Sheep are not afraid to graze away from the herd.

____ Sheep will follow anyone who gives them a command.

If you answered true to any of these, you're wrong! The actual characteristics of sheep are the exact opposite of the ones described here. When Jesus said that we are like sheep, He was not paying us a high compliment.

Sheep are simpleminded, but they respond immediately to the love and tender care of their shepherd—and only their shepherd. Jesus said, "The sheep hear his [the shepherd's] voice, and he calls his own sheep by name, and leads them out. When he puts forth all his own, he goes before them, and the sheep follow him because they know his voice" (John 10:3–4 NASB).

The sheep have security and direction because they know their shepherd and respond to his commands. Do you know your Shepherd's voice?

Precious Lord, You give me spiritual food and water, You aid me when I am wounded or stuck, and You carry my burdens. Thank You for being my Shepherd.

How to Listen to God

SCRIPTURE READING: Isaiah 30:15–18   KEY VERSE: Isaiah 50:4

The Lord GOD has given Me the tongue of the learned, that I should know how to speak a word in season to him who is weary. He awakens Me morning by morning, He awakens My ear to hear as the learned.

The center of the Christian life is a relationship with Jesus Christ—personal, unique, and rewarding. At the core of this relationship is communication—expressing ourselves to God in prayer and His speaking to our spirits.

We must admit, though, we are usually far better at the former than the latter. Listening to God is a realm in which we are sometimes uninformed and frequently uncomfortable. *Is that God I am hearing or just the echo of my own thinking?* we wonder.

It helps to demystify the terminology. He usually doesn't speak to us audibly as He did to the Old Testament characters. Today, He speaks through the Scriptures, the sound advice of other Christians, and the presence of the Holy Spirit who lives within each believer. We hear His voice as we meditate on the truth of His Word, listen and sift through the counsel of others, and commit each day to His sovereign control, trusting Him to order our ways and thoughts.

God communicates His will to us so that we might comprehend His truth and be conformed to it. He always takes the initiative to make it happen. Our best move is to quiet our busy souls and allow Him to speak (Isa. 30:15).

There is so much God wants to share with you. He has something to say about everything that touches your life. Who wouldn't want to hear from Him?

Dear heavenly Father, speak to me through Your Word today. Communicate Your will to me so that I can be conformed to the truth. Quiet my busy soul so that I can hear Your voice.

Learning to Listen

SCRIPTURE READING: Matthew 13:10–17   KEY VERSE: Matthew 13:16

Blessed are your eyes for they see, and your ears for they hear.

One of the qualities that drew people to Jesus was His ability to listen. He listened with His entire being. That is why we see Him mingling with crowds of people and healing the ones who are sick. Jesus was the greatest communicator the world has ever known. He wasn't worried about getting equal time in conversations or impressing others. He was interested in building relationships. So He listened.

Jesus could sense the hurts and the frustrations on the faces of the people He met. He gave them freedom to express their deepest needs. Two of man's basic needs are love and acceptance. That's how the Savior listens to us, with eyes of love and acceptance.

How do you listen to Him? Do you long to be near Him, to study His Word, and to hear His heart about certain situations? Or do you rush through prayer, afraid of what He might say and require of you?

Until we learn to truly listen, first to God and then to others, we will never know the deeper side of Christ's love. Only in listening for His voice can we truly experience the intimacy of His presence.

Ask Him to help you become the kind of listener that He is to you. If you will listen, you will hear His voice.

Almighty God, I long to be near You, to study Your Word, to hear Your heart about the situations in my life. Forgive me for rushing through my time with You. Help me learn to listen so that I can experience the intimacy of Your presence.

Take Out Your Earplugs

SCRIPTURE READING: 1 Samuel 3:1–10   KEY VERSE: 1 Samuel 3:10

The LORD came and stood and called as at other times, "Samuel! Samuel!"
And Samuel answered, "Speak, for Your servant hears."

Visit a major airplane construction plant and you will be amazed by two things: the size of the airplanes under construction and the noise level.

Much of the machinery used to assemble aircraft is driven by air-pressure devices. Because of this, a person in the assembly plant is subjected to constant noise pollution. Safety is a top concern, and workers are given earplugs and safety glasses for protection. Plant managers also have keen eyes as to potential dangers. Once the earplugs are in place and the machinery turned on, there is no way you can yell to a coworker and be heard.

Many of God's people are like employees in an airplane production plant. They cannot hear God's voice because they are too busy assembling the pieces of their lives. They wear the earplugs of worldly thinking, becoming complacent toward the things of God. When the bottom drops out, they wonder why God allowed it. But in actuality, God spent months and in some cases years shouting warnings that went unheeded.

In your life, is it time to take out the earplugs, turn off the machinery of the world, and listen to God's voice?

O Lord, I'm too busy trying to assemble my life. Please help me to take out
my earplugs, turn off the machinery of the world, and listen to Your voice.

He Speaks in Silence

SCRIPTURE READING: Psalm 42   KEY VERSE: Psalm 44:1

We have heard with our ears, O God, our fathers have told us, the deeds You did in their days, in days of old.

One of the most precious privileges we have as believers is the privilege of hearing God speak to us. In her book *No Pat Answers,* Eugenia Price wrote,

We rush at God with our questions and firmly believe that He welcomes them. Indeed, I imagine He expects them. After all, no one but God knows us as we really are inside. Still, when we get back only what we, in our sorrow, fear, or panic, recognize as silence, what of that?

It may be all we can expect by way of understanding the reason for our grief, shock, or fear. Could this be where we make our big mistake? Do we fall victim to time itself? Do we rush at God in our extremity, demanding an immediate answer in understandable words, not according to God's time schedule, but because we want our question answered now with a pat answer?

How could we expect to be able to hear the voice of God in our distress when we have long ago forgotten, or never learned, to be quiet before Him? . . . There is no time element involved in divine mystery, but there is silence in it. And we can't bear silence. We fear it. The radio or TV is turned on the minute most of us enter a room. Yet we are told that the voice of God is "a still, small voice." He waits for our inner silence before He speaks on any subject. Possibly because He wants what He says to be heard.

Dear God, teach me to be quiet—to still the noise around me, to calm my soul and spirit, to wait in Your presence. I want to hear what You have to say.

A Hearing Ear

SCRIPTURE READING: Revelation 3:14–22   KEY VERSE: Revelation 3:22

He who has an ear, let him hear what the Spirit says to the churches.

Jesus spoke these words to the Laodiceans, but they are just as relevant to us. Don't make the mistake of thinking they apply only to nonbelievers. They're spoken to a believing church that had slipped into thinking of themselves as spiritually elite.

Warren Wiersbe remarked, "These people couldn't see themselves as they really were. Nor could they see their Lord as He stood outside the door of the church. Nor could they see the open doors of opportunity. They were so wrapped up in building their own kingdom that they had become lukewarm in their concern for a lost world" (*The Bible Exposition Commentary*).

God speaks to those who listen for His voice. But if we are not listening, we won't hear a sound. The Laodiceans were convinced they were on the right track. But their self-sufficiency and arrogance led Christ to say they were neither hot nor cold; therefore, "I will spit you out of My mouth" (Rev. 3:16 NASB).

It has been said that if you are going be cold in your relationship with God, then be cold. But if you are going to love Him and serve Him, then be hot in your devotion to Him. In other words, be committed. Don't allow the devotion of your heart to become callous. Pray that your life will remain open and sensitive to His Spirit.

Precious heavenly Father, strip me of self-sufficiency and arrogance. I don't want my devotion to become callous. Keep me open and sensitive to Your Spirit. Give me a hearing ear.

Seeking God's Guidance

SCRIPTURE READING: Psalm 16:7–11   KEY VERSE: Proverbs 8:11

Wisdom is better than rubies, and all the things one may desire cannot be compared with her.

When we talk about the wisdom of man, we're usually referring to mental ability, the capability to know and to achieve. We also use the word *wisdom* to refer to spiritual perception and insight on living.

The wisdom of God encompasses a far different realm. As Paul expressed it, His wisdom is so far above ours, there is no rational comparison: "The foolishness of God is wiser than men, and the weakness of God is stronger than men" (1 Cor. 1:25 NASB). Paul was speaking in figurative terms to say that if there were anything about God's thinking that could be called foolishness, even that would be superior to our highest wisdom.

Jerry Bridges explains the significance of God's wisdom to our faith in his book *Trusting God:*

> When we stop and think about it, we know in our heart of hearts that God does not make any mistakes in our lives . . . God does know what He is doing. God is infinite in His wisdom. He always knows what is best for us and what is the best way to bring about that result . . .
>
> We all recognize that human wisdom at its best is fallible . . . All of us from time to time agonize over some important decisions, trying to determine the best course of action. But God never has to agonize over a decision . . . His wisdom is intuitive, infinite, and infallible . . . (Psalm 147:5).

Father God, Your wisdom is intuitive, infinite, and infallible. I need wisdom for my spiritual journey. On the basis of Your Word, I claim it right now!

Waiting on God

SCRIPTURE READING: Psalm 106   KEY VERSE: Psalm 106:13

They soon forgot His works; they did not wait for His counsel.

Psalm 106 records the bleak history of the Israelites' wilderness journey following their exodus out of Egypt. Many negative episodes are chronicled, and one glaringly deficient trait was their inability to wait on God. In one incident, the Hebrews complained about their steady diet of manna, God's daily, supernatural provision. The psalmist recounted, "They quickly forgot His works; they did not wait for His counsel, but craved intensely in the wilderness, and tempted God [put Him to the test] in the desert" (vv. 13–14 NASB).

Failing to wait on God for His answer is usually coupled with a memory lapse of God's past help. The intensity of our needs often fogs our vision of God's faithfulness and power. Keeping God's character in sharp focus is crucial to waiting for His response. When God's ability to supply our needs is obscured, we too readily rely on our wisdom instead of seeking His counsel.

If you are tempted to move ahead without God's guidance, pause and reflect on His perfect timing in meeting previous demands. The less you desire to wait on God, the greater your craving for instant solutions. You look for shortcuts instead of traveling the road of trust and dependence on God.

> *Dear Lord, thank You for Your help in the past. I need to remember these times as I travel down the road of trust and dependence on You. Help me bypass the shortcuts.*

Waiting Is Not in Vain

SCRIPTURE READING: Mark 4:26–29   KEY VERSES: James 5:7–8

Be patient, brethren, until the coming of the Lord. See how the farmer waits for the precious fruit of the earth, waiting patiently for it until it receives the early and latter rain. You also be patient. Establish your hearts, for the coming of the Lord is at hand.

The good earth of America's breadbasket has done its job. Once vacant silos stand ready for the year's harvest.

Today's promising bounty, however, was buried in the spring in soft furrows. For weeks, the vision of fertile fields could be seen only in the farmer's mind.

Then seedlings peered out of the darkness and eventually matured into stalk and produce. Patience and perspiration were daily companions of the tiller.

James, the half brother of Christ, compared waiting on God to this scenario: "Behold, the farmer waits for the precious produce of the soil, being patient about it, until it gets the early and late rains. You too be patient; strengthen your hearts" (James 5:7–8 NASB).

Waiting on God is not being resigned or idle. There are things we must do, tasks that are required. But like the farmer, we work and wait for God to bring forth the fullness of His answer. There are days of stillness and days of labor. Both are necessary.

The motivation to persist is knowing that God is actively preparing our hearts to receive the right answer at the right time. The waiting is not in vain. Both the process and the outcome can be to the praise of God's grace.

Heavenly Father, help me realize that days of stillness and labor are both necessary for harvest. My waiting is not in vain. Both the process and the outcome will be for Your glory.

When the Timing Is Right

SCRIPTURE READING: Acts 16:1–15   KEY VERSE: Acts 16:9

A vision appeared to Paul in the night. A man of Macedonia stood and pleaded with him, saying, "Come over to Macedonia and help us."

Paul spent a lot of time seeking God's guidance for his missionary journeys. In Acts 16 after revisiting the churches at Derbe, Lystra, Iconium, and Pisidian Antioch, Paul decided to continue westward to Ephesus. However, God stopped him. Scripture tells us he was "forbidden by the Holy Spirit to speak the word in Asia" (Acts 16:6 NASB).

This change had to be disappointing to Paul, who was prepared to go into a city that was in deep spiritual need. No one knows why God stopped Paul, but thanks to Luke we have a record of what happened next. Rather than becoming sullen, Paul turned northwest to the borders of then Asian territory, hoping to evangelize the cities of Bithynia. However, he was stopped once again. Therefore, Paul passed through the region and turned toward Troas. At any point, Paul could have resisted the Spirit of God and forcibly preached the gospel. However, his message would have been empty and without the power of the Holy Spirit.

In Troas, Paul had a vision that God wanted him to go to Macedonia. Because of his obedience, the gospel spread throughout Europe and later the Western world. Perhaps God is calling you to stop or wait before you make the next move. You think all looks perfect; Paul did too. Only God knows what lies ahead. Refuse to make a move until He says the timing is right.

Father, only You know what lies ahead on this road I travel. I don't want to make a move until the timing is right. Help me watch for the STOP as well as the GO signs.

Time Spent in Waiting

SCRIPTURE READING: Psalm 27   KEY VERSE: Psalm 27:14

Wait on the LORD; be of good courage, and He shall strengthen your heart; wait, I say, on the LORD!

All of us know the feelings that accompany making a quick decision. After we walk away, we wonder whether we did the right thing. Many times we have a nagging sense inside that we didn't. How can we avoid this?

How and when to wait on God is one of the wisest things you can learn about the Christian faith. At times doing this may seem difficult, especially in a society where faxes, E-mail, and overnight mail services are a way of life, but it's a principle that brings great reward.

Too many people ignore God's plea to wait. They push ahead of Him in the decision-making process. Impulsive spending is one area that is abused regularly. Ron Blue, founder of Ronald Blue and Company, a financial advisory firm, reminds us, "You can spend money any way you want, but you can only spend it once." Bad decisions have consequences. When we fail to wait for God's best, we often end up making horrendous mistakes.

If God is blocking you from making a certain decision, consider it a blessing. He is saving you from hurt—physical or emotional. See this as an opportunity to draw closer to Him. Make it a goal not to move ahead until you hear Him say, "This is the way, walk in it" (Isa. 30:21).

God uses the time you spend in waiting to prepare you for His future blessings. Therefore, you don't have to worry about missed opportunities. When the timing is right, God will open the door.

Lord, I want to wait for Your best in every area of my life. Thank You for the tremendous doors of opportunity that lie ahead—doors I don't yet see. I know You will open them in due time.

Positioned to Hear His Voice

SCRIPTURE READING: 2 Samuel 5:22–25   KEY VERSE: Psalm 62:5

My soul, wait silently for God alone, for my expectation is from Him.

David had just been anointed king over Israel when the Philistines attacked. The first thing he did was to go to God in prayer and inquire: "Shall I go up against the Philistines? Wilt Thou give them into my hand?" (2 Sam. 5:19 NASB). The Lord affirmed the victory to David.

Israel captured the Philistine camp. In desperation, the Philistines attempted another raid. David could have looked at the situation from a human perspective. His army easily won the first victory; what was there to stop them from repeating the same action? Plenty, and David knew it. Joshua failed to seek God at Ai and lost to a much smaller army than the one David faced (Josh. 7:1–12). Making decisions such as that one apart from God invited defeat. David immediately went back to God for the solution.

The Lord told him *not* to attack the enemy! Instead, he was to wait until he heard the sound of marching in the tops of the balsam trees. Try to imagine what David felt. He knew the enemy was poised and ready to strike, but he had to wait for God's timing.

Times of waiting are times of great blessing. When we learn to wait on the Lord, we position ourselves to hear His voice. God's timing is always perfect. And when you commit yourself to following His lead, you will never be disappointed.

> *O God, help me wait for Your timing, even when I frantically feel I must do something. I commit myself to follow You. I know I won't be disappointed.*

Test the Words by the Word

SCRIPTURE READING: Galatians 1:11–24   KEY VERSE: 1 John 4:1

Beloved, do not believe every spirit, but test the spirits, whether they are of God; because many false prophets have gone out into the world.

D on't believe everything you read" is just commonsense good advice. It is always wise to read with a wary eye and try to verify facts before you repeat them. The same is true about spiritual information. Scripture warns us to "test the spirits" (1 John 4:1) to make sure that what we are hearing or reading squares with God's Word.

The people of the Galatian church had similar concerns about the accuracy of the information they were receiving. Some even doubted Paul's authority to be a teacher. That was why Paul spent so much time defending his authority as an apostle. In other words, Paul furnished them with the basis for his knowledge: "For I would have you know, brethren, that the gospel which was preached by me is not according to man. For I neither received it from man, nor was I taught it, but I received it through a revelation of Jesus Christ" (Gal. 1:11–12 NASB).

Paul had a one-on-one encounter with the Messiah on the road to Damascus and then spent several years in careful study of God's Word. If the words he spoke were his own or supported by a self-generated philosophy, then Paul's ministry would have been groundless and false.

Make it a personal habit to test the words you hear against the infallible, inerrant Word.

Master, give me the wisdom to test everything I hear against Your infallible, inerrant Word. Let Your Word be the plumb line against which I measure all other voices.

Moving God's Direction

SCRIPTURE READING: Psalm 51   KEY VERSE: Psalm 51:10

Create in me a clean heart, O God, and renew a steadfast spirit within me.

Have you ever felt a silent time in your walk with the Lord, a time when you did not feel in close fellowship with Him? Maybe it had been weeks since your last devotional and prayer time, or perhaps you were so busy in general that your thoughts never turned to God during the bustle of the day.

This is not such an unusual problem; many believers have the same experience over the course of their relationship with Christ. And the old saying is true: "God hasn't moved; you have." God is the same yesterday, today, and forever, and His love never diminishes.

The feeling of distance is the result of an unquietness in your heart, which may stem from many spiritual causes. As you pray for understanding, God will show you the heart blockage. In her book *When God Whispers*, Carole Mayhall offers a prayer, based on Psalm 51, which helped her move in God's direction again:

Create in me a caring heart—tender toward the hurts and happenings of others, more concerned with their needs than with my own.

Create in me an attentive heart—able to hear Your whisper, and moment by moment to listen to Your voice.

Create in me a contented heart—at peace with the circumstances of life.

Create in me a hungry heart—longing to love You more, desiring Your Word, reaching . . . stretching . . . for more of You.

Lord, even in the silent times I am still moving in Your direction. Create in me a caring, attentive, contented, hungry heart that will listen for Your whisper.

Failing to Listen to God

SCRIPTURE READING: 2 Samuel 11:1–12:13   KEY VERSE: Psalm 52:1

Why do you boast in evil, O mighty man? The goodness of God endures continually.

I magine you are driving along a narrow two-lane road, and you come upon a warning sign. The sign warns of possible rock slides ahead, and a detour sign points to a good alternate route. Would you ignore the warning sign and drive on?

King David ignored many of God's warning signs along his path, and he plunged deeper and deeper into sin. He knew that the Lord did not approve of lust, adultery, or murder. But one sin led to another as David deliberately ignored his conscience, which God uses to remind us of His truth.

David had done such a remarkable job of not listening to God that God had to use the bold voice of the prophet Nathan. Perhaps David was puzzled as Nathan began to tell him a story about a poor man's pet lamb. At the end of the tale, David still did not hear God's message. Nathan had to spell it out for him: "You are the man!" He then recounted everything David had done and how the Lord felt about his sin.

When David's ears finally heard the truth, he repented immediately. David said, "'I have sinned against the LORD.' And Nathan said to David, 'The LORD also has taken away your sin; you shall not die'" (2 Sam. 12:13 NASB).

If you have been turning a deaf ear to what the Lord has been trying to tell you, it is never too late to ask forgiveness and travel on His road.

Dear heavenly Father, sometimes I have ignored warning signs along the way. Forgive me. Put my feet back on the right path.

Discerning False Voices

SCRIPTURE READING: 1 John 2:18–27   KEY VERSE: 1 John 2:26

These things I have written to you concerning those who try to deceive you.

The story is told of a young boy who believed that he would one day inherit a beautiful piece of land. His father told him about it continually and promised one day to take him to his future land. When that day came, he realized he had been the victim of a cruel family joke—the promised land was a boggy swamp in the middle of nowhere.

That little boy was none other than P. T. Barnum, the famous circus man of the late 1800s. In bitterness of heart, he coined the statement about suckers, saying, "There's a sucker born every minute."

Some people are out to deceive, and they seek the gullible, weak, and uninformed and prey on them for their own selfish purposes. John the apostle warned the believers in the early church to look out. The church is not immune to infiltration by opportunists and liars.

How can you discern these false voices? John explained, "You have an anointing from the Holy One, and you all know. I have not written to you because you do not know the truth, but because you do know it, and because no lie is of the truth . . . As for you, let that abide in you which you heard from the beginning" (1 John 2:20–21, 24 NASB).

You have the direction of the Holy Spirit and God's unchanging Word. Nothing God says will ever contradict His Word. When you rely on this truth as the test of accuracy, you will not be swept away by error.

Almighty God, thank You for the anointing of the Holy Spirit that enables me to know the truth. Deafen my ears to the deceptions of the world around me. Let me abide continually in Your Word of truth.

The Spirit of Truth

SCRIPTURE READING: John 16:7–15   KEY VERSE: John 14:26

The Helper, the Holy Spirit, whom the Father will send in My name, He will teach you all things, and bring to your remembrance all things that I said to you.

The disciples were worried. Jesus was talking more and more about the time when He would leave them. Who would tell them what to do and how to act? Who would answer the tough questions?

Jesus put their fears to rest: "I tell you the truth, it is to your advantage that I go away; for if I do not go away, the Helper shall not come to you; but if I go, I will send Him to you . . . But when He, the Spirit of truth, comes, He will guide you into all the truth; for He will not speak on His own initiative, but whatever He hears, He will speak; and He will disclose to you what is to come" (John 16:7, 13 NASB).

Jesus was not leaving them to muddle about in confusion and uncertainty; on the contrary, He promised them revelation and understanding of His truth beyond their current experience.

The Holy Spirit is actually the One who takes the words of the printed page of God's Word and reveals the meaning to your heart and mind. He uses many human "tools" as aids in the process, including pastors, teachers, and your personal traits. But without the Spirit, the words would remain just that—words.

If you've ever avoided a difficult passage because you feel you won't understand it, don't turn away. God promises to enlighten your heart (1 Cor. 2:14). You are the intended recipient of every meaningful word.

O Lord, how I thank You that You did not leave me to muddle about in confusion and uncertainty. You promised revelation and understanding beyond my abilities. I receive it!

Building a Close Relationship

SCRIPTURE READING: Psalm 84   KEY VERSE: Psalm 88:2

Let my prayer come before You; incline Your ear to my cry.

In the Old Testament, God spoke to His people through the prophets. Men such as Moses, Isaiah, Jeremiah, and others exhorted Israel to return to purity and worship of the Lord. God gave these men the ability to see and proclaim truth.

God's reason for speaking today is much as it was then; however, His method has changed drastically. In seeking to build an intimate relationship with us, God now speaks directly to the hearts of those who believe in Him through the Scriptures and the illuminating presence of the Holy Spirit. The birth of Jesus Christ turned an important page in history by opening the way for us to establish and enjoy a personal relationship with the heavenly Father.

While God still speaks through spiritual leaders, He delights in communicating with you one-on-one. From the beginning of your life, He has sought your fellowship. Now it is your decision. God waits for you to come to Him. He has already come to you through the person of Christ. You may know Him as your Savior, but do you know Him as Lord and intimate Friend? Building a close relationship with God takes time. As you pray, ask Him to guide you into an even deeper relationship, so you may know His ways and find eternal glory in His blessings.

Precious Father, I am overwhelmed that You desire to communicate with me. Help me set aside the time to meet with You. I want to know Your ways and find eternal glory in Your blessings.

God's Goal in Speaking

SCRIPTURE READING: Luke 24:44–49   KEY VERSE: Isaiah 52:10

The LORD has made bare His holy arm in the eyes of all the nations; and all the ends of the earth shall see the salvation of our God.

When God speaks to us, He has these goals in mind:

He wants us to understand His truth. God has written the Bible in such a way that we cannot read through it and think we know everything about Him. The more you read God's Word, the more He reveals Himself to you. The more He reveals, the more you will understand His will for your life.

He seeks to conform us to the image of Jesus Christ. God wants us to take His truth and apply it to our lives. As we do, He molds us and conforms us to the likeness of His Son. Jesus is our example. In Him we discover we are wonderfully accepted and loved.

He wants us to communicate His truth to others. As we grow in Christ, God empowers us to teach others about Him. He may not call you to be a pastor or missionary, but He calls each of us to share His love with others. Our communication does not begin and end with words. It goes much deeper to our attitudes, values, convictions, and desires. What does your life say to others about Christ? Do they see a God who loves, forgives, and encourages all people?

Father God, help me to understand Your truth. I want to be conformed to the image of Your Son, Jesus Christ. I want to communicate Your truth to others.

Alive to God

SCRIPTURE READING: Romans 6   KEY VERSE: 2 Timothy 2:22

Flee also youthful lusts; but pursue righteousness, faith, love, peace with those who call on the Lord out of a pure heart.

The poster showed a sleeping dog and cat, and the sentence below them read, "The trick to overcoming temptation is to play dead." It was followed by the Scripture, "Even so consider yourselves to be dead to sin, but alive to God in Christ Jesus. Therefore do not let sin reign in your mortal body" (Rom. 6:11–12 NASB).

Sin blocks us from hearing the voice of God. In Romans 12:1–2 (NASB), Paul told us to present our bodies as living and holy sacrifices to God. He continued, admonishing, "And do not be conformed to this world, but be transformed by the renewing of your mind, that you may prove what the will of God is, that which is good and acceptable and perfect."

Christians who toy with sin play a deadly game. Sin not only brings static into our communication with God, it divides and separates us from other believers while dimming our view of God's principles. That was why Paul wrote that when temptation comes, flee from it (2 Tim. 2:22)!

God's goal in speaking to you is to conform you spiritually, emotionally, and mentally into the image of His Son. However, Satan's goal in tempting you to sin is to see that you never become all God wants you to be. The choice is yours, and you are free to make it now that you are "alive to God."

> *Dear Lord, I do not want sin to reign over me! Clear up any static that prevents me from hearing Your voice. Help me flee when temptation comes. Make me dead to sin and alive to You.*

The Voice of Accusation

SCRIPTURE READING: Genesis 3:1–7   KEY VERSE: John 8:44

You are of your father the devil, and the desires of your father you want to do. He was a murderer from the beginning, and does not stand in the truth, because there is no truth in him. When he speaks a lie, he speaks from his own resources, for he is a liar and the father of it.

Jesus called Satan "a murderer" and "the father of lies" (John 8:44 NASB). In the book *The Bondage Breaker,* Neil T. Anderson observes,

> One of the most common attitudes I have discovered in Christians . . . is a deep-seated sense of self-deprecation. I've heard them say, ". . . I'm no good." I'm amazed at how many Christians are paralyzed in their witness and productivity by thoughts and feelings of inferiority and worthlessness.
>
> Next to temptation, perhaps the most frequent and insistent attack from Satan to which we are vulnerable is accusation. By faith we have entered into an eternal relationship with the Lord Jesus Christ . . . Satan can do absolutely nothing to alter our position in Christ and our worth to God. But he can render us virtually inoperative if he can deceive us into listening to and believing his insidious lies accusing us of being of little value to God and other people.

When God speaks, He always uses words of hope, encouragement, direction, and promise. Even in times of discipline, He is quick to restore and renew our fellowship. If the voice you hear within your heart is one of accusation, know it belongs to the deceiver. Therefore, take your stand against the enemy and ask God to fill your heart with His truth.

> *O God, the accuser often tries to condemn me, but I realize there is no condemnation because I am Your child. I reject the accuser's voice and his deceptive lies.*

God's Message to You

SCRIPTURE READING: Hebrews 10:35–39   KEY VERSE: Jeremiah 29:11

I know the thoughts that I think toward you, says the LORD, thoughts of peace and not of evil, to give you a future and a hope.

God's message to you is always consistent with His Word. Therefore, the apostle Paul instructed the churches to read and study God's Word, knowing it would produce an abundance of righteousness: "Let the word of Christ richly dwell within you, with all wisdom teaching and admonishing one another with psalms and hymns and spiritual songs" (Col. 3:16 NASB).

Early believers didn't have the Scriptures as we know them. They had the Law of Moses and the words of the prophets. Letters (our books of the New Testament) from the apostles were circulated to the churches who taught the words and principles of Christ. Paul knew if the people studied them, they would be equipped to face all temptation and trouble.

Many times we face emergencies that leave us little time to go to the Scriptures and hunt for God's answer. However, when we study God's Word, we have the spiritual tools needed to face the conflict.

You may be facing a deep personal loss. God wants you to know He is a God of comfort (2 Cor. 1:3). He has a plan for your life that goes past the immediate hurt (Jer. 29:11). Therefore, do not throw away your confidence, because it will be rewarded (Heb. 10:35).

Father God, Your plan goes beyond the immediate hurts and trials of my life. I am confident in it. I know I will not be disappointed.

Seeking God's Guidance

SCRIPTURE READING: Psalm 131   KEY VERSE: John 11:41

They took away the stone from the place where the dead man was lying. And Jesus lifted up His eyes and said, "Father, I thank You that You have heard Me."

The result of seeking God is a life abandoned to Him. Oswald Chambers asserted,

The destiny of my spiritual life is such identification with Jesus Christ that I always hear God, and I know that God always hears me (John 11:41). If I am united with Jesus Christ, I hear God, by the devotion of hearing all the time. A lily, or a tree, or a servant of God, may convey God's message to me. What hinders me from hearing is that I am taken up with other things.

It is not that I will not hear God, but I am not devoted in the right place. I am devoted to things, to service, to convictions, and God may say what He likes but I do not hear Him. The child attitude is always, "speak, Lord, for Thy servant is listening" (1 Samuel 3:9). If I have not cultivated this devotion of hearing, I can only hear God's voice at certain times; at other times I am taken up with things.

In seeking God, we make a choice either to take time to listen or to spend our lives frantically working in our own strength. God's guidance is always clear. There may be valleys and hills along our way; but because we have spent time with Him, we can know He is near. As you open His Word today, pray that He will speak specifically to your heart.

Precious Lord, I am devoted to things, service, and convictions—but I need more devotion to You. Help me listen for Your direction rather than spend my life working in my own strength.

A Guide for Life

SCRIPTURE READING: 2 Timothy 3:14–17 KEY VERSE: Romans 12:2

Do not be conformed to this world, but be transformed by the renewing of your mind, that you may prove what is that good and acceptable and perfect will of God.

When it comes to using Scripture as the guide for life, the most common question is not *why* to use it, but *how* to use it.

Many people use the "hop, skip, jump" method; that is, they wait until a crisis hits and then try to flip through their Bibles quickly for fast answers. They want the words to leap off the page. True, God does work this way at times; He has ministered to many in their need by underscoring a specific promise of Scripture to sustain even the feeble and doubting heart.

However, the Lord wants His Word to be your sustenance and source of direction on a daily basis, not just an occasional respite when the going gets rough. Romans 12:2 (NASB) explains the key to making the Bible your moment-by-moment support: "Do not be conformed to this world, but be transformed by the renewing of your mind, that you may prove what the will of God is, that which is good and acceptable and perfect."

Renewal is not an overnight process; the word itself implies an ongoing change and development. As you study and dig into its deeper meaning, you understand the interrelationship of His principles and how God works in the lives of His people. This process prepares you to sense His leading.

Dear heavenly Father, I need a guide for my journey. Thank You for the road map of Your Word. Let it do its work in me.

DECEMBER

THEME

Journey Down the Damascus Road

REPRESENTING: Moving toward our divine destination

KEY VERSE: Proverbs 9:10

The fear of the LORD is the beginning of wisdom, and the knowledge of the Holy One is understanding.

Paul's trip down the Damascus Road led to a divine destination—a life-changing encounter with Jesus Christ (Acts 9).

Paul was never again the same after this journey. His personality, his plans, his life purpose—everything was impacted by the Damascus Road experience. Years later, he stood before King Agrippa with a powerful testimony: "Therefore, King Agrippa, I was not disobedient to the heavenly vision" (Acts 26:19).

This month, as we conclude our spiritual journey together, we focus on our own divine destination. Devotions emphasize the importance of setting proper goals, finishing well, and fulfilling God's plan for your life.

When you complete the final reading on December 31, your spiritual journey really will not end. It will continue in the everyday challenges, opportunities, and adversities of life. Keep learning. Be obedient to the heavenly vision. Keep traveling in faith and at the end of your trip you will be able to echo the words of the apostle Paul: "I have fought the good fight, I have finished the race, I have kept the faith" (2 Tim. 4:7).

Spiritual Slippage

SCRIPTURE READING: Psalm 31:19–24   KEY VERSES: Colossians 2:6–7

As you therefore have received Christ Jesus the Lord, so walk in Him, rooted and built up in Him and established in the faith, as you have been taught, abounding in it with thanksgiving.

No-till farming has become a standard practice in the Midwest. To prevent the loss of fertile topsoil, crop stubble is left after harvest instead of plowed under, maximizing dirt and moisture retention.

Spiritual slippage can likewise be minimized and steady growth fostered as the Holy Spirit applies these time-tested principles to the soil of our souls:

A renewed concentration on the Word of God. We become firmly rooted in Christ as the principles and power of God's Word are implanted into our minds and woven into our behavior. Regular reading, studying, and meditating upon the Scriptures add solid layers of Christlike character to our lives, which act as invisible seawalls against the forces of spiritual erosion.

A heightened attention to worship and praise. The less awesome God becomes in our eyes, the easier it is to drift. Praise and adoration lead to an exalted view of God and restore our spiritual passion.

A revived focus on service to others. Ministering to the practical needs of others is a great stimulus for reversing spiritual erosion because it releases the power and love of God.

You can regain the joy, peace, and confidence you once had in your relationship with Christ. Apply at least one principle today, and watch God rebuild your life.

Dear Lord, I pledge renewed consecration to Your Word. Show me ways I can minister to practical needs of others. Reverse the effects of spiritual erosion in my life.

Getting God's Viewpoint

SCRIPTURE READING: Psalm 139   KEY VERSES: Proverbs 3:5–6

Trust in the LORD with all your heart, and lean not on your own under-
standing; in all your ways acknowledge Him, and He shall direct your paths.

In some elaborate English gardens, the gardeners cultivate hedgerows
arranged in the shape of a maze. A person wandering between the lines of
bushes is forced to find his way by trial and error; the bushes are too high to
see over, and it is almost impossible to remember the twists and turns.
Someone watching from the balcony of the manor house, however, can see the
leafy pathways clearly and give direction to the one wandering below.

It's all a matter of perspective, and that saying applies to your life as well.
You can see where you have been and where you are now, but the Lord can see
the entire span of your life, every step along the way (Ps. 139). You might feel
surrounded by a maze of bewildering details, but you are not lost when you
trust Jesus Christ to lead the way.

Of course, leaning on Him comes more naturally when you cannot see the
road ahead, but it is just as crucial to rely on His direction even when you think
you have the whole picture. God's perspective is vital at all times.

Do you seek God's guidance every day, or do you turn to Him only when
your resources and common sense are not enough?

Give me Your perspective, heavenly Father, whether or not I can see the
road ahead. Make my paths straight. I am not depending on my own
understanding. I trust in You.

Live Free in Him

SCRIPTURE READING: John 15:4–7 KEY VERSE: John 14:23

Jesus answered and said to him, "If anyone loves Me, he will keep My word; and My Father will love him, and We will come to him and make Our home with him."

The young woman spent days working on her presentation, but her superiors only gave a casual nod of approval. Later in the quiet of her office, she broke down and cried. Why was there not more praise for her work? Had they failed to notice her effort?

Our world is performance crazy. Computers push the limits on technology. The one you buy today will be out of date in six months. This type of thinking leads to a lifestyle that pushes in an effort to get higher and closer to an imaginary goal. But sooner or later, it all comes crashing down.

A child's story tells of a caterpillar longing to find out what was at the top of a huge pile of caterpillars. He pushes and shoves his way to the top, but when he reaches his goal, he finds nothing there. Immediately he returns to what he was before, and a marvelous thing occurs. The desire to become all God intends for him to be takes over, and he becomes a beautiful butterfly.

You may spend years striving and pushing to get more out of life, but all you gain is a sense of being burned out. The mind-set that adheres to the thought, *I'm good, but not good enough,* is the mark of performance-based living. God's way is life lived to the fullest in the light of His grace and acceptance. Lay down your expectations and fears, and allow Him to bless you abundantly as you live free in Him.

Father, I want to live free in You. Help me lay down my expectations and fears so that You can bless me abundantly. Thank You for unconditional acceptance.

Readiness for Rough Times

SCRIPTURE READING: 1 Peter 1:13–21   KEY VERSE: 1 Peter 1:13

Gird up the loins of your mind, be sober, and rest your hope fully upon the grace that is to be brought to you at the revelation of Jesus Christ.

The importance of "girding your mind for action" cannot be emphasized enough, especially when you consider the likelihood of trials in your everyday experience. If you are not maintaining your spiritual strength all along, the rough times can hit even harder.

In her book *Lord, Where Are You When Bad Things Happen?*, Kay Arthur explains what this strength looks like:

Faith recognizes that God is in control, not man. Faith does it God's way, in God's timing, according to His good pleasure. Faith does not take life into its own hands, but, in respect and trust, places it in God's hands . . . Faith waits and trusts, taking God at His Word.

When life is difficult to understand, when doubt pounds on the door of your mind calling you a fool for not letting him in, when believing God seems insane, when human reasoning lays before you the rational choices of the majority of thinking men and women, what will you do? Will you follow the logical choices of man, or will you seek God in prayer, waiting to see what He will say?

When things become difficult, even unbearable, will you change your mood with the tide of circumstances, or will you rejoice in the God of your salvation? . . . Will you stumble in the darkness of your own reasoning . . . or will you let God help you walk above the difficulties of life?

O God, You are in control of my destiny. Help me walk in faith, doing it Your way, in Your timing, according to Your plan. I place my life in Your hands.

Power to Persevere

SCRIPTURE READING: Romans 8:35–39   KEY VERSE: Romans 8:2

The law of the Spirit of life in Christ Jesus has made me free from the law of sin and death.

You've heard the funny saying, "When the going gets tough, the tough get out of there!" That's actually a fairly accurate picture of how many react when life gets rough. What many fail to see, though, are the benefits of standing strong. Cynthia Heald explains the importance of perseverance in her book *Abiding in Christ:*

> After visiting a close friend and listening to her ongoing heartaches, I felt that the only thing I could do was encourage her to persevere—to face her pressures and trials with a steadfast commitment to do right and to maintain a godly life. In the Greek, perseverance means "to patiently endure." Our English definition means "to persist or remain constant to a purpose, idea, or task in the face of obstacles." . . .
>
> Persevering and enduring are not exactly cheerful words! Yet they are powerful and necessary in our lives. No matter who we are, who we know, or what our status is in life, we all go through trials. How encouraging to know that persevering through these experiences produces a beautiful result: Our character matures, and so does our ability to place our hope in God and to experience God's love. It is much easier to persevere when we remain closely connected to our source of strength and grace. Abiding in Christ enables us to endure, even rejoice in, the hardship that God allows in our lives.

> *Lord, give me the power to persevere. I want to face pressures and trials with a steadfast commitment to maintain a godly life. Enable me to endure and rejoice in hardships.*

A Candle of Hope

SCRIPTURE READING: Genesis 39; 41   KEY VERSE: Genesis 45:5

Now, do not therefore be grieved or angry with yourselves because you sold me here; for God sent me before you to preserve life.

M any times in our spiritual walk with the Lord, we do not know where He is leading or why. Often we may misunderstand why He has allowed certain circumstances to invade our otherwise safe and appointed world.

More than likely, Joseph did not understand why God allowed his brothers to treat him with such deep animosity. He had faithfully worshiped the Lord, yet God did not save him from the trial of being sold into Egyptian bondage. Once Joseph was there, his life became a drama of ups and downs, good and bad. If we think about it, Joseph's story may remind us of our own lives at times.

Because he could not escape captivity, he was forced to trust God throughout his Egyptian days. Think about it; he never again walked through his beloved homeland of Canaan. Even after God blessed him and Pharaoh appointed him over all the land, Joseph remained in Egypt. But God had a plan. He used Joseph's banishment to save Israel from starvation when a famine struck.

Had Joseph not gone into Egypt, Israel would have perished. God used Joseph's suffering to bless others. The years from the time of his arrest until the time of his family's arrival were not explained in detail to Joseph. God's servant walked through the darkness with only one candle of hope—his faith in a changeless God. And guess what? It was more than enough light!

Master, help me walk through the darkness with the candle of hope—my faith in a changeless God. Your light is enough for my journey.

The Victory Is Near

SCRIPTURE READING: Psalm 23   KEY VERSE: Psalm 23:4

Yea, though I walk through the valley of the shadow of death, I will fear no evil; for You are with me; Your rod and Your staff, they comfort me.

The above Scripture reading is a favorite. It also is one that children can easily learn. Many who memorize Psalm 23 early in life find themselves repeating it later, especially when trouble arises. The most outstanding feature of this psalm is the sense of trust and safety it brings.

David spent much of his young life as a shepherd in his father's field. There he encountered all kinds of dangers. His love and devotion to God stabilized his heart. When the temptation to become fearful arose, David focused on God's sovereign ability to protect and keep him.

Are you facing a particularly difficult situation? Maybe there has been a change in your home or work environment. Perhaps someone has attacked your personal reputation, and it seems that no amount of words or explanation can change his opinion.

What do you do when things go wrong or turn out badly? How do you cope when your loved one dies or leaves home? How do you handle the teenager whose course in life seems set on destruction?

There is only one way. It may sound simple or trite, but it works each and every time. Lay down your expectations. Be still in your heart and quiet in your spirit, and listen for God's word to you. Trust Him as David did to lead you through the valley and back out into the light of His eternal hope. The victory is near.

Precious Lord, I lay my expectations at the foot of the cross. Quiet my heart and spirit so that I can hear Your word to me. Lead me through the valley and back into the light of Your eternal hope. I rejoice because victory is near!

Your Source of Hope

SCRIPTURE READING: Psalm 42   KEY VERSE: Psalm 42:1

As the deer pants for the water brooks, so pants my soul for You, O God.

Hope brings an anticipation of blessing. We live in hope of our wedding day, the birth of a child or grandchild. We have hope over graduation from college or the day we can finally place a "Dr." in front of our names. There are as many reasons to hope as there are people.

To know hope, you must endure times of hopelessness. Hope represents an end to desperate longing—a need that begs to be satisfied and in the end is fulfilled. When hope burns within your heart, it cries out to be heard.

The psalmist declared, "As the deer pants for the water brooks, so my soul pants for Thee, O God . . . My tears have been my food day and night, while they say to me all day long, 'Where is your God?'" (Ps. 42:1, 3 NASB).

What is your hope, your dream, the cry of your heart? Take a moment and go to Jesus with your deepest, most earnest plea. The psalmist cried out, "Why are you in despair, O my soul? And why have you become disturbed within me?" (Ps. 42:5 NASB). Nothing is known about the man's struggle other than that it was critical to him.

Realize that whatever is important to you is even more important to the Lord. Let Him be your Source of hope for the future.

> *Dear heavenly Father, You hear the cry of my heart. The things that are important to me are important to You. You are my hope for the future. I rest in that knowledge.*

The Great Encourager

SCRIPTURE READING: James 1:1–12   KEY VERSE: James 1:12

Blessed is the man who endures temptation; for when he has been approved,
he will receive the crown of life which the Lord has promised to those who
love Him.

Though all that surrounds you seems lost in a misty sea of confusion, God is with you. He never leaves your side. Some may say, "There is nothing wrong in my life." However, each of us faces times of uncertainty when sorrow or dread covers the pathway before us and leaves us feeling helpless.

There is no greater blessing than beginning and ending each day with Jesus. Don't let doubts cloud the reality of His indwelling presence in your life. God tests your faith to make sure that it is deeply rooted within His truth. He allows adversity to brush across your life sometimes with great intensity so that the level of your trust will be exposed.

You learn to endure in the testing of your faith. And godly endurance, not human ability, makes you strong. James wrote, "Consider it all joy, my brethren, when you encounter various trials, knowing that the testing of your faith produces endurance. And let endurance have its perfect result, that you may be perfect and complete, lacking in nothing" (1:2–4 NASB).

To have the faith that conquers all doubts and fears, you must look to Christ as your Hope and Guide in every situation. Don't allow yourself to be drawn off course by the criticism or lack of support of others. God is your greatest Encourager, and when your faith is firmly fixed in Him, you can be sure He will lead you to victory.

Almighty God, give me the faith that conquers all doubts and fears. I look
to You as my Hope and Guide in every situation. Don't let me be drawn off
course by others. I fix my focus on You.

A Great Beginning, a Tragic End

SCRIPTURE READING: 1 Samuel 18–19   KEY VERSE: Proverbs 29:23

A man's pride will bring him low, but the humble in spirit will retain honor.

Saul was clearly a king out of control. He was consumed by jealousy of young David, whom God had clearly selected to be His earthly representative of leadership to the chosen people. Saul did not want to acknowledge God's decision, and he demonstrated his inner rebellion many times through disobedience.

A king who was once the admiration of all for his physical strength and spiritual vigor allowed the desire for personal power to consume him, and at great expense. God removed him from all position of authority and used David to carry on His work.

You have probably seen this principle at work in the lives of some believers today. When someone gets off course and refuses to let the Lord guide him back into His truth, very often God removes him from the situation that he is not submitting to His authority. God's decisions are examples of His love, ultimately, because the Lord cannot allow His children to continue on a course of self-destruction.

The problem with striking out on your own course and ignoring His direction is that such fleshly "pioneering" only desensitizes your heart to His direction even further. If you think this hardening may be present in your heart today, ask God to reveal the truth about how you're walking with Him. He wants you to live in His guidance for all of your years.

Dear God, reveal the truth of how I am walking with You. Sensitize my heart to Your direction. Lead me. Guide me.

Try, Try Again

SCRIPTURE READING: Luke 10:1–24   KEY VERSE: Galatians 6:9

Let us not grow weary while doing good, for in due season we shall reap if we do not lose heart.

I f Tom had given up the first time he failed, the world would not be the same. He labored in his workshop day after day, trying an endless stream of materials. With each option that did not work, he carefully cataloged the failure and moved on to the next substance with the sense he was that much closer to the answer. Finally the light turned on—quite literally. Thomas Alva Edison had found the secret to building a filament for the first incandescent light bulb.

In your walk with the Lord, failures and mistakes can cause you to have one of two reactions. Either you crumple under feelings of worthlessness, with the belief that things will never change, or you move forward and try again in confident faith.

That is what Jesus encouraged the seventy disciples to do when they met with discouragement and failure. If the people of a town or village welcomed them with open arms and listened to their teaching, Jesus told them to stay there for a while. However, if they met with resistance, they were to go into the streets and proclaim God's message of judgment against the city before they left.

Jesus was not commanding them to be quitters. They were on a special mission, and negative response was not to be a deterrent to the disciples' obedience.

O Lord, don't let me crumple in the face of failure. Help me use my failures as stepping-stones to the future. Give me the strength to try again in confident faith.

Beyond Ourselves

SCRIPTURE READING: 2 Corinthians 1   KEY VERSE: 2 Corinthians 1:12

Our boasting is this: the testimony of our conscience that we conducted our-
selves in the world in simplicity and godly sincerity, not with fleshly wisdom
but by the grace of God, and more abundantly toward you.

Many secular books and talk shows feature individuals who have made a comeback of some kind. Men and women who were once trapped in a bad situation dug themselves out of despair through sheer willpower and made themselves what they are today.

Many say something such as, "I just reached within myself to discover a strength I didn't know I had. When you understand how much power you really have, how much potential is locked within, you can release an inner force that helps you be successful."

Does this lingo sound familiar? It is the cry of modern man depending on himself and making himself the measure of all things. These speakers don't discuss, however, what to do when this self-generated energy runs out, when the problem gets too big for simple do-it-yourself answers. Human effort and power go only so far.

Can you imagine the apostle Paul saying that he had survived merciless beatings and shipwreck and public rejection through his own willpower? Absolutely not. Instead, Paul said this: "Our proud confidence is this, the testimony of our conscience, that in holiness and godly sincerity, not in fleshly wisdom but in the grace of God, we have conducted ourselves in the world, and especially toward you" (2 Cor. 1:12 NASB). This is your one sure hope as well.

Precious heavenly Father, I can't do it in myself. I don't have the energy or
the wisdom. My confidence is in You. I am depending on Your power.

Tugging at Your Heart

SCRIPTURE READING: 1 Timothy 1:18–20   KEY VERSE: 1 Timothy 1:19

Having faith and a good conscience, which some having rejected, concerning the faith have suffered shipwreck.

The ship plunged through the wild waves. The captain standing on deck spotted the yellow flash from the lighthouse on shore. But instead of steering a straight course in its direction, the captain ignored its warning and veered away. Unless he changed his course, his ship and crew faced almost certain destruction on the surrounding rocks.

Does that seem to be an insane response? It's something that people do all the time when they ignore the "flashes" of their God-given conscience.

The apostle Paul wrote to the young pastor Timothy about what happens to those who ignore the spiritual light of their consciences: "This command I entrust to you, Timothy, my son, in accordance with the prophecies previously made concerning you, that by them you may fight the good fight, keeping faith and a good conscience, which some have rejected and suffered shipwreck in regard to their faith" (1 Tim. 1:18–19 NASB).

The believers who rejected the messages of their consciences experienced a period of brokenness because they didn't pay attention to the spiritual danger signs along the way. Have you ever felt a tugging at your heart when you were about to move in a wrong direction? That is the action of the Holy Spirit, and He will never force you to pay attention. You must turn toward God's light and heed His call.

Father God, help me turn toward Your light and heed Your call. Make me alert to danger signs along the way. Keep me from moving in the wrong direction. Guide my spiritual journey.

A Fresh Touch from God

SCRIPTURE READING: Psalm 77   KEY VERSES: Isaiah 43:18–19

Do not remember the former things, nor consider the things of old. Behold, I will do a new thing, now it shall spring forth; shall you not know it? I will even make a road in the wilderness and rivers in the desert.

H ave you ever felt as if your life was a dry, barren desert? In the opening passage, Israel felt spiritually and emotionally desolate. In their disobedience, they had wandered from God, and He had allowed them to go. When they came to their senses, they cried out in evidence of the burden they bore in their hearts. They were alone and needed a fresh touch from God.

The wonderful thing about Christ is He is never at a distance. He is always beside us. Because faithfulness is a part of His nature, He cannot be unfaithful and still be God. When we are faithless, He is still faithful. And in the case of Israel, He proved true to His nature.

God commissioned the prophet Isaiah to record and report His words to His people. In Isaiah 43:18 (NASB), God told Israel: "Do not call to mind the former things, or ponder things of the past." In other words, "Don't spend a great deal of time looking back over past failures. Today is today. Up ahead is where we are going, and this is what I plan to do."

God always works in the present but looks to the future. Life at its best is not lived in the past, worrying over what happened or what once was. Instead, it is lived in the here and now, aware of one thing: God is a God of love, and He is always at work in your life to do something for your good and His glory.

Dear Lord, keep my focus off the past and on the future. Up ahead is where I am going. You are at work in my life, opening the way for me. I embrace tomorrow with joy and anticipation.

Class Six White Water

SCRIPTURE READING: Psalm 25   KEY VERSE: 1 Peter 5:8

Be sober, be vigilant; because your adversary the devil walks about like a roaring lion, seeking whom he may devour.

Two friends were alone on vacation and totally unprepared for what they were about to face. Looking forward to returning to college in the fall, they wanted to experience one last adventure before hitting the books. So they chose rafting down what was supposed to be a slow-moving river.

They had been told there would be an occasional white-water rapid. But they were convinced it would be nothing more than what rafters call "a Class Two on a scale of one to six." However, what they heard in front of them was much more than a Class Two, and the churning mist rising above the rushing waters confirmed their fears.

Even as they sprang to action, they realized there was little hope of controlling their raft. Neither possessed navigational skills, but the story's ending is more embarrassing than tragic. Wet and disoriented, they reached the shore and thankfully retrieved their boat from a cluster of low-lying limbs. After a few silent moments, the truth sank in. They were ill prepared for the journey. Never once had they seriously inquired about the nature of the river. Their expectations were false assumptions.

We think we are beyond sin's enticement, but we are not. Peter admonished us to remain on guard at all times (1 Peter 5:8). That way when we do run into Class Six white water, we won't be tempted to dismiss it as Class Two.

> *Heavenly Father, help me be on guard against the enemy at all times, spiritually alert to dangerous waters ahead. Protect me from Class Six white water.*

Who Is in Charge?

SCRIPTURE READING: Ephesians 5:11–21   KEY VERSE: Galatians 5:25

If we live in the Spirit, let us also walk in the Spirit.

Have you ever asked a question and gotten the runaround? One person passes you to the next, who passes you to someone else, who calls a representative in another department, and so on. With all that confusion, you wonder who is really in charge.

Paul addressed this issue of authority in Ephesians 5:18 (NASB): "Do not get drunk with wine, for that is dissipation, but be filled with the Spirit." The word *filled* here is translated from a Greek word meaning "controlled by" or "mastered by." The question God wants you to ask is, Who is in charge of my life?

Even though the Holy Spirit came to live in you when you trusted Christ as your Savior, He does not necessarily control and guide you. You must first yield to His authority, acknowledging His power as necessary for living as Jesus wants you to live.

The Holy Spirit is His guidance system for your life. A pilot may have the most advanced navigational equipment at his disposal, but it's useless if he does not turn it on. You must allow the Holy Spirit to turn you in the right direction, trusting in His infallible wisdom.

And this yielding isn't merely a one-time action; each day you need to make the conscious decision to rely on Him in spite of what your emotions may tell you. Are you ready to let Christ call the shots? He longs to lead you.

O God, regardless of what this day brings, You are in control. Lead me. Guide me. I yield every event of this day to You. You are in charge.

God's Perfect Timing

SCRIPTURE READING: 1 Samuel 13:1–14   KEY VERSE: Psalm 128:1

Blessed is every one who fears the LORD, who walks in His ways.

All of us know the feeling; a decision must be made, and from our point of view God seems to be dragging His feet. That was what Saul was feeling just before battling the Philistines. Samuel had instructed him to wait seven days. At the end of that time, he would come and make the appointed sacrifice.

But by the morning of the seventh day, Samuel had not arrived and Saul made a spiritually devastating decision to make the sacrifice himself:

> Saul's motivation . . . seems genuine and appropriate: the Philistines were gathering for battle against Israel, his men were deserting him, and Samuel had not arrived . . . Saul therefore felt the urgent need to seek God's favor— or at least that was his excuse. What he apparently failed to realize, however, is that animal sacrifice is not a prerequisite for entreating God . . . The fact is that Saul had not heeded the divine word through the prophet, and obedience is always better than sacrifice. *(The Expositor's Bible Commentary)*

Shortcuts are never an acceptable alternative to God's chosen plan. Before you make the decision to go ahead of Him, think of the consequences and how they will affect your life at a later date. At that point Saul lost his right to the kingdom. Remember, whatever you think needs to be done now can wait for God's perfect timing.

Father, Your timing is perfect. Don't let me be diverted by shortcuts. Your way is best, even when it seems longer. Give me patience to wait.

Some Assembly Required

SCRIPTURE READING: Hebrews 4:1–10   KEY VERSE: Hebrews 4:12

The word of God is living and powerful, and sharper than any two-edged sword, piercing even to the division of soul and spirit, and of joints and marrow, and is a discerner of the thoughts and intents of the heart.

Have you ever bought something with these words on the box: *Some assembly required?* You have to rely on the enclosed directions to make sure that slot A fits into tab Λ, and so forth. Even with careful instructions and diagrams, putting it together can be a challenge, so you know how hard it would be without any help from the manufacturer.

When someone tries to live without the direction of God's Word, essentially he is attempting to put together the complex pieces of his life minus the benefit of the Lord's perfect and wise guidance. Nothing else is a substitute.

Why? We learn the answer from Hebrews 4:12 (NASB): "For the word of God is living and active and sharper than any two-edged sword, and piercing as far as the division of soul and spirit, of both joints and marrow, and able to judge the thoughts and intentions of the heart."

God knows exactly how you are put together. He made you and knows what you need to function properly. In one sense, the Bible is the ultimate Manufacturer's Guide, one that does not lie, never beats around the bush, and cannot fail to fashion you as God intends. Best of all, the wisdom of Scripture is available at all times, no restrictions applied. Are you a reader of life's Instruction Book?

Master, thank You for Your Instruction Book for life. Your Word is living and active in me. You made me and know what I need to function properly. I praise You that my life is in the process of being assembled in perfect, divine order.

Trusting God

SCRIPTURE READING: Hebrews 4:11–16   KEY VERSE: Hebrews 4:14

Seeing then that we have a great High Priest who has passed through the heavens, Jesus the Son of God, let us hold fast our confession.

The Hebrew Christians were wavering in their faith, and thoughts of returning to their former ways of worship were both tempting and inviting. Along with that came the enticement to return to Jerusalem to offer sacrifices. There they could see the priest performing the ritual duties of the priesthood, which were the very tangible elements they missed in their new faith.

Those people were facing the same temptation we face each day, and that was to place their trust in what was visible rather than invisible. But faith is not a matter of seeing and then believing. It is a matter of trusting God, regardless of whether or not He shows us something.

The great men and women of the Bible trusted God not because He provided material evidence of His existence, though He did that on many occasions, but because He was faithful and true in His nature. A benefit of faith is watching God work in the circumstances of our lives to bring about the answers to our prayers. He is ever mindful of those who follow Him.

An even greater benefit of trusting God is developing an intimate relationship with the Lord Jesus Christ, who is the foundation of our faith. He is our great High Priest, and because of His death at Calvary, there is no longer a need to travel anywhere other than to Him in prayer.

> *Lord, help me look beyond the visible to see the invisible. I trust You, O God. Let me realize that faith is not seeing and believing; rather, it is believing when I cannot see.*

An Investment in Your Future

SCRIPTURE READING: Luke 9:23–26   KEY VERSE: Matthew 16:26

What profit is it to a man if he gains the whole world, and loses his own soul?
Or what will a man give in exchange for his soul?

The young woman went to a financial counselor to get help in constructing a livable budget. Part of her expenditures included putting money into a savings account and certain long-term investments as well. Is this woman unwise for setting aside money that she could spend and enjoy today? Of course she isn't. No one would criticize her for judicious planning; it is always wise to invest in the future.

This concept of looking ahead is part of what Jesus had in mind when He told His disciples to deny themselves each day in favor of following Him alone: "If anyone wishes to come after Me, let him deny himself, and take up his cross daily, and follow Me. For whoever wishes to save his life shall lose it, but whoever loses his life for My sake, he is the one who will save it" (Luke 9:23–24 NASB).

Following Jesus means sacrificing your personal agenda to His will, submitting obediently to His desires and plans for your life. Yielding to Him in this life means receiving the unending reward of eternal life. However, those who refuse to give up self-control or self-reliance and refuse to admit they need Him suffer in the end. What they thought they could hold on to often slips through their fingers, and they receive nothing in its place.

To which life-savings plan do you belong? Trusting Jesus is the best investment in the future you will make.

Precious Lord, here's my agenda—it's Yours. Please take control. I want to deny myself, take up my cross, and follow You.

Consider the Options

SCRIPTURE READING: John 6:53–69   KEY VERSE: John 6:69

We have come to believe and know that You are the Christ, the Son of the living God.

Jesus' earthly ministry up to John 6 mainly focused on healing the sick, teaching about the kingdom of God, and bringing insight to the words of the prophets. However, this changed with the introduction of John 6:53–69: "Unless you eat the flesh of the Son of Man and drink His blood, you have no life in yourselves. He who eats My flesh and drinks My blood has eternal life" (vv. 53–54 NASB).

Warren Wiersbe explained, "All Jesus said was, 'Just as you take food and drink within your body and it becomes a part of you, so you must receive Me within your innermost being so that I can give you life.'" Jesus' words were not meant to be taken literally. They were spiritual in nature and, if heeded, would lead His followers into a closer walk with God.

Realizing that many were turning from Jesus discouraged the disciples. Jesus confronted their fears: "You do not want to go away also, do you?" Peter answered for the group: "Lord, to whom shall we go? You have words of eternal life. And we have believed and have come to know that You are the Holy One of God" (vv. 67–69 NASB).

There will come a time in your life when you will have to decide whom you will follow. At times, God's Word may seem difficult; but remember, He has the larger picture in mind. Can you trust Him as Peter did and say with him, "Lord, You have the words of eternal life, and I believe in You"?

Dear heavenly Father, there are no options for me. I choose Your way. I choose the way of the Word. To whom else can I go? You have the words of eternal life.

The Truth About Consequences

SCRIPTURE READING: Proverbs 26:23–28   KEY VERSE: Galatians 6:7

Do not be deceived, God is not mocked; for whatever a man sows, that he will also reap.

Think about what life would be like if the consequences of all our actions were immediate, just as in the story of Pinocchio. If you lied, your nose would grow. If you gossiped, your mouth would get bigger. In such a scenario, one thing is for certain—there would be a great number of funny-looking people.

In the real world, however, consequences don't always come at the exact moment an offense is committed, yet the long-term results of going against one of God's principles are there nevertheless. Proverbs 26:27 (NASB) makes this connection clear: "He who digs a pit will fall into it, and he who rolls a stone, it will come back on him."

The reaction may not be immediate, but it will come; this is God's way. In a sense, you can never truly violate one of His immutable principles, in the same way that you cannot go against the natural law of gravity.

Ultimately the Lord has set up boundaries and guidelines for your life to be a source of protection and blessing (Ps. 119). What many nonbelievers interpret as the negative "don'ts" of Christianity are really positives, as though God were saying: "Do live according to My plans, and then you will find real reward."

Almighty God, I realize there are consequences to my actions. Give me wisdom and understanding to walk Your way. Take my hand and guide me on my journey.

Living Above Your Circumstances

SCRIPTURE READING: Philippians 1:21–26   KEY VERSE: Philippians 1:21

For to me, to live is Christ, and to die is gain.

Paul's letter to the Philippians wasn't written in elegant or secure surroundings, nor was it penned in the comfort of a cozy study. Instead, it was composed under the most difficult circumstances.

The very thing that led to the letter's writing, sharing the gospel, eventually led to its author's death. Yet Paul was confident: God's redemptive message must be told, and those who follow Christ must be shown the way.

Spiritually Paul learned to live above his circumstances by focusing on something much grander than his earthly existence. Yet for a moment, we sense his desire to leave the pain and suffering behind: "For to me, to live is Christ, and to die is gain. But if I am to live on in the flesh, this will mean fruitful labor for me; and I do not know which to choose . . . Yet to remain on in the flesh is more necessary" (Phil. 1:21–24 NASB).

Are you facing a time of deep discouragement? Each of us does at some point. When troubles come, Jesus remains at your side. You have a lot to live for because Christ lives in you. Never be afraid to ask Him for a fresh sense of His hope and peace. He is faithful and will answer the prayers of His children.

> *O Lord, help me live above the circumstances of my life. Let me realize that when trouble comes, You are at my side. You live in me. Give me renewed hope and peace.*

Life Is an Adventure

SCRIPTURE READING: Acts 8:26–40   KEY VERSE: Psalm 37:23

The steps of a good man are ordered by the LORD, and He delights in his way.

Philip had no way of knowing what was about to happen. All he knew was that God told him to go down the road from Jerusalem to Gaza, and he obeyed without a single question. Imagine his amazement when he found an Ethiopian eunuch, riding in his chariot and reading a passage from the book of Isaiah. In the forefront of his mind was an unanswered question—who was the Lamb of whom the prophet spoke?

God put the two men on that path together for a special reason. Philip knew the gospel, and the Ethiopian was ready to receive it. Then the two experienced the wonders of God's perfect plan.

It has been said that there is no such thing as coincidence, just God's plan unfolding in unexpected ways. Certainly that is true in the lives of believers. Have you been a part of a miracle of God's timing? Maybe you ran out of gas by the side of the road and someone came along with a gas can before you had to seek help. Maybe it was an unanticipated meeting with an old friend, who really needed your encouragement in the Lord.

When you understand that God's ways are perfect and that He is continually working, you will begin to see your life as the adventure that it is. You may not know exactly what's ahead or when change will occur, but you can know that every experience is from Him.

> *Dear Lord, Your way is perfect. Thank You for being continually at work in me. I may not know what is ahead or what changes will come, but I rejoice in the confidence that each experience is from You.*

The True Colors of God's Nature

SCRIPTURE READING: John 1:1–24   KEY VERSE: Matthew 5:16

Let your light so shine before men, that they may see your good works and glorify your Father in heaven.

For years, poinsettias have been a favorite plant at Christmas. But in order for their brilliant color to be revealed at just the right time, nursery growers make sure the plants spend a certain amount of time in darkness. When the plants grow to maturity, large amounts of light are then introduced into their environment.

The poinsettia is native to Florida, and many who have them in their yards tell how the poinsettia must be planted on a certain side of the house in order for the plant's leaves to turn a brilliant color. Again, the secret lies in the amount of sunlight the plant receives. The more sun at the right time, the more brilliant the color.

God calls us to be lights in a world of darkness. However, we can never forget that He is our Source of light. Without the light of His presence we become dull and colorless. Christ said, "Let your light shine before men in such a way that they may see your good works, and glorify your Father who is in heaven" (Matt. 5:16 NASB).

The true colors of God's nature are released within us by spending time in His Word. If we fail to read and study His principles, our lights will never reflect the brilliance of His love, forgiveness, and grace to others. We must have contact with the Father of Lights in order for our light to have purpose.

Precious heavenly Father, the true colors of Your nature were reflected in Your Son, who came to this earth to share Your light. Let my life be a reflection of Your divine gift of love.

Focus On the Finish Line

SCRIPTURE READING: 1 Corinthians 9:24–26   KEY VERSE: Philippians 1:6

Being confident of this very thing, that He who has begun a good work in you will complete it until the day of Jesus Christ.

A key to living above your circumstances is leaning on the faithfulness of Christ while refusing to be caught up in the instability of your surroundings. Paul used the analogy of a runner to explain how you are to respond to life's circumstances (1 Cor. 9:24–26).

You are to fix your gaze on the finish line and race with all your might toward that goal. Once God places a goal in your heart, never give up. Instead, move toward it with swiftness and courage.

Paul's goal was to take the gospel message to Asia. Three completed missionary journeys proved he had a plan and purpose. Personal testimonies bear witness he achieved his goal, but not without cost. No one completes the race of life without facing many trials and tribulations.

Paul had a wonderful system for bypassing negative thinking and potential defeat. He looked beyond his circumstances to the sovereignty of God. He focused on the positive results of his ministry, not the personal pain.

In the end, the trials of Paul matured and strengthened his spiritual walk. Even though you are hard-pressed on every side, Jesus will bring light to all you are facing. Trust Him, and you will see His victory.

Dear God, fix my gaze on the finish line. Help me race with all my might toward the goal. I rebuke negative thinking and potential defeat. I will finish my journey in victory.

Your Spiritual Pilgrimage

SCRIPTURE READING: 1 Corinthians 9:26–27   KEY VERSES: 2 Timothy 4:6–7

I am already being poured out as a drink offering, and the time of my departure is at hand. I have fought the good fight, I have finished the race, I have kept the faith.

Literally and figuratively it is the final chapter of Paul's life. Writing from the dungeons of Rome and nearing his execution, Paul closed his second letter to his understudy Timothy with a ringing manifesto: "I am already being poured out as a drink offering, and the time of my departure is at hand. I have fought the good fight, I have finished the race, I have kept the faith" (2 Tim. 4:6–7).

The aged campaigner for the gospel was facing death just as he had faced life, boldly and fearlessly. His trademark confidence was still at full mast. Paul understood the significance of ending well. He had compared the spiritual life to a race, the goal of which is to finish (1 Cor. 9:26–27).

Do you have the long-term goal in mind of ending with a solid testimony for Christ? If so, you can deal with momentary afflictions from a perspective of endurance and steadfastness. You may be perplexed, but you will move on. You may be bruised, but you will recover for the next leg of the journey.

What would you like others to think and say when you conclude your spiritual pilgrimage? What do you need to do now to make that possible? You can run well and end well when knowing Christ is your consuming passion.

Father God, I want to end my spiritual pilgrimage with a solid testimony. Strengthen me for the next leg of the journey. Help me to continue to run the race and end well.

God-Given Goals

SCRIPTURE READING: Philippians 2:13–16   KEY VERSE: Isaiah 64:4

Since the beginning of the world men have not heard nor perceived by the ear, nor has the eye seen any God besides You, who acts for the one who waits for Him.

A my Carmichael wrote,

We have often taken the above verse to mean that our God so guides and controls our outward affairs that confusion ends in peace; and this is true, but taken with Philippians 2:13, we find an even deeper comfort.

We want to be sincere. We do earnestly desire to mix salt [our commitment] in our incense of devotion to Christ at all times, but we fear we might fail. However, you have not to do it in your unaided strength: it is God Who is all the while supplying the impulse, giving you the power to resolve, the strength to perform, the execution of His good pleasure.

Amy explained that while our commitment and devotion to Christ are of utmost importance, so is our willingness to trust God for His goodness by acting on the opportunities He places before us.

Many people miss the blessings of God simply because they hesitate and fail to trust God to give them good things. During the coming year, when you have an idea or see an opportunity unfolding, don't be so quick to dismiss it. Instead, test its validity by going to God's Word. Does your dream or goal contradict Scripture? Is it in line with God's will for your life? If it passes the test, pray for God to continue to make His way clear. The impulse, the inner strength, or the peace is evidence of His good pleasure.

Heavenly Father, let me set goals that honor You and are in harmony with Your plan for my life. Give me the impulse, inner strength, and peace as evidence that my plans are approved. Help me set proper goals, then live out their reality by faith.

Facing the Future

SCRIPTURE READING: Romans 5:1–2   KEY VERSE: Romans 5:5

Hope does not disappoint, because the love of God has been poured out in our hearts by the Holy Spirit who was given to us.

A popular bumper sticker reads, "No God, no peace. Know God, know peace." The message is short and simple, but it's absolutely true.

Thousands of Christian counselors would attest to this fact every day, as hurting people approach them with problems that stem from a lack of peace on the inside. A great many counselees are believers who have never really embraced the security and love of God's grace. They lack an understanding of how His plan of reconciliation in the Cross bears on their real lives.

The following are some self-diagnostic questions to help you determine your own "peace factor":

- Do I feel restless or apathetic about spiritual things or life in general, even when circumstances are going fine?
- Do I still feel a cloud of guilt hanging over my head for things I did wrong in the past?
- Am I easily infuriated by the weaknesses of people around me?
- Do I secretly resent those who seem happy or content, believing they are just faking it?
- Do I wish I were someone else?
- Am I afraid that God is going to punish me when I mess up?

If you answered yes to any of these questions, you may be experiencing a lack of peace. Ask the Lord to show you the root of the problem. He will help you embrace the tender wonder of His love today and give you peace and power to face the future.

O God, free me from restlessness, apathy, guilt, and resentment. Make me more tolerant of weaknesses of others. Give me peace and power to face the future. Help me embrace Your forgiveness, Lord, and rest in it fully.

Looking for a Shortcut?

SCRIPTURE READING: Matthew 6:25–34   KEY VERSE: 1 Thessalonians 5:24

He who calls you is faithful, who also will do it.

The sign read: DANGER! STAY ON PATHWAY. But the four hikers ignored the warning and began their climb. Their reasoning: the sooner we get to the top, the more time we will have to explore the cavelike overhangs along the rocky face of the mountain.

Halfway up the precipice, the third man back lost his footing on some loose rocks. In an instant, the last two men went tumbling backward down the steep incline. On their way down, they frantically grabbed at small bushes and weeds, hoping to slow their descent. But nothing worked.

Finally they came to a stop. Cut, bruised, and one suffering from a broken arm, they concluded that taking the shortcut had not been worth their effort. In fact, they had almost cut short the lives of two best friends.

Very few shortcuts in life are worth the time and energy to travel them. We may get by here and there; but in the end, if we decide to take a way other than what God has mapped out for us, we come out the losers.

If you feel God is taking a long time in fulfilling His promises to you, think again about how much He loves you and is dedicated to your growth and success. Don't get in a hurry. Whatever He has for you, it's worth the wait. Eternity is His, and you can trust this fact: He won't forget His promises to you (1 Thess. 5:24).

> *Lord, sometimes it seems it is taking a long time for Your promises to be fulfilled. Help me not to be in a hurry. Your plan is worth the wait. Let me travel the way You have mapped out for me.*

The Journey of Faith

SCRIPTURE READING: Hebrews 11:8–10   KEY VERSES: Romans 8:28–29

We know that all things work together for good to those who love God, to those who are the called according to His purpose. For whom He foreknew, He also predestined to be conformed to the image of His Son, that He might be the firstborn among many brethren.

You can't reach the mountaintop unless you scale its slopes. You can't reach your destination unless you hazard the journey. That's what it means to take a step of faith, to risk the comfort of the familiar and trust God to take you to new places. Doing anything less is a form of compromise.

At the beginning of his trip of a lifetime, Abraham could not say with certainty that he understood God's reasons or methods. But he did grasp God's good purpose and knew that the only way to live it was to surrender himself to the experience.

In her book *Faith: The Substance of Things Unseen*, Penelope Stokes describes the value of the risk of faith:

It's a frightening concept, new birth . . . to be catapulted like helpless infants into an unfamiliar, perhaps hostile world . . . to give ourselves over, heart and soul, to the God who calls us out into new life, into new experiences, into deep spiritual waters.

Both before and after my experience of surrender to Christ on September 15, 1970, I can see the hand of God working in my life, drawing me toward spiritual consciousness, leading me on the journey of faith . . . And all along the way, I see altars of sacrifice, times in which God called me to a new place, a different level of intimacy, continued growth . . . We must take the risk to go forward as God leads us to new levels of life in the Spirit.

Lord, thank You for being my Guide on this spiritual journey. I rejoice to see how You directed my footsteps during this past year. I face the future in faith and confidence.

About the Author

Dr. Charles Stanley is pastor of the 14,000-member First Baptist Church in Atlanta, Georgia. He is well known through his In Touch radio and television ministry to thousands internationally and is the author of many books, including *Our Unmet Needs, Enter His Gates, The Source of My Strength, The Reason for My Hope, The Glorious Journey, How to Listen to God,* and *How to Handle Adversity.*

Dr. Stanley received his bachelor of arts degree from the University of Richmond, his bachelor of divinity degree from Southwestern Theological Seminary, and his master's and doctor's degrees from Luther Rice Seminary. He has twice been elected president of the Southern Baptist Convention.

Other Best-Selling Books by Charles Stanley

Enter His Gates

Spiritual gates are much like the gates of a city. They are vital to your well-being as a Christian and, if not maintained, leave you open to attack by the enemy. *Enter His Gates* is a daily devotional that encourages you to build or strengthen a different spiritual gate each month.

0-7852-7546-0 • Hardcover • 400 pages • Devotional

In Touch with God

This unique gift book is filled with inspirational Scriptures as well as thoughts and prayers from Dr. Stanley. It will help you know God's heart on a variety of topics, including forgiveness, relationships, Spirit-filled living, Christian character, and God's plan for your life.

0-7852-7117-1 • Printed Hardcover • 208 pages • Gift/Devotional

The Power of the Cross

Using inspirational Scriptures as well as personal insights and heartfelt prayers, Charles Stanley encourages you to see the transforming power of the Resurrection for salvation, victory over temptation, healing of emotional pain, and restoration with the heavenly Father.

0-7852-7065-6 • Printed Hardcover • 208 pages • Gift/Devotional

The Reason for My Hope

Dr. Stanley shares his personal struggles to remain focused on Christ and keep hope alive in the middle of difficult circumstances. In his warm and insightful style, he reveals the promises and resources God provides His children, identifying nine key reasons for all believers to have unshakable hope.

0-8407-7765-5 • Hardcover • 256 pages • Christian Living